The Last of the Knights
The Regent
Earl Birger of Bjälbo

The Last of the Knights
The Regent
Earl Birger of Bjälbo

By August Strindberg

TRANSLATIONS AND INTRODUCTIONS
BY WALTER JOHNSON

University of Washington Press   Seattle and London

Preface

THE THREE PLAYS in this volume are the last plays August Strindberg wrote about figures from the Swedish past. So far as I know they have never appeared in American or British translation; yet they deserve consideration from anyone who wants to understand Strindberg's contribution to the historical drama. These folk dramas illustrate Strindberg's remarkable skill in making the historic dead come alive in highly playable dramas, and they illustrate, too, his skill in varying his technique to suit his subject and his ideas.

The Last of the Knights and *The Regent* were deliberately designed as companion plays and, in part at least, as contributions toward the completion of the cycle of plays about Gustav Vasa, the king Strindberg admired above all others. That these two plays and *Earl Birger of Bjälbo* were written long after the greatness of his Vasa trilogy—*Master Olof* (1872), *Gustav Vasa* (1899), and *Erik XIV* (1899)—had been acknowledged helps to account for the relatively little attention these three last plays have received from critics and students of Strindberg.

Aside from its genuine merits as a folk drama, *Earl Birger of Bjälbo* is interesting for the light it throws on Strindberg's attitude toward history and the historical drama as well as on Strindberg's thinking toward the close of his life. He never wrote more fully or more frankly about any of his post-Inferno * historical plays than

---

* The Inferno experiences consisted of the emotional, mental, and physical agony which led to Strindberg's conversion. For information about the Inferno experiences, see any biography of Strindberg or Strindberg's *The*

he did about *Earl Birger of Bjälbo;* in the introduction to that play
I have paid attention to these matters in some detail.

Following the procedure used in *Strindberg's Queen Christina,
Charles XII, Gustav III* (University of Washington Press and the
American-Scandinavian Foundation, 1955), I have provided after
each play brief notes on the period, on major and secondary characters, and on various passages. I have presented this material as
far as possible from the points of view of Strindberg and his major
sources—Anders Fryxell's *Berättelser ur svenska historien* (*Stories
from Swedish History*) (Stockholm, 1900 edition) and Starbäck
and Bäckström's *Berättelser ur svenska historien* (Stockholm, 1885
edition; SB in the notes).

WALTER JOHNSON

Inferno (New York, 1913). The major study of Strindberg's Inferno period,
Gunnar Brandell's *Strindbergs Infernokris* (Stockholm, 1950), is, unfortunately, not available in English translation.

Contents

The Last of the Knights
The Regent
Earl Birger of Bjälbo

Introduction to
'The Last of the Knights'

THE WRITING of a realistic drama about Sten Sture the Younger, regent of Sweden from 1512 to 1520, provided Strindberg with a challenge, the like of which he had faced only to a degree in *The Saga of the Folkungs* (1899) and *Engelbrekt* (1901). For Sten Sture, according to the popular sources Strindberg regularly used and the scholarly historians as well, surpassed both Magnus the Good and Engelbrekt as the epitome of the good man, i.e., a knight without fear and beyond reproach. Fryxell's comments are typical (II, 182-184):

> Lord Sten Sture the Younger, like his father, was a very noble and distinguished man in many respects. Upright but humble before God, honest and loyal toward his fellow men, wise and sharpwitted in counsel, grave and unafraid in battle: like his father, he was all this, but in addition, he was much more gentle, friendly, and good-hearted than Lord Svante. As a young boy he was often seen, his eyes filled with tears, kneeling to propitiate his father when the latter's violent temper lashed out against cowardly, false, or negligent servants; and in that way, he saved many from the severest of punishments. When he grew up, he retained the same gentle, conciliatory turn of mind, and the people loved him for it warmly. But his best friends, who loved him for this very quality, complained that his gentleness misled him to the point of gullibility and altogether too much forbearance for his enemies. . . . He traveled regularly throughout the country to learn about the circumstances of the people, and both his ears and heart were open to the complaints the people had to offer; for he wanted to protect everyone, the learned

3

as well as the layman, the powerful as well as the humble, so that no one would have to suffer injustice under his administration. Without hypocrisy, he considered himself the father of his countrymen; he did not seek his own pleasure and his own advantage, but sacrificed for the welfare of the people his time and his energies, yes, eventually his life itself.

This interpretation, expanded and embellished by legend and historical fact, could hardly be anything but challenging to a dramatist whose observation of human nature had found few if any equals to Sten Sture in the use to which men put their dual capacity for good and evil.

Strindberg's examination of the sources gave him a clue. When Sten Sture became regent in 1512, he was little more than nineteen years old. He was the exceptional product of two related civilizing forces, chivalry and the church, and he was a thoroughly good example of what happens to the idealist and the good man in a thoroughly human environment. In other words, Strindberg saw Sten Sture's journey through the eight years of his regency as the pilgrimage of a very young idealist who has to learn the bitter lessons that life has to teach about oneself and one's fellow men.

In his realistic interpretation of the young regent, Strindberg has followed his sources in placing emphasis on chivalry as the primary formative factor in Sten Sture's life. A product of the thirteenth century in Sweden, initiated and controlled by the Swedish kings (only the king could dub a man knight), chivalry had complemented the church's doctrine of brotherly love by attempting to indoctrinate young aristocrats with the code of honor. It must be kept in mind when one considers *The Last of the Knights* that honor was the major fact of knighthood, that one could achieve it in open and honest combat for what is just and good: the defense of one's country, the church, women, the defenseless, and the victims of oppression and brute force.

The knight who, theoretically, was to dedicate himself to an en-

thusiastic love of good and to hatred of evil was exposed to a training designed to develop him physically, socially, and, above all,
morally. Strindberg's Sten Sture has not only been exposed to all
this but *it has taken:* physically, the training has developed his body
which is to serve the spirit by means of military skills (the desire
for military prowess and glory was considered highly justified);
socially, the ideals of courtesy, gallantry, and romantic love have
made him a model of social conduct; morally, he has developed
those traits of chivalric (and Christian) conduct that make him
a good man, constantly aware of his own weaknesses and ever
struggling against them, and applying the doctrine, "Do unto
others as you would have others do unto you." He has been imbued with the ideals of self-sacrifice, service as a goal, liberality and
generosity toward friend and foe alike, opposition to injustice, pro-
motion of peace, and defense of law and order. The training included, to be sure, recognition of the presence of evil in the world,
in oneself, and one's fellows, but it did not call for frank, open
analysis and blunt discussion of evil in all of its manifestations; it
gave the other man the benefit of the doubt and frequently frustrated the good and gentle knight's endeavors to forward good and
curb evil.

Such a historic figure, placed near the end of the turbulent period of more than a century's futile attempt at uniting Sweden
with its fellow Scandinavian countries, interested Strindberg very
much, as the fate of the good in the midst of a dominantly egotistic
community had always interested him. As both his favorite sources
and the recognized historians told him, neither chivalry nor the
church had ever succeeded in securing much more than protective
and otherwise self-advantageous lip service from the vast majority
of the human beings exposed to them. "The misfortunes of the
realm in the last hundred years" had involved the struggle for
power between nationalists and unionists: on the one hand, patriotic Swedes had seen advantages to Sweden in independence,
and, on the other, many of the prominent lords had tried hard to

secure the real power for themselves through a loose and nominal control by a union king with his major residence in then distant Copenhagen. The environment in which Sten Sture was to work was consequently one filled with bitterness, hatred, divided loyalties, selfish ambitions. The princes of the church, it should be noted, were among the most worldly and realistic. It was an environment in which knightly conduct, idealistically conceived and idealistically applied, would, except for the very young either in age or in spirit, seem stupidly quixotic.

Minimizing the fairly extended lapse of time by deliberately not mentioning it in too specific terms, Strindberg uses the realistic technique to demonstrate in dramatic terms what happened to the young idealist who attempted by means of applied chivalry and applied Christianity to govern Sweden and to defend its independence. Sten Sture surrounds himself with a group of enthusiastic but realistic followers, a loving and faithful wife who in most respects is his feminine counterpart, devious and selfish lords, one wise but wily old councillor, and, in general, a motley group of humanity. Following history, Strindberg makes Sten Sture's primary antagonist the infamous archbishop, Gustav Trolle. In a broad sense, the drama tells the story of the struggle between a man who is a knight and a Christian in spirit and act as well as in name and a man who is a Christian and a knight in name alone. In none of his other historical plays did the sources, both popular and authoritative, provide Strindberg with such a clear-cut dramatic struggle between good and evil, between selfishness and self-restraint, as in the story of the knightly regent and the Machiavellian archbishop.

Yet Strindberg the realist did not succumb to predecessors' example either by making Sten Sture a flawless human being or by making Gustav Trolle a devil incarnate without saving human qualities. Products of their environment and heredity, they exhibit —at opposite poles, to be sure—two striking possibilities of human development.

Lady Mätta, the stepmother, explains how the son of her husband, Lord Svante Sture, could reach the age of nineteen without losing his childlike innocence:

> I have always admired good people, because they could do what I couldn't: love!—When I had to bring up an angelic child with blue eyes and blond hair, I loved that child more than my own children, and I took care that from me he never heard or saw anything but good! I, the bride of hate and vengeance, I taught him to love, to believe good, and to forgive! What I couldn't become myself, he was to become! But, just the same, I was forced to harm him!

Mistress of the regent's court, Lady Mätta has supplemented the chivalric and Christian training of young Sten; she has overprotected the already protected son of a regent by keeping him from discovering the less pleasant facts of human nature and human society. In so doing she has harmed him by not equipping him with the knowledge required in actual life and by giving him false notions that have kept him childlike in a highly adult world.

Strindberg traces the development of Sture from the start of his career as a young idealistic regent, setting out to create in Sweden a sort of Utopian state based on the code of honor, until, after one failure after the other in his attempts at converting his major adversary, and after wasting one opportunity for victory after the other because of unrealistic knightly behavior (the impulsive promise given to Erik Trolle, the knightly sparing of the archbishop's life, the feeding of his starving enemies, for example), he faces inner defeat. The gradual shock of awakening to rude reality culminates in the ban of excommunication proclaimed against him by the church whose faithful member and servant he had been. Anna Bielke says, "Sten is lying smiling like the sleeping child he was all his life." That, briefly, suggests the drama that Strindberg saw in Sten Sture's career as regent. When the good man awakens from his sleepwalking, he learns the nature of his environment: "In the final analysis, it's only you and I. Out-and-out disloyalty, dissension, greed; every one of them's for sale, and there's no lack of buyers"; and, having discovered that his major adversary is evil beyond hope: "That there can be a being in this world like Gustav Trolle! In whom one can't find one human trait . . . He has robbed me of my faith in people."

In a world dominated by people who consider applied chivalry and applied Christianity quixotic, the idealist cannot help feeling: "I don't know if I can be happy any more; it's as if a veil had been dropped over my life! . . . All that's happening is foreign to me; if it's good or evil, I don't know . . ." Sten Sture's tragedy stems from his unrealistic idealism which results in gullibility, impulsiveness, and self-deception. Strindberg has amply illustrated all this in his skillful demonstration of Sten Sture's pilgrimage from innocence to knowledge of a world that is Swiftian in its human environment. It is part of the irony of life, as Strindberg saw it, that it is the good son of the church, the knight without fear and beyond reproach, who is excommunicated and who loses his life in the defense of what is good.

History indicated to Strindberg that the one who is likely to inherit in such a world is either the Machiavellian man of evil or the practical realist with attainable goals: either Sten Sture's bitter opponent, the aristocrat Gustav Trolle, who became archbishop of Sweden at twenty-six largely because of the intrigues of leading unionists and the gullibility, impulsiveness, and self-deception of Sten Sture; or Gustav Vasa, the practical realist who knows life even though he is one of the youngest men about Sten Sture.

Strindberg's presentation of the technically secondary character Archbishop Trolle is restrained in comparison to that in some of the earlier accounts. Strindberg carefully interprets him in terms of his heredity and environment. The son of Erik Trolle, Sten Sture's predecessor as regent, and member of the family that resented and hated the Stures, Gustav Trolle is the brilliant and ambitious product of an environment of hate and intrigue:

> ERIK TROLLE: I've taught you that!
> GUSTAV TROLLE: You have taught me a great deal!

ERIK TROLLE: If I could only teach you to forget the evil I've taught
  you!
GUSTAV TROLLE: Don't say that. What you call evil has benefited me
  most in life!

He wants power, position, prestige, and possessions. He has become
a priest not because he believes in Christ but because he sees in
the church the surest means to secure his ambition. He lives in the
old dispensation, as he tells his father. He has lived in Rome and
has learned much from the brilliant but corrupt Rome of Luther's
day. Nominally a Christian and a knight of the Holy Sepulchre,
he takes the ideals of both the church and the order as mere words,
but useful ones.

Strindberg gives us a remarkably detailed portrait of this highly
important secondary character. By exposition and by action, Strindberg reveals the archbishop as the unhappy, inwardly disharmoni-
ous product of his environment. Feeding on hate, ever mindful of
himself, in rapport with no one, he thwarts Sten Sture at every
opportunity, misjudges him, and makes sure that Sten Sture is excommunicated. The Lübeckers summarize what the historians (and
Strindberg) have to tell:

BREMS: Who is Gustav Trolle?
ISRAEL: He's a French, no, an Italian bandit, like Alexander VI
  Borgia, a fat fish like the eel. If you try to seize his head, you get
  hold of his tail, if you manage to get hold of him at all.

The haughty condescension, the offensive familiarity, and the rude-
ness with which he speaks to Sten Sture bear out wise Heming
Gad's early warning to Sture: "You want to talk with him; he
never talks; he only hears, listens, steals every word and converts it
into a promise, which he'll force you to keep later . . ." Strindberg
has made brilliant use of comparison and contrast in his interpretations of his central character and his major antagonist. For those
who feel that the thoughts, words, and deeds of a good man are

relatively tame, Strindberg has provided an opposite who should be found, by the same token, highly interesting.

Strindberg has concentrated the larger as well as the personal conflicts in the struggles between these two strikingly different knights. In Act I, he not only introduces Sten Sture and makes both the man and his ideas fairly clear but prepares the audience for the role Gustav Trolle is to play in Sten Sture's regency. In Acts II and III, the archbishop destroys every attempt by Sten Sture to secure cooperation for the general good. In Act IV, Sten Sture wastes his greatest opportunity to achieve his goal by behaving like a knight toward his captive antagonist. In scene 2 of Act V, Sten Sture is dead, and Trolle is among those who are besieging the castle in which the late regent's body lies.

The very young Gustav Vasa, Strindberg's favorite Swedish king —he appears in three other plays as well—and the very old Heming Gad add a great deal to the play. The former provides a highly interesting and convincing contrast to the man whose loyal follower he is by seeing human beings as they are, even though he himself is very young; the latter provides effective contrast to Sten Sture as an old man who has the wisdom of old age and has been schooled in the ways of the world. Neither of them is crippled in action, as Sten Sture is, by false evaluations of human individuals or of human society.

One of the striking facts about *The Last of the Knights* is the effect of youthfulness that Strindberg conveys. In fact, the majority of the secondary characters as well as the central character are little more than boys, with the enthusiasm and the fervor of the very young. Even Archbishop Trolle is only twenty-six when he first appears. The very young men and women struggling for the independence of their country lend a freshness to this play that helps much to make it the very effective folk drama it is.

The Last of the Knights

· A Play in Five Acts

Characters [1]

STEN STURE THE YOUNGER
KRISTINA STURE, *his wife*
MÄTTA STURE, *his stepmother, widow of Svante Sture*
GUSTAV VASA
JOHAN NATT-OCH-DAG *of Göksholm, the son of Engelbrekt's murderer Måns Natt-och-Dag*
ANNA BIELKE, *later his wife*
ARCHBISHOP GUSTAV TROLLE
ERIK TROLLE, *his father, first regent, then councillor*
LARS SPARRE
GÖRAN SPARRE, *his brother*
ERIK LEJONHUVUD
HEMING GAD, *elected but not inducted as bishop*
NIKLAS (NILS) BREMS, *burgomaster of Lübeck*
HERMAN ISRAEL, *councillor of Lübeck*
CORD KÖNIG, *councillor of Lübeck*
CASTELLAN (*governor of the castle*)
GUSTAV TROLLE'S CHANCELLOR
MAGNUS GREN

TAVERN KEEPER, SENTINEL, GIRLS, MAYOR, and MINOR CHARACTERS

Settings

ACT I: *The Rathskeller in Stockholm's Town Hall*
ACT II: *A room in Stockholm Castle; the Hanseatic warehouse*
ACT III: *The sacristy in Uppsala Cathedral*
ACT IV: *Stäke Castle*
ACT V: *The Blockhouse; the same room in the castle in Stockholm as in Act II*

ACT I

The vaulted sections of the Rathskeller in the Town Hall.

To the right, the Grapevine and the Ivy; to the left, the Rose, which is just as large as the two others combined. The Grapevine is decorated with vine leaves and grapes; it is the regular meeting place of the members of the city council; a golden seven-armed candlestick, a little banner with the figure of St. Erik, and gold and silver tankards and drinking cups are on the table reserved for them.

The Ivy is the Lübeckers'; this section is decorated with ivy; the table has Rhenish flagons and tankards, glass, etc. The banner has a three-headed black eagle, holding a shield in red and white.

In the Rose, there is a painting of St. George and the dragon; the horse is white, and St. George's armor silver and gold; white and red roses on the walls.

In the background an archway to the wine cellar stands open, with barrels, casks, etc.

Small tables with benches here and there. Unimpeded exits to the right and left and at the back.

When the curtain goes up, the regent ERIK TROLLE *is standing in the middle of the floor speaking quietly with the* KEEPER. ERIK LEJONHUVUD *is standing behind them. The regent's* GUARDS *can be seen in the exit at the back.*

From the right enter LARS SPARRE *and his younger brother* GÖRAN.

LARS SPARRE (*half-aloud, to* GÖRAN): The regent—Erik Trolle—is conferring with the keeper! What can that mean?

GÖRAN SPARRE: That he's sure he'll be re-elected . . . and so he's arranging a banquet . . . free food—musicians—tar barrels and heralds! *Saperlotte!*

LARS: Silence, boy!

GÖRAN: Don't be impudent, brother!

LARS: Silence!

(ERIK TROLLE *looks cheerful; pats the* KEEPER *on the back, gestures toward* ERIK LEJONHUVUD, *and then goes out with his* GUARDS.)

ERIK LEJONHUVUD (*to the* KEEPER): So then—as the regent has pleased to arrange—free drinks down here in the vaults—yes, a tun of Eimbecker and two of Rostock. (*Pause*)

KEEPER: Only beer! That won't do!

LEJONHUVUD: Won't beer do? Oh yes, it'll flow like a stream . . .

KEEPER: I mean some wine ought to be served, too! Beer has something of a bad reputation since the meeting at Arboga [2] . . .

LEJONHUVUD: Take a little poor Spanish wine then, down here, but at the table up in the large hall it'll have to be claret and Rhenish!

KEEPER: For how many shall I set the table up there?

LEJONHUVUD: We aren't so many as the Stures, but say two hundred . . . And there are to be red-and-white flags on the table; no blue ones.[3] You understand?

KEEPER: I have both kinds . . .

LEJONHUVUD: Smart fellow, keeper! You never know . . . Lord Erik Trolle was elected in January, and now it's July!

KEEPER: Yes, but this is another election . . .

LEJONHUVUD: What's that? Lord Trolle's election was confirmed by king and council.

(KEEPER *moves his mouth but does not dare to speak.*)

LEJONHUVUD: Chew dry, you, and keep your bit in your mouth!

(GÖRAN SPARRE *wants to rush up but is held back by* LARS.)

LEJONHUVUD: I've spoken. So, then—two hundred up there, and hoist the Danish flag.

(KEEPER *moves his mouth.*)

LEJONHUVUD: If you're through chewing, swallow it, and your tongue, too! But don't forget the musicians and the tar barrels! Understand? Now you may answer. (*Gives him a good shaking*)

KEEPER: I understand. But don't shake me, or I'll forget . . .

LEJONHUVUD: Yes, I'll shake you so what's thick will come up; you are thick-headed, but I'll pull out the corks! (*Strikes him across the ear and goes*)

(GÖRAN SPARRE *rushes up. The* KEEPER *prevents him from running after* ERIK LEJONHUVUD.)

KEEPER: Hold it, knight!

GÖRAN: "Tar barrels!" he said. Powder barrels! Under the floor!

LARS: Not so hot! You're very hot-headed, boy.

GÖRAN: Good God, but you're cold. A person could chill wine on you.

LARS (*takes him by the ear*): Come on, sit down.

GÖRAN: Erik Lejonhuvud, our kinsman, a Swedish subject, pro-Danish, Erik Trolle's table setter, King Hans's platelicker [4] . . .

(LARS *makes him sit down at a table toward the front of the stage.*)

GÖRAN: You're pinching me! Quit it! Knights! We're only squires, because regents can't knight anybody—that's why they want kings.[5] Only traitors who become knights! Go to the powder makers and buy a barrel of powder, and I'll light it myself. I'll let North Stream into the vaults here.

LARS (*puts his hand over* GÖRAN's *mouth*): Keeper, bring us some Rhenish wine! Göran, calm down! (*Steps on* GÖRAN's *foot under the table*)

(KEEPER *goes to get the wine.*)

GÖRAN: Why are you stepping on my foot?

LARS: So that you'll watch out.

GÖRAN: For the keeper, who just got a doozer! That fellow isn't dangerous.

LARS: He *is* dangerous! He'll take a kick in his rear for five bits and say thanks, too—he always has two flags to run up; today he'll hoist the three crowns, tomorrow the white cross on the field of red . . .

GÖRAN: Then you can't depend on anyone!

LARS: No, you can't! Well, on one . . .

GÖRAN: Say two, then. Sten Sture is one.

LARS: And you're two, I suppose.

GÖRAN: Heming Gad's three.

LARS: You're not counting me!

GÖRAN: I don't know where I have you!

LARS: You'll see, I suspect! And Gustav Vasa's five.

GÖRAN: Vasa? Vasas and Oxenstjernas have always been pro-Danish foxes! [6]

LARS: Until now, yes. But everything changes, fortunately.

GÖRAN: You go ahead and change, but I'll never change.

LARS: Sh-h!

KEEPER (*comes up with wine*): Is it true, gentlemen, that the election's over?

LARS: No, it's just being held at the monastery of the Gray Friars. (GÖRAN *becomes listless.*)

KEEPER: Will it be Trolle?

LARS: It *is* Trolle; who it *will* be, that's what we don't know.

KEEPER: You never can tell.

GÖRAN: That's what he said—Erik Lejonhuvud the Muttonhead! [7]

(JOHAN NATT-OCH-DAG [8] *enters from the right. Dark and hesitant, he greets* LARS SPARRE *and wants to approach him, but draws back when* LARS *nods coldly to him; he sits down alone at a table to the right. The* KEEPER *stares at him, recognizes him, disregards his signal, and goes to the back.* JOHAN *becomes even more hesitant and makes embarrassed gestures.*)

GÖRAN: Who's that fellow you nodded to?

LARS: Don't you know him?

GÖRAN: No!

LARS: I'll tell you later!

GÖRAN: What an odd-looking fellow!

LARS: He knows it, too, poor devil, but beware of him!

GÖRAN: A spy?

LARS: No-o. I don't think so.

GÖRAN: Looks like a murderer!

LARS: Sh-h! He's to be pitied. The keeper doesn't want to wait on him.

GÖRAN: Who is he?

(NATT-OCH-DAG *taps on the table.*)

GÖRAN: Don't tap on the table!

(NATT-OCH-DAG *stares at* GÖRAN.)

GÖRAN: Yes, it's an old custom, but we have new ones nowadays.

(NATT-OCH-DAG *gets up and goes out to the* KEEPER *to place his order.*)

LARS (*to* GÖRAN): Don't torment the man—he's an unfortunate.

GÖRAN: Who is he, then?

LARS: I don't want to tell you, because you're so cruel.

GÖRAN: Then I'll have to guess.

(NATT-OCH-DAG *comes back discreetly and sits down silently to wait.* LARS *and* GÖRAN *put their heads together and speak inaudibly.*)

GUSTAV VASA (*enters from the back, without noticing* LARS *and* GÖRAN, *who do not notice him;* VASA *goes up to* JOHAN NATT-OCH-DAG's *table, takes hold of a chair, and says*): May I? [9]

NATT-OCH-DAG: You may; my pleasure.

GUSTAV VASA: Excuse me, I thought you were Danish.

NATT-OCH-DAG: I thought the same thing about you.

GUSTAV VASA: About me? Think what the hell you want to, but not that about me! (*They stare at each other.*)

NATT-OCH-DAG: It seems to me I've . . .

GUSTAV VASA: Isn't it . . .

NATT-OCH-DAG: Yes, it is . . .

GÖRAN (*calls*): Gustav!

(NATT-OCH-DAG *extends his hand.* GUSTAV VASA *has involuntarily extended his hand, but jerks it back.*)

GÖRAN: Gustav, come over here!

(GUSTAV VASA *leaves* JOHAN NATT-OCH-DAG, *who collapses in despair.*)

LARS (*to* GUSTAV): What's new? Where did you come from?

GUSTAV VASA: I came from the Gray Friars and the castle—I've heard Heming Gad talk for two hours about the misfortunes of the realm in the last hundred years.

LARS: He can really pour it on; he . . .

GUSTAV VASA: The Kalmar Union was a piece of trickery, because they promised us a Danish king, but we got a German one by the name of Erik of Pomerania [10] . . .

GÖRAN: That devil!

GUSTAV VASA: Then Engelbrekt [11] came along and freed us from the Danes—twice he took the same castles and fortresses, because he let them fool him the first time; and then we became Danes again, and so we have Erik Trolle—that's how far we've come in a hundred years . . .

LARS: It's hopeless, then?

GUSTAV VASA: Hopeless! Take out the cards!

NATT-OCH-DAG (*with uncertainty in his voice*): It's not hopeless!

(*The three to his left stare at* JOHAN NATT-OCH-DAG *but do not speak to him.* MÅNS NILSSON *of Aspeboda and* ANDERS PERSSON [12] *come in from the back with the* KEEPER.)

GUSTAV VASA (*to his companions*): Shall we play?

LARS: Should we play on a day like this?

GUSTAV VASA: Yes, what else can we do? At least we don't have to think about the mess. Let's have the cards, Göran!

GÖRAN (*takes cards from a drawer in the table and they begin to play listlessly*): Are those Dalesmen who just came in?

GUSTAV VASA: I suspect! Come a little too late and ought to have
been more!

KEEPER (*shows the vaults to the* DALESMEN): You've never been here
before, gentlemen? No! Here's a vault called the Grapevine; the
mayor and the council sit there, well, not just now, of course;
and here the Lübeckers sit—we call that the Ivy, and then we
have the Rose, that's St. George's Guild—he sits there himself
with the dragon and everything . . .

MÅNS NILSSON: That was mighty fine! (*Points at the table where
the men are playing cards*) Do those gentlemen live here?

KEEPER: No, not at all.

MÅNS NILSSON: Then why are they sitting here gambling?

KEEPER: Gentlemen do what they please.

GUSTAV VASA: Don't talk so loudly, farmers!

ANDERS PERSSON: I recognize that voice!

GUSTAV VASA: You won't forget it very soon, I promise.

ANDERS PERSSON: Gustav Vasa of Rydboholm.[18]

GUSTAV VASA: Lindholm, Rävsnäs, and so on, and you're Anders
Persson of Rankhyttan and a mineowner; we've drunk and fought
together as students at Uppsala, what's more, eh? Aren't you
going to say hello? Hello, hello! Now that that's done, sit down,
boys, over there.

ANDERS PERSSON: So young! And already—so old . . .

GUSTAV VASA: And sensible. Go and be likewise! We're so wise that
we're looking for the shifts in fortune in the cards instead of in
an uneven struggle.

ANDERS PERSSON: . . . and to conceal the game.

(GUSTAV VASA *stares at him.*)

ANDERS PERSSON: Look at me, and I'll say the word . . . (*Pause*)
With God and St. George.

(*The three players get up;* GUSTAV VASA *throws the cards into
the drawer.*)

GUSTAV VASA: Keep talking!

ANDERS PERSSON: No, here comes the man who can tell us everything.

GUSTAV VASA: Who's he?

ANDERS PERSSON: Herman Israel from Lübeck.

(HERMAN ISRAEL *and* TWO COLLEAGUES *enter from the back. They sit down in the Ivy and examine papers.*)

GUSTAV VASA (*to* ANDERS PERSSON): So I didn't have to be ashamed of the cards . . . Now we'll talk! (*Places himself in the center of the floor*) *Wer da?*

ALL PRESENT: "Three crowns! With God and St. George!"

GUSTAV VASA (*to* NATT-OCH-DAG): Will you, my lord, or whatever I should call you, please go out since the destiny of the realm is to be decided right now?

NATT-OCH-DAG: Why should I? What have I done that people refuse me a drink when I'm thirsty, a place to sit when I'm tired?

ISRAEL: Who is that man?

GÖRAN: His name's Natt-och-Dag, but mostly Natt.[14]

NATT-OCH-DAG: Yes, that's my name. The outlawed son of Måns Natt-och-Dag of Göksholm.

GÖRAN: The murderer of Engelbrekt!

NATT-OCH-DAG: That's right, young man. May God forgive you as he has forgiven my unfortunate father, who lost his mind from remorse and regret, but who afterward served his country when he had gained peace . . .

ISRAEL: Time's passing . . . We have understood with sympathy who you are, and we deplore your fate, but the moment isn't suitable for clearing up private matters . . . We beg you not to awaken discord at a moment like this and that you'll find another place in which to pour out your justified sorrows.

NATT-OCH-DAG: Just one word.

GUSTAV VASA: Go, man! Go!

LARS: What is it? Quickly!

NATT-OCH-DAG: It's Kalmar—

GUSTAV VASA: What do you know about Kalmar? Go, go! We aren't angry with you.

NATT-OCH-DAG: And I won't avenge myself, because I don't dare to; I'm a victim of vengeance. Well, that's how it is. (*Goes out at the back*)

ISRAEL: You know who I am, and we all know each other. At this moment Sten Sture may be elected, since he controls all but a couple of the castles in the realm.

MÅNS NILSSON: Would that please Lübeck?

ISRAEL: Lübeck has always . . .

GUSTAV VASA: Lübeck has never loved Sweden.

ISRAEL: Lübeck has never loved anyone, and is not loved. The free city does not concern itself with love but with commerce.

GUSTAV VASA: But it does go acourting occasionally!

LARS: Gustav, control yourself!

ISRAEL: May I go on? By the way, it isn't the patriotic Sture party that has won this election . . .

GUSTAV VASA: . . . but Lübeck! That's a lie! Let me talk now, who knows the most, though I'm the youngest.

(KEEPER, MONKS, SOLDIERS, BURGHERS *can be seen in the background.*)

GUSTAV VASA: It isn't actually the Sture party which has forced through the election; nor is it Lübeck with its false goods, poor money, and rotten ships; but it's the Lord, the God of Hosts, who has controlled and ordained matters for poor Sweden. (*Noise*) King Hans has become ill; the heir apparent Prince Christian has thrown off his mask and has behaved like a Nebuchadnezzar in Norway so that, at the very moment he dares to sail to Sweden, he'll have the Norwegians at his back.[15] (*They shout.*) Quiet! I'm not done! But Prince Christian, who's courting the sister of Emperor Charles V, has taken a Norwegian mistress in Bergen and made her mother Sigbrit lord high steward in Denmark. This has made the Danes rebel against the heir apparent, and the whole country's working to get a new ruler, Fredrik of Holstein!

All this, which isn't the work of men, brought about the election of Sten Sture as regent half an hour ago. It was to have been a secret until we'd heard . . .

ISRAEL: That the last castles have been taken . . .

GUSTAV VASA: Not the very last, but here's the key to Stockholm Castle. (*Throws a large key onto the table*)
(*Shouts at the back*)

ISRAEL: But Västerås is left, and Kalmar! Above all, Kalmar!

GUSTAV VASA: Right! That pleases you, Lübeckers; at least it doesn't make you unhappy!

ISRAEL: Right! (*Pause. Ironically*) Perhaps one of you gentlemen has the key to Västerås Castle?

MÅNS NILSSON: Yes, if it's a matter of showing off . . .

ANDERS PERSSON: A person surely doesn't have it in his pocket, surely . . .

ISRAEL: No, I shouldn't think so.

MÅNS NILSSON: Do you have it in your bag, Anders?

ANDERS PERSSON: You must have it yourself, Måns!

MÅNS NILSSON: By my life and knife, if I don't . . . Yes, gentlemen, here's the key to Västerås! Now you can go on the Brunn Brook ferry to Long Heath; then you won't have far to Stora Tuna, where the Dalesmen live.[16] Do you know them?

GUSTAV VASA: We know them. (*To the people*) Cheer them! Hail them!

ALL: Hail, Dalesmen!

HERALD: The mayor and the councillors of the city of Stockholm.

(*The* MAYOR *and the* COUNCILLORS *enter and go into the Grapevine.*)

MAYOR: Bishop Heming Gad, that noble old man, has asked us to announce his impending arrival at the Town Hall. Next to God and the commons of Sweden, we have him to thank for a happy end to a peaceful struggle. And the only reward he asks for himself is that he may announce that Sten Sture has been elected regent of Sweden!

(*Solemn silence; all look toward the back.*)

August Strindberg. By R. Borgh

Anders de Wahl as Sten Sture

MAYOR (*to* HERMAN ISRAEL): The bishop is tired—eighty years tell.
He has spoken for six hours as he alone can!

(ISRAEL *speaks inaudibly.*)

MAYOR: Twenty years in Rome—papal chamberlain and statistician
—a soldier besides! Isn't that right, Squire Vasa?

GUSTAV VASA: Bishop Heming Gad once took both Kalmar's castle
and Stockholm's by *arte propugnatoria.*[17]

MAYOR: Yes, yes, a mighty man—sh-h—he's coming! (*Silence*)

HERALD: The royal councillor, Bishop Heming Gad. (*Pause*)

HEMING GAD (*at the back, escorted by two* PAGES, *whom he leaves
at the door. He is tired and feeble at first, but his spirits gradually
rise*): My dear children—I say children because I am so old; I do
not see you, for the light of my eyes is going out; but I perceive
you with my heart, and I can hear you breathe, I feel your
warmth as a sunny spring day . . . (*Is overcome by his tears; the
rest are moved.*) No, I can't go on . . . (*A chair is carried forward;
he sits down. Controls himself*) We have followed faithless shepherds for a hundred years, and the latest one was false and led us
astray. Therefore sayeth the Lord: "Awake, O sword, against my
shepherd, and against the man that is my fellow . . . smite the
shepherd, and the sheep shall be scattered: I will turn mine hand
to the little ones." [18]

Recently we anointed a conqueror, "but the Lord said unto
Samuel" (it was about Elias), "Look not on his countenance . . .
because I have refused him . . . for man looketh on the outward
appearance, but the Lord looketh on the heart." [19] And then he
came to the last, the smallest, the youngest one. And he was fair,
had beautiful eyes, and was goodly to look at. "And the Lord
said: Arise, anoint him: for this is he!"

(STEN STURE *has appeared at the back; now he steps forward.*)

ALL (*shout*): This *is* he!

MAYOR: Sten Sture, the regent! Hail! Hail!

ALL: Sten Sture. Hail! Hail!

(*Trumpets, drums, ringing of bells.* HEMING GAD *does not see*
STURE, *so he stands amazed, staring with sightless eyes.*)

STEN STURE (*goes to the* BISHOP, *kneels, places the* BISHOP's *hand on his own head*): Bless me, father, as you were a blessing for *my* father, for my country, and for my people.

HEMING GAD:

Blessed is every one that feareth the Lord. . . .
Thy wife shall be as a fruitful vine
by the sides of thine house:
Thy children like olive plants
round about thy table.
Behold, that thus shall the man be blessed
that feareth the Lord.
The Lord shall bless thee out of Zion! [20]

(*Music outside. All go up and shake* STEN STURE's *hand. He says an inaudible word to each of them. The music ends.*)

HERALD: Councillor Erik Trolle requests an audience.

STEN STURE: Erik Trolle?—Wait!

HEMING GAD: Don't let him in!

STEN STURE: You should be kind to your adversary, bishop, and, when a defeated enemy asks to shake your hand, you should give it to him!

HEMING GAD: Then he'll bite it!

STEN STURE: He's my kinsman.

HEMING GAD: Your Danish kinsman!

STEN STURE: Admission of defeat is noble.

HEMING GAD: Or arrogant; he ought to be put in prison.

STEN STURE: He has done no wrong.

HEMING GAD: Trolles are always doing wrong.

STEN STURE: Don't be bitter in this hour, old friend; instead be a little curious, as I am, because I very much want to know what Erik Trolle can want on a day like this.

HEMING GAD: Let's see him, then.

STEN STURE (*to the* HERALD): Let Lord Erik enter! (*Pause*)

ERIK TROLLE (*enters, looks about as if he were counting and examining the gathering; then he speaks to* STURE): As a Swedish sub-

ject, a former member of the national council, and until just now
the regent, I come only to render homage to my successor and to
confirm the validity of the election. When I say that Sture is the
good name of very good people, I say it with the profoundest sin-
cerity, and the one who bears the hated name of Trolle has nothing to gain thereby, and I least of all, who most undeservedly was
advanced, merely because I was not a Sture. Lord Sten, I congratulate you, and I congratulate the country in Lord Sten, our
best man.

STEN STURE (*touched*): Lord Erik Trolle, kinsman, may I believe
that the ancient feuds between our clans are over? May. I place
my hand in yours and say: friend?

ERIK TROLLE: With God and St. George! I'm a man of peace, Lord
Sten, and I've never sought high positions; the days of my life are
almost over, and this is my farewell. I entered unarmed; I place
my head in my enemy's lap (*falls to his knee*)—without seeing
one friend to support me in this room; take me up among your
men, let me and mine be guests at the banquet I ordered before
you dared hope to be host; we want to rejoice with you, and seal
our new friendship, which has only one goal: the welfare and the
honor of our country!

STEN STURE: Rise, Lord Erik. The first request I grant is yours; you
shall all be welcome at the banquet when you are so noble that
you can celebrate a defeat which benefits the fatherland.

ERIK TROLLE: Your word?

STEN STURE: My word! Done! (*They embrace each other.*) But,
Lord Erik, I'd rather have had you ask for something other than
a valueless gift, which is not a gift . . .

ERIK TROLLE: I ask nothing of this turbulent life but the peace of old
age. Can you give me that?

STEN STURE: Perhaps! You have a son, Lord Gustav . . .

(HEMING GAD *becomes uneasy; twists and turns.*)

STEN STURE: If he wants to place his great gifts in our and the nation's service, he shall have me as an advocate.

ERIK TROLLE: I'm not my son's advocate—(*pause*) because Gustav and I are not friends.

STEN STURE: Then you should be, and I'll be the mediator; we must all become friends, and Lord Gustav Trolle shall be my man, if he will or not!

ERIK TROLLE: All *he* wants now is to be archdeacon . . .

STEN STURE: He has my recommendation even if it were to succeed Jakob Ulvsson as archbishop.[21]

(HEMING GAD *clears his throat loudly.*)

STEN STURE: Enough of words! The ladies are coming. In a little while we'll meet again at the banquet upstairs.

HEMING GAD: . . . which Lord Erik Trolle ordered.

(*Kettledrums are sounded. All groups break up, and they prepare to go out, but at a sign from* STURE *these remain:* HEMING GAD, LARS *and* GÖRAN SPARRE, *and* GUSTAV VASA.)

HEMING GAD (*to* STURE): Gustav Trolle?

STEN STURE: My enemy who shall become my friend.

HEMING GAD: *Gustav* Trolle!

STEN STURE: Don't be unkind today, Father Heming! Don't you think that Lord Erik Trolle was sincere, either?

HEMING GAD: Half-sincere; everything about him is half-and-half; half-Danish and half-Swedish, half true, and half false . . .

STEN STURE: Hush, old friend. You may think things like that, but you musn't say them. Believe good of God and men, and they'll be good—to you.

HEMING GAD: May be, may be! But, Lord Sten, write nothing either on paper or parchment to anyone whose name is Trolle. I've known father and son and grandfather and uncle.

STEN STURE: My spoken word's as good as my written one! Here come the ladies! The sun's rising; come and cheer me up, Kristina darling; everything became so cold in here; come quickly.

(KRISTINA STURE *and* ANNA BIELKE *come in from the left, accompanied by* PAGES.)

KRISTINA (*hurries into* STURE's *arms*): Sten! my dear; now every-

thing's right! May time stand still and life, too, but no more part-
ings, never to be away from each other. Where have you been?
What have you been doing?

STEN STURE: You ask; I ask: Is my linden playing? Is my nightingale singing? Is my little son crying?

KRISTINA: Your son isn't crying at all, and now you're to be happy.

STEN STURE: Yes! Go and kiss the old man first; he's the one who
has worked the hardest.

KRISTINA: No, you have—and I! But I'll thank the bishop, even if
he doesn't like me . . .

HEMING GAD: As a priest I may not like women—oh, a little, of
course! I was in Rome too long . . . and saw too much [22] . . .

KRISTINA (*kisses* HEMING GAD's *hand rather coldly*): But one may
kiss a bishop's hand.

STEN STURE (*embraces* ANNA BIELKE): Anna, just as beautiful, just as
sad as always. Is life that hard?

ANNA BIELKE: It isn't easy, Sten, and joy makes it more difficult.

(JOHAN NATT-OCH-DAG *comes in without being noticed and sits
down at the same table as before.*)

(LARS *and* GÖRAN SPARRE *and* GUSTAV VASA *greet the ladies in
turn and proper form.*)

(LARS, GÖRAN, *and* GUSTAV *go up to* JOHAN NATT-OCH-DAG *and try
to persuade him to leave.*)

STEN STURE (*notices them*): Who is that? What are you doing?
(*Goes up to them*) It's Johan, Natt-och-Dag. Don't be cruel,
Göran.

NATT-OCH-DAG (*rises*): It's I . . .

STEN STURE: Unfortunate friend, why are you here? And at this moment! I'm not insensible to your difficulties, but when you can't
enter your country's service . . .

NATT-OCH-DAG: Why not?

STEN STURE: Will you force me to answer? I can't but you know
why yourself.

NATT-OCH-DAG: Because no one will serve with me any longer, even though I've done no wrong.

STEN STURE: That's right. But can I change it? Go into foreign service, abroad, win honor for yourself, and come back ... Can I help you? Do you need anything? Why are you here?

NATT-OCH-DAG: I need nothing, but I lack everything; I came here, driven out of every inn in the city, to sun myself in your happiness, to get a drink, which no one gives me, a meal, which is denied me. I should be somewhere; I'll go, but I don't know where ... Yes, now I know!

ANNA BIELKE (*comes up*): Let me speak with Johan; he's my kinsman and my friend from childhood—though he's older than I— you go along and talk—time drags when you wait for pleasure. Dear friends, go.

(STEN *and* KRISTINA STURE *go into the Rose;* GUSTAV VASA *goes over to* HEMING GAD; LARS *and* GÖRAN *to the table on the left.*)

ANNA BIELKE (*to* JOHAN NATT-OCH-DAG): You're a child of sorrow, born innocent but guilty, with blood guilt, you as well as I. Yes, I! My grandfather Ture Turesson was sentenced to lose his life, honor, and property, because he carried on treasonable correspondence with the Danes; he fled, but returned with Christian I, bore weapons against his country in such a way that they called him the butcher of the commoners.[23] At the battle of Brunkeberg, he joined the Danes against Sten Sture. It wasn't fun to be a Bielke when I was a child. That's why I've never really been a child—you remember that.

NATT-OCH-DAG: Anna Bielke.

ANNA BIELKE: I've borne this, but I'm not bitter, and you can see that I have friends. Why can't you bear your fate? ...

NATT-OCH-DAG: Anna Bielke ... you have such a beautiful name that I have to say it, and, when it crosses my lips, it's like a rose.

ANNA BIELKE: You musn't talk like that; I can't bear it. I know you have other things to say. Where have you been? Why are you so poorly dressed? You're rich.

NATT-OCH-DAG: Really?

(*They continue talking softly.*)

(STEN STURE *and* KRISTINA *in the Rose*)

STEN STURE: Here lie the keys to Stockholm and Västerås, but Kalmar's isn't there.

KRISTINA: Is Kalmar so important?

(NATT-OCH-DAG *becomes attentive every time Kalmar is mentioned.*)

STEN STURE: Kalmar's the gateway to the land north of the forests. If I had that, I'd give half . . .

KRISTINA: You mustn't give away what you don't have.

HEMING GAD (*to* GUSTAV VASA): Believe me, this isn't over; there's a lot left. Prince Christian is a devil from hell, and now he's the brother-in-law of the emperor; the emperor is the friend of the pope—at times. You who are young will see a lot; it's no art to prophesy when one's eighty, because everything's alike, repeats itself, and the same cause has almost the same effect. If those of us here could see our future . . . You, Gustav, are gifted, and you're realistic about the evil in people. Sten's too soft-hearted and believes they're better than they are; that's why he's always deceived. You're too frank, on the other hand, and impatient, too. You should be something of a fox, Gustav, a fox!

GUSTAV VASA: A wolf, rather, but not a fox. I can't!

(LARS *and* GÖRAN SPARRE *are standing beside them.*)

HEMING GAD: Lars Sparre is good, firm of body, a bit slow but persevering; Göran, well, there's powder in that fellow, but, if it gets wet, it'll only fizzle; yes, you'll see a lot, you men, and I don't feel happy when I think about the future. Prince Christian ruled like a Satan in Norway . . . he's crazy at times, you know, absolutely insane . . . (*They continue the conversation softly.*)

ANNA BIELKE (*to* JOHAN NATT-OCH-DAG): Can't you tell me your secret?

NATT-OCH-DAG: Life has frightened me, people still more so, they're cowardly and cruel—you're the only one, Anna.

ANNA BIELKE: Don't say that. Are you so hungry that you can't talk coherently? . . .

NATT-OCH-DAG: Yes, that, too—no one wants to give me any food, and I have no money left.

ANNA BIELKE: But you were rich!

NATT-OCH-DAG: I was . . .

ANNA BIELKE: So that's your secret. (*They continue talking softly.*)

STEN STURE (*to* KRISTINA): What are Anna and he talking about? Do you think maybe . . .

KRISTINA: I don't know. They've always been friends.

STEN STURE: Poor Johan . . . he's a handsome man, but he looks lost, and he's a little crazy, I think . . .

KRISTINA: Poor Johan! Poor souls who have to suffer innocently!

STEN STURE: Anna should get married and have children; then she'd be happy . . . They say that Gustav . . .

KRISTINA: Not that! Anna can't stand him because he jokes so much.

HEMING GAD (*to the three men*): Believe me, young men, that fellow Gustav Trolle who has studied in Rome is an ugly fish . . . You'll have to scale 'im if you can. Now they could announce dinner.

NATT-OCH-DAG (*to* ANNA): You alone, Anna, may hear this. Come closer. (*Pause*)

ANNA BIELKE: Quickly, they'll announce dinner soon, I heard them say.

NATT-OCH-DAG: When I saw that I was in no position to re-enter the service of my country, I wanted to restore my family name by means of a praiseworthy deed. Like the wealthy young man, I went away and sold everything I possessed, land and goods. I went to Lübeck, bought a ship, powder, and lead and guns, recruited marksmen—then I sailed to Kalmar, for I had sworn I would take Kalmar or die.[24] When I got there, they took the gift, but they didn't want the giver. Because of the soldiers, they were afraid of my name, my damned name!

ANNA BIELKE (*rises and kisses* JOHAN NATT-OCH-DAG *on the forehead*):

This you have done and get rewarded like this . . . sit like a beggar by the door, and no one asks you to step forward . . . They
took the gift but drove the giver away. Cruel people! I must tell
Sten . . .

NATT-OCH-DAG: No, for heaven's sake, no! Then they'll be angry
with me for they'll have to invite me, and Sture mayn't associate
with a Natt-och-Dag. Anna, I'll leave . . . and besides, I don't
know if the siege has succeeded, but they can get here with word
at any time . . .

ANNA BIELKE (goes up to STURE): Sten, they've got help for the siege
of Kalmar.

STEN STURE (gets up): Oh, lord!

HEMING GAD: What are you saying? Has the Kalmar army been
relieved? How much does it amount to?

ANNA BIELKE: A whole shipload from Lübeck . . .

HEMING GAD: Lübeck! Ask Herman Israel to come in. He's out there
pretending to listen to the music . . .

    (GÖRAN hurries out.)

HEMING GAD: Forgive me, Sten Sture, but I know Kalmar . . . A
whole shipload! Then Kalmar has fallen and is ours right now,
because the last message said that the garrison was almost de-
pleted from hunger and sickness.

    (ANNA BIELKE tries in vain to get a word in.)

STEN STURE: Then we must go to the Great Church to celebrate
Te Deum! For now Sweden is ours.

ISRAEL (enters, followed by GÖRAN SPARRE): Your Grace has summoned me.

STEN STURE: Yes! Is it true that a ship from Lübeck has relieved the
besieging army at Kalmar?

ISRAEL: A large caravel with German soldiers and marksmen left
Lübeck long ago, and I assume Kalmar has already fallen.

STEN STURE (comes up to ISRAEL and embraces him): And this
Lübeck has done—to tell the truth, unexpectedly—but I'll not be
ungrateful.

HEMING GAD: I would never have believed that Lübeck would help us again.

ISRAEL: One can confuse friend and enemy sometimes.

ANNA BIELKE (*to* HERMAN ISRAEL): May we regard this as a friendly gift from Lübeck?

ISRAEL (*ambiguously*): Lübeck has had such long and advantageous relations with this country . . .

ANNA BIELKE: . . . that . . .

ISRAEL: . . . assume that it's a gift or not a gift, a gift that awaits a gift in return . . .

ANNA BIELKE: Do you call payment a gift in return?

ISRAEL: Well, from a certain point of view payment can be considered a gift in return . . .

ANNA BIELKE: Shame! You speak like a serpent, Herman Israel, with a flapping tongue and with poison at the root of it. But this is how we speak our language. Sten, listen! Listen to me. The Lübeck caravel with soldiers and marksmen was bought with resounding Hungarian coins by Johan Natt-och-Dag, who wanted thereby to restore the good name of his family and his clan.

STEN STURE: Is this true, Johan?

(JOHAN NATT-OCH-DAG *looks down.*)

ANNA BIELKE: And it's also true that they drove away the giver, who had sacrificed everything he had.

STEN STURE: Well! At the moment the confirmation of the fall of Kalmar arrives, Johan Natt-och-Dag is commander of the castle. Herman Israel himself will have to discover an honorable way out.

HEMING GAD: If there's still such faith in and love for our poor country, then I want to live for many years yet! (*Rises; goes up to* JOHAN NATT-OCH-DAG) May I look at you? Natt-och-Dag, your day has begun and your night is over. (*Looks into his eyes*) Poor fellow, life has had little happiness to give you . . . you've been ostracized, you as I, but you are blameless. Let that comfort you.

NATT-OCH-DAG (*speaks with difficulty*): . . . I am not . . . blameless, not completely . . .

HEMING GAD: He's suffering from sickly thoughts . . .

ANNA BIELKE: He thinks he has killed a man . . .

(*The trumpet sounds for the banquet to start.*)

LEJONHUVUD (*comes in at the back*): The banquet begins.

HEMING GAD: Is *that* the table setter?

GUSTAV VASA: He's certainly Erik Lejonhuvud, but he ordered the banquet for Erik Trolle.

HEMING GAD: And I'm to sit at the same table with that person?

STEN STURE: Peace, Father Heming, and the word after that is reconciliation!

(*All prepare to go up;* JOHAN NATT-OCH-DAG *stands at a loss.*)

STEN STURE: Anna Bielke. Place Johan at my right. He's my guest! Mine!

LEJONHUVUD: Excuse me, I bring another message. King Hans is dead.

HEMING GAD: King Hans in Denmark. I'm not weeping.

STEN STURE: But he was a good man.

HEMING GAD: So-so. Well, now King Christian starts. And Gustav Trolle!

STEN STURE: Now the banquet starts.

HEMING GAD: Erik Trolle's!

STEN STURE: Peace! Peace!

HEMING GAD: Strife! . . . Strife!

CURTAIN

ACT II

SCENE 1

A room in Stockholm Castle. At the back is a door to the balcony where treetops can be seen. To the right and left are large open arcades without doors.

JOHAN NATT-OCH-DAG *and* ANNA BIELKE *are standing on the balcony.* ERIK LEJONHUVUD *is in the middle of the room spying and listening.*

MÄTTA STURE (*Svante Sture's widow,* STEN STURE'S *stepmother, comes in from the left*): Erik Lejonhuvud! What are you doing here?

LEJONHUVUD: I'm a courtier, gracious lady . . .

MÄTTA STURE: May we close the doors?

LEJONHUVUD: There aren't any doors, my lady. Here everything's open.

MÄTTA STURE: As in an inn. When I was the chatelaine here for my noble husband the late Lord Svante Sture,[25] it was different, and I was something other than widow—and stepmother. Aren't there any doors?

LEJONHUVUD: No, but that's why we may speak frankly, since no one listens, and people can say anything they please, because no one believes it. People go out and in . . .

MÄTTA STURE: Is Sten crazy?

LEJONHUVUD: Not at all! Lord Sten's an angel, and so is his lady . . .

MÄTTA STURE: What *is* he?

LEJONHUVUD: A child, if you will, two children who know no evil; they walk in the midst of evil and deceit, and understand nothing.

MÄTTA STURE: You seem to me to have changed your likes and inclinations, Erik.

LEJONHUVUD: Yes, a person becomes a better man when he's among pure-minded people . . .

MÄTTA STURE: . . . but your nature remains the same, like the roots of weeds . . . As my stepson Lord Sten was beyond reproach, so I'm not complaining; but now everything's changed . . .

LEJONHUVUD: Well, everything *has* changed since Lord Svante died.

MÄTTA STURE: I can't talk with you—you're distant . . . Who are standing on the balcony?

LEJONHUVUD: Johan Natt-och-Dag and Anna Bielke.

MÄTTA STURE: Engelbrekt's Natt-och-Dag! Sten made his first and biggest stupid blunder when he had that fellow sit down at the banquet table in Stockholm's Town Hall—why, he's a fool who makes up songs—and he's to have charge of Kalmar Castle . . .

LEJONHUVUD: He has defended castles before this . . .

MÄTTA STURE: Göksholm,[26] yes. And Anna Bielke's going with him. She's too good for that . . .

LEJONHUVUD: She doesn't think so.

MÄTTA STURE: What are they trying to see out there?

LEJONHUVUD: Like all the rest of us, they're waiting to catch sight of the pennants of Gustav Trolle's ship . . .

MÄTTA STURE: The new archbishop's?[27]

LEJONHUVUD: Yes, Lord Sten recommended his election, and now he has invited him here; the whole apartment in the Green Walk is ready . . .

MÄTTA STURE: Sten! Sten Sture! What have you done?

LEJONHUVUD: Lord Sten has promised himself that Gustav Trolle's going to be his friend!

MÄTTA STURE: What have you done, Sten? (Pause) Gustav Trolle!

LEJONHUVUD: Conquer evil with good, says Lord Sten.

MÄTTA STURE: He? Yes! But what do you say?

LEJONHUVUD: I'll wait to see the outcome.

MÄTTA STURE: That's the first sensible word I've heard in Stockholm Castle since Lord Svante died. Now I'll go to my rooms and wait for the outcome. (Goes to the right)

(ANNA BIELKE and JOHAN NATT-OCH-DAG enter.)

NATT-OCH-DAG (childishly): Coming, not coming, coming, not coming.

ANNA BIELKE: Are you counting your buttons, Johan?

NATT-OCH-DAG: Yes. He's not coming! Anna Bielke.

ANNA BIELKE: What do you think, Erik? Isn't Trolle coming?

LEJONHUVUD: You never can tell.

ANNA BIELKE: That's your motto.

LEJONHUVUD: And this, too: A person never knows where he'll end up.

NATT-OCH-DAG: Anna Bielke.

ANNA BIELKE: Won't you know my name soon, Johan?

NATT-OCH-DAG: No, never! Your name is so beautiful that it *can* never be learned, and never forgotten, either; it says who you are, and it sings your praises, it utters a prayer and a plea, it is as soft as wool, and it caresses the cheek when it passes by, Anna Bielke!

ANNA BIELKE: Sh-h-h! You may not say anything like that; you mustn't. Erik, isn't the archbishop coming? You never can tell, you said, of course. Who was in here just now?

LEJONHUVUD: The stepmother.

ANNA BIELKE: How unkind you are, Erik! You only go about stirring up people and mixing poison . . .

LEJONHUVUD: No one speaks of poison in Mätta Sture's house.[28]

ANNA BIELKE: Shame! Come, Johan; we won't listen to him.

NATT-OCH-DAG: I didn't hear what Erik said.

ANNA BIELKE: You never hear any evil; your ear isn't made for it. Come, Johan, we'll leave him . . . There's Kristina!

KRISTINA STURE (*enters from the left*): Anna! I was looking for you; you're to help me take my birds out of the Green Walk. The archbishop doesn't like birds and flowers—he can't help that —but we must be polite to a guest, and to such a guest!

LEJONHUVUD: Such a guest!

KRISTINA: Yes, such an honored guest . . . who comes from his journey to Rome and is tired; he has to sleep, and the birds wake him too early . . . Come, Anna!

ANNA BIELKE: Do you think he'll come?

KRISTINA: Of course he'll come when he's invited . . .

ANNA BIELKE: Come along, Johan; you may carry the bird cages.

NATT-OCH-DAG: Anything you wish, darling!

(*They go out to the right.* ERIK LEJONHUVUD *shakes his head and then, in deep thought, goes out to the right.*)

(*The stage stands empty for a moment; then* GUSTAV VASA *comes in from the right, violently.*)

GUSTAV VASA: Is the regent here? (*Goes to the balcony door*) Is the regent here? (*To the left door*) Is the regent here? (*Goes, impatient, out through the door at the right*)

(*The stage stands empty for a moment; then* STEN STURE *comes in from the left, violently.*)

STEN STURE: Is Bishop Heming here? (*Pause*) Bishop Heming? (*Pause*)

HEMING GAD (*enters, fit and lively, from the left*): Why, I'm running after you!

STEN STURE: What is this?

HEMING GAD: This is the result of a sufficient cause: your naïveté. How could you make Trolle archbishop?

STEN STURE (*firmly*): I gave my word to his father.

HEMING GAD: To make him archdeacon, but not archbishop.

STEN STURE: You heard what I unfortunately added—that was conditional, though: when Jakob Ulvsson retires.[29] You see, I didn't believe that he'd resign so soon. But since it's done, it's done.

HEMING GAD: You'll keep your word?

STEN STURE: Keep! And since Trolle's the most learned and worthiest candidate, he's the obvious choice; nepotism and favoritism may not control my administration.

HEMING GAD: And you've invited him here! Your enemy!

STEN STURE: I'm no one's enemy . . .

HEMING GAD: But all are yours! You want to talk with him; he never talks; he only hears, listens, steals every word and converts it into a promise, which he'll force you to keep later . . .

STEN STURE: Keep your evil thoughts to yourself; they're yours, not his . . .

HEMING GAD: Fortunately, he won't come.

STEN STURE: But he's invited.

HEMING GAD: He's invited! Has he answered and said thank you?

STEN STURE: No, he hasn't had time.

HEMING GAD: The Dane!

STEN STURE: The Dane's a human being even as you and I!

HEMING GAD: No, the Danes are "sworn enemies of the state, the church, and humanity; the descendants of robbers, thieves, and criminals who seek the ruin of every other people, and for that reason are rightly hated and despised by the whole world." [30]

STEN STURE (*smiles*): It's amusing to listen to you, Father Heming, and people do laugh a little at you behind your back.

HEMING GAD: But not to my face, as they do to you! Then there's this. Why have you taken Lady Mätta into your house?

STEN STURE: My father's widow, my own stepmother, who brought me up . . .

HEMING GAD: And who corresponds with Denmark! Now, Sten, our ways part; the devil himself can't live in an insane asylum which hasn't any strait jackets and handcuffs!

STEN STURE: Let's part for a while; we'll meet again when need knocks on the door, because you, Heming Gad, won't desert your country even if you don't love Sture.

HEMING GAD: Are you sure?

STEN STURE: Sure!

HEMING GAD: Thank you! You know me—I hear! Take your young squires and let this old man rest; govern by means of sportsmanship and persuasion, and you won't govern long . . .

STEN STURE: Stern rulers don't govern long, I've been told . . .

(HEMING GAD *speculates on an answer.*)

STEN STURE: But don't be against me, Father Heming, and—we'll meet again.

HEMING GAD (*goes toward the left door*): Not in a hurry.

STEN STURE: Oh, yes.

HEMING GAD: What irritates me most is that . . . that you can't get angry! And that . . . that one can't get angry with you! (*Goes*)

(STEN STURE, *alone for a moment, sits down at the table in the center of the stage.*)

(GUSTAV VASA *enters from the right.*)

STEN STURE: Now it's we! Sit down, Gustav.

GUSTAV VASA: Has the old man left?

STEN STURE: He has run off, in anger, as usual. Is Trolle in sight?

GUSTAV VASA: He isn't coming.

STEN STURE: How do you know?

GUSTAV VASA: Spies.

STEN STURE: What do they say?

GUSTAV VASA: He has passed Vaxholm, landed, and gone directly to Stäke.[31]

STEN STURE (*rises; paces the floor*): Sit down, Gustav.

GUSTAV VASA: Now you have set the devil loose!

STEN STURE (*calmly*): No, I have him in bonds.

GUSTAV VASA: He has had Stäke fortified.

STEN STURE: But I had it confiscated for the crown just before that.

GUSTAV VASA: Then he's a traitor at once. To think that you had that much foresight.

STEN STURE: I always think before I act.

GUSTAV VASA: He'll tear that bond.

STEN STURE: That's why I've yet another. You see, I made it a condition with Pope Julius that the new archbishop should swear allegiance to the regent.

GUSTAV VASA: That'll hold.

STEN STURE: He's not coming. How discourteous . . . think of it! And Kristina, who has gone to so much trouble! (*Pause*) People are strange.

GUSTAV VASA: Then we'll take Stäke, eh?

STEN STURE: We're going to speak with him first, and speak courteously. You're to go to Trolle.

GUSTAV VASA: I? Talk! No, I'll hit him!

STEN STURE: But talk first.

GUSTAV VASA: Write.

STEN STURE: I don't like what's written. You're going now. What are you going to say? That Stäke belongs to the crown. He can grasp the rest himself.

GUSTAV VASA (*gets up*): That *is* your command!

STEN STURE: When a decision's reached, it's to be executed.

HEMING GAD (*in the left doorway*): That wasn't badly managed.

Without pen and paper on the table . . . To think that Sture is that sly!

STEN STURE: Are you standing there listening?

HEMING GAD: Where there are no doors, one doesn't listen. Imagine: little Sture could tie up the big Trolle's tail! Keep on as you've started. Now I'm calm, and am not needed. (*He nods and leaves.*)

LEJONHUVUD (*comes in from the right with a letter*): Here's a letter.
   (STEN STURE *takes the letter.*)

GUSTAV VASA: From Trolle.

STEN STURE (*reads*): From his chancellor. He already has a chancellor! (*Reads*) But this is shameless. Not a word by way of excuse! He reminds me about the ransom of *pallium,* that is . . . his symbol of authority, which is very expensive, and which . . . for the sake of the honor of the country must be paid in gold, immediately.[32]

GUSTAV VASA: Do you intend to?

STEN STURE: I'm not forced to, but I must . . . because I want to win his heart. That hard man.

GUSTAV VASA: He says that the heart lies in the stomach.

STEN STURE: But you're to tell him . . . that I'll pay—that should crush him.

GUSTAV VASA: Yes, hm. I don't believe that, but all the same.

LEJONHUVUD: There's an oral message, too.

STEN STURE: Is it reliable?

LEJONHUVUD: One never knows.

GUSTAV VASA: By my soul, you're right about that . . .

STEN STURE: Tell us.

LEJONHUVUD: On his trip up here, Trolle stopped in Denmark to visit King Christian.[33]

STEN STURE: That's so ugly I don't believe it!

GUSTAV VASA: And you intend to pay for him?

STEN STURE: Yes! But I'll have to go to Herman Israel to borrow the money.

GUSTAV VASA: Has Johan Natt-och-Dag been put in command of Kalmar Castle?

STEN STURE: Yes, he has.

GUSTAV VASA: Is he the man to defend a castle?

STEN STURE: Yes, just he! There's no trick to it if the man's loyal, and besides he's a soldier, though he's not at ease with people or in a tavern. He was twelve years old when he defended Göksholm Castle.

(KRISTINA STURE, ANNA BIELKE, *and* JOHAN NATT-OCH-DAG *come in from the right.*)

STEN STURE (*going up to* KRISTINA): Dear, he isn't coming.

KRISTINA: He isn't coming, and we've got ready for him . . .

STEN STURE: He wasn't able to—but now, Johan, you're going to leave, and take Anna with you!

KRISTINA: Right away?

STEN STURE: This evening! King Christian's getting active; Trolle's unruly; a papal legate has arrived and is spinning his webs; the Lübeckers are beginning to pack up. We're in for trouble! Every man to his post!

(NATT-OCH-DAG *wants to speak.*)

STEN STURE: Is there anything to hinder you?

NATT-OCH-DAG: Anna Bielke has to know who I am before she accepts my hand.

STEN STURE: She knows that you're a brave man . . .

NATT-OCH-DAG: It's Jeppe Bagge.[34]

STEN STURE: Hush! And control yourself. Come into our apartment so that we may say good-bye, my friends. Kristina, bring Anna; and Johan, you come with me. Good-bye, Gustav. Erik, stay here and look after the house.

KRISTINA: To think that he didn't come!

STEN STURE: Yes, they're unkind to us, dear, but we must bear it.

(*They go.* GUSTAV VASA *and* ERIK LEJONHUVUD *stay. The stage has become darker.*)

GUSTAV VASA (*to* ERIK LEJONHUVUD): You've come here like Saul among the prophets.

LEJONHUVUD: Yes, one has to be somewhere, and, when a person like me has been sent back and forth from right to left and back again, one doesn't know on what foot one should stand.

GUSTAV VASA: Well, my forefathers were always pro-Danish, but I'm Swedish! A person has to take a stand; otherwise, everything gets unreliable and false.

LEJONHUVUD: Yes, false! The two Stures are walking about here like children in the midst of falseness, understanding nothing. They're too good for this world. Are you going out to see Trolle?

GUSTAV VASA: I wish he had sent Heming Gad instead.

LEJONHUVUD: Yes, Gad. Who is that man?

GUSTAV VASA: He's thoroughly honest . . .

LEJONHUVUD: But it seems to me he isn't properly serious.

GUSTAV VASA: That's his manner; he conceals his plans under his mockery . . .

LEJONHUVUD: It seems to me he's always hiding something . . . Do you see who's walking out there?

GUSTAV VASA: Lady Mätta, Sten's stepmother. Is she walking in her sleep?

LEJONHUVUD: No one knows. But she's so hated for everything she's done that she doesn't dare to show herself in the daytime—that's why she walks at night.

GUSTAV VASA: She looks as if she were asleep.

LEJONHUVUD: Perhaps she is, or she may be sick . . . It looks as if she were hunting for treasures or testaments in the walls. See, she's coming . . . stand still; she neither sees nor hears.

(MÄTTA STURE *enters without noticing the two men; first she walks back and forth; then she begins to search for cabinets in the walls.*)

GUSTAV VASA: Is she still corresponding with the Danes?

LEJONHUVUD: Well, she's a Dane . . .

GUSTAV VASA: And Svante Sture lived with her.

LEJONHUVUD: That's why he died, too!

GUSTAV VASA: Sh-h!

LEJONHUVUD: See, she's going out on the balcony . . . She must be walking in her sleep.

GUSTAV VASA: Sten should see her now . . .

LEJONHUVUD: What good would that do? He wouldn't believe anything bad anyway.

GUSTAV VASA: But the guards might shoot at her!

LEJONHUVUD: That'd be fine!

GUSTAV VASA: No, now I'm going to leave you! Why, you talk as if you were depraved . . .

LEJONHUVUD: Now she's starting to wander . . . See!

(MÄTTA STURE *enters, walks irresolutely back and forth.* GUSTAV VASA *and* LEJONHUVUD *withdraw to the right.*)

GUSTAV VASA: God save us all! Good night, Erik.

LEJONHUVUD: Good night, Gustav. Look! Look at her!

CURTAIN FALLS SLOWLY

SCENE 2

The Lübeck office. A large table on a dais under a canopy; on the table are an assay balance and a box.

HERMAN ISRAEL, CORD KÖNIG, NIKLAS BREMS *at the table standing behind the chairs. A* CLERK *is at the door.*

NIKLAS BREMS (*chairman, at the end of the table*): Are the doors guarded?

CLERK: Yes, they are.

(BREMS *strikes the table with his gavel; they sit down.*)

ISRAEL: When the burgomaster of Lübeck has honored our office with his special presence, we beg leave to welcome him.

BREMS: It isn't without a very important reason that the free city has sent me to your office. I thank you for your welcome, and I want to explain my mission briefly.

ISRAEL AND KÖNIG: We're listening.

BREMS: I'll begin. With King Christian II's accession to the throne, Lübeck and the whole Hanseatic world have been struck a blow, which—to speak plainly—threatens us with ruin. King Christian has become the brother-in-law of the emperor, and both of them have sworn to ruin us with the intention of opening the Baltic to Holland and introducing that upstart into world commerce. This is the question: What is Sweden's policy toward Lübeck since the latest election of a regent? Herman Israel, who is Sten Sture the younger?

ISRAEL (*contemptuously*): He's a mere youngster!

BREMS: Cord König. Who is Sten Sture?

KÖNIG: We haven't seen what he really has yet. But he was discourteous to Herman at the Town Hall.

BREMS: A merchant has to bear that with patience and make up for it in something else. Can one *do* anything with him?

ISRAEL: He's definitely in the Swedish party.

BREMS: Not pro-Danish, then. There we have a rip in the sail.

KÖNIG: He's a statesman, but he's a man of honor.

BREMS (*smiles*): *But* he's a man of honor! That was well put. Does he like money?

ISRAEL: Not particularly; the Stures have always been unselfish; Svante was considered stingy, though; but he contributed from his own means to the welfare of the kingdom.

KÖNIG: Here the water's clear, and we won't need to fish in it.

BREMS: Who is Gustav Trolle?

ISRAEL: He's a French, no, an Italian bandit, like Alexander VI Borgia,[35] a fat fish like the eel. If you try to seize his head, you get hold of his tail, if you manage to get hold of him at all.

BREMS: Yes, but is he Danish?

ISRAEL: Hide and hair!

BREMS: Then I have the warp; now we'll weave! On the way up here, I happened to meet the Italian agent with the horrible name Arcimboldus[36] . . .

KÖNIG: What does he deal in?

BREMS: He deals in the forgiveness of sins.

ISRAEL: That's a dog!

KÖNIG: Oh-h, it's the pardoner?

BREMS: He is a dog, but he has credentials from and credit with Fugger of Augsburg, the pope's banker! [37]

ISRAEL: That changes the matter . . .

KÖNIG: Definitely!

BREMS: At all events, the man is a papal legate with very broad powers—I have seen his credentials. He can sit in judgment in ecclesiastical cases, award certain positions, grant doctors' degrees and forgive sins in return for *contantibus in manibus* . . .

ALL THREE: Naturally!

BREMS: But . . . the said legate has honored me with a secret mission—unbelievable but true! To ask Lord Sten Sture—now don't fall off your chairs!—if he, in case, and to bring to an end the dissension in the North, would want, in case, of course, to accept the crown of Sweden!

ISRAEL: Through Lübeck! That's excellent!

KÖNIG: The burgomaster of Lübeck distributing crowns!

BREMS: That is our trump card.

(*Someone knocks three times on the door.*)

BREMS: Don't let anyone in. With that, Sweden is Lübeck's vassal and Denmark's eternal enemy!

(*Again someone knocks three times on the door.*)

BREMS (*to the* CLERK): Go and see who it is. (*The* CLERK *goes out; a bell rings.*) Has fire broken out? (*All get up.*)

ISRAEL: The dogs are barking, and the guards are blowing their horns.

KÖNIG: A distinguished guest is coming!

CLERK: The regent!

(*General amazement. They look at each other.*)

BREMS: He came just at the right time. (*To* HERMAN ISRAEL) How shall I talk to him?

ISRAEL: Like a twenty-year-old. Condescendingly.

BREMS: Is he stupid?

ISRAEL: He believes everything one tells him, always keeps his word, is a happy giver, and thinks good of everyone.

BREMS: You call that stupid? Shame! Bring a chair, clerk.

KÖNIG: I wonder what he wants.

ISRAEL: He wants to borrow money, of course; otherwise, he wouldn't come here.

BREMS: Now!

STEN STURE (*enters, gentle but firm*): Burgomaster and councillors of the free city of Lübeck, my greetings.

BREMS: We are honored, lord regent. In what can we serve you? (*Indicates the chair that has been brought forward*)

STEN STURE (*sits down*): I come on an errand that is anything but pleasant for me.

BREMS: If it can lighten Your Grace's cares, let us guess the nature of the errand.

(STEN STURE *smiles.*)

BREMS: It's about money.

STEN STURE: It really is about money—the fact is that I'm going to pay for the *pallium* or symbol of authority for Lord Gustav Trolle's appointment . . .

BREMS: That's very noble, but if it's very wise . . . and, besides, money is scarce.

STEN STURE (*smiles*): It isn't, but the merchant always says that— Here are deeds to three of my houses in Munklägret . . . Can I get a few thousand Hungarian *guilders* on them?

BREMS: Munklägret with beach property, that is good. We like water. Legal and complete purchase. We'll say three thousand. Herman, look at these.

(ISRAEL *takes the papers and reads.*)

BREMS: Gustav Trolle. A learned man, a big name, archbishop, universally liked . . .

STEN STURE: I don't believe the last is so, if we should be truthful . . .

BREMS: No? I have heard only good things about that man . . .

STEN STURE: Then I'll not say anything bad . . . and he'll most likely become good.

BREMS: Well, Herman, are they sound papers?

ISRAEL: Perfect.

BREMS: Weigh up the gold, then.

STEN STURE: No gold's needed. We'll make out a draft on Fugger in Augsburg, which you'll kindly send to the papal curia's chancellery in Rome.

BREMS: Excuse me, Your Grace, it's unsafe to go by way of Denmark [38] . . .

STEN STURE: Why?

BREMS: King Christian has bared his teeth at Lübeck . . .

(KÖNIG *winks at* BREMS.)

STEN STURE (*sits down*): That's a precious bit of information you gave me . . .

BREMS: Yes, that is to say . . . But we have better connections with Rome; why, a papal legate has arrived, and he can deliver the sum as a draft . . .

STEN STURE: That's true! What sort of man is the legate?

BREMS: He's a man with excellent credentials, with exceptional influence, exceptional; I have seen his letters of authority, and I believe the mission in question would make a good impression, especially in consideration of—certain projects—which—

STEN STURE: Does the legate have any secret mission on his trip up here?

BREMS: Yes! He has! And I have accepted as just as secret a mission to present the matter to Your Grace!

STEN STURE: Many secrets. Let me hear it now, because I'm always in a hurry.

BREMS: In the presence of these men who are sworn to silence, I have no secrets, and this one, the very greatest, they already know.

STEN STURE: Fine. Speak out!

BREMS: It's a great moment when the burgomaster of the free city of Lübeck has received the undeserved honor to—from His Holiness—to offer the noble Lord Sten Sture the royal crown of Sweden.

STEN STURE (*after a pause*): What would be gained by that?

BREMS: This, as His Holiness himself says: the dissension in the north would thereby end.

STEN STURE (*calmly*): Experience has shown that the dissension has never been greater than under the native dynasty to which Karl Knutsson belonged.[39]

BREMS: Your Grace . . .

STEN STURE: Besides, and this you know: a Sture will never accept a crown. (*Rises*)

BREMS: That was unknown to us . . .

STEN STURE: Then you know it—now! It is the destiny of our family to serve, not to reign, to unite, not to divide, with the people, against the lords! Is the draft ready?

BREMS: Think of your poor fatherland . . .

STEN STURE: I never think of anything else!

(*Three knocks on the door*)

BREMS (*to the* CLERK): See who it is, but don't admit anyone.

STEN STURE: Now I'll not disturb you any longer.

BREMS: Can't I tempt Your Grace?

STEN STURE: No, burgomaster, you can't.

CLERK (*enters*): Lord Gustav Eriksson Vasa of Rydboholm requests permission to deliver an important message without delay.

STEN STURE: With your permission, I'll receive Gustav Vasa here. He comes from Stäke Castle.

BREMS: Gustav Trolle's?

STEN STURE: We can say that, for the time being.

BREMS (*to the* CLERK): Bring in the gentleman.

(GUSTAV VASA *enters.*)

STEN STURE: Speak out in these gentlemen's presence. What did Trolle say?

GUSTAV VASA: He said nothing.

STEN STURE: What's that?

GUSTAV VASA: He shot at me!

STEN STURE (*after a pause*): Then I'll go to talk with him. How unkind!

GUSTAV VASA: There you have your reward for your generosity. No, go to Stäke with powder and lead and tear down that robber's hangout.

STEN STURE: I'll summon him to a meeting first.

GUSTAV VASA: He won't come, because you lack royal authority, he says.

STEN STURE: Is that what he says?

BREMS: There you are—excuse me! Yes, royal authority! Now Lord Gustav's going to hear how the pope in Rome's offering the regent the crown of Sweden.

GUSTAV VASA: Is that true?

STEN STURE: It may be true!

GUSTAV VASA (*on his knees*): But, in the name of God, take the crown, Sten, and bring this hundred-year mess to an end!

STEN STURE: Do not tempt me!

GUSTAV VASA: To save our country, for our sake, for everybody's, in the name of Jesus, accept the crown! You Stures have earned it.

(STEN STURE *hesitates.*)

GUSTAV VASA (*gets up*): Sten, now or never, and you're going to . . .

STEN STURE: Leave me!

GUSTAV VASA: My king!

STEN STURE: Get thee behind me, tempter!

GUSTAV VASA: No, I shan't, before you've said amen.

STEN STURE: Then I'll go! Give the draft to the legate. Farewell, gentlemen. (*Goes*)

BREMS: Was he serious?

GUSTAV VASA: That was the word of a Sture. He'll never change it!

CURTAIN

ACT III

The sacristy in Uppsala Cathedral.

GUSTAV TROLLE, *who is alone on the stage, stands deep in thought; then he walks over to the window and taps with his fingers on a pane.*

CHANCELLOR *enters.*

GUSTAV TROLLE: Has Sture arrived?

CHANCELLOR: The regent has arrived in the city, but hasn't shown up here yet.

GUSTAV TROLLE: Then I'll let him wait. What do you have in your hand?

CHANCELLOR: A letter and package.

GUSTAV TROLLE: From Sture? Wait! (*Reads the letter and throws it to the floor. Opens the package, smiles contemptuously, and throws a rosary on the table*)

GUSTAV TROLLE: Bring in my father, Lord Erik Trolle.

CHANCELLOR: Isn't the regent going to . . .

GUSTAV TROLLE: Yes, later, since he has made me wait for him.

(CHANCELLOR *goes out.* GUSTAV TROLLE *goes to the window and taps with his fingers on the pane.* ERIK TROLLE *enters.*)

GUSTAV TROLLE: Welcome, father!

ERIK TROLLE: I sense I'm not welcome.

GUSTAV TROLLE: That's the customary greeting at any rate.

ERIK TROLLE: And it's the custom to say: Sit down. I've taught you that.

GUSTAV TROLLE: *You* have taught me a great deal!

ERIK TROLLE: If I could only teach you to forget the evil I've taught you!

GUSTAV TROLLE: Don't say that. What you call evil has benefited me most in life!

ERIK TROLLE: What have you gained in life, really?

GUSTAV TROLLE: I'm the archbishop of Sweden . . .

ERIK TROLLE: Even if you won the crown, and your soul were injured, what would be gained by that?

GUSTAV TROLLE: *Soul!*

ERIK TROLLE: That's Rome, that's Borgia, that's heathendom, that's Johanna of Naples and Lucrezia, the *Decameron* and Leo, who paid five thousand ducats for the manuscript of Plato [40] . . .

GUSTAV TROLLE: Won't you sit down? Sit down!

ERIK TROLLE: Soul? You most likely don't have any.

GUSTAV TROLLE: You must have had such a little one there wasn't enough to give me one.

ERIK TROLLE: Reproach me! But I, too, was the child of my time and . . .

CHANCELLOR (*enters*): The regent!

GUSTAV TROLLE: Let him wait.

ERIK TROLLE: Gustav! Be human!

GUSTAV TROLLE: Oh, no! He has made me wait, and an eye for an eye, a tooth for a tooth.

ERIK TROLLE: Can't you forgive?

GUSTAV TROLLE: No! When I get a grudge against anyone, I never forgive him!

ERIK TROLLE: That's beautifully put by a servant of the Lord.

GUSTAV TROLLE: I live in the old dispensation and can't serve two masters.

ERIK TROLLE: Let Sture come in, and I'll mediate between you.

GUSTAV TROLLE: You'd say he's right.

ERIK TROLLE: He *is* right!

GUSTAV TROLLE: That you don't understand, and I'll save my answers until he's allowed to come in, if that sheep can grasp what I say.

ERIK TROLLE: Sture isn't stupid, only gullible.

GUSTAV TROLLE: Isn't the person who writes letters like this stupid? (*Touches the letter on the floor with his foot*)

ERIK TROLLE: What did he write?

GUSTAV TROLLE: *He* asks *me* if *I* want to be the godfather of *his* son!

ERIK TROLLE: Why, that's fine, but may look childish; why, that's offering you his hand . . .

GUSTAV TROLLE: He sent me a gift, too . . . St. Birgitta's rosary [41]— (*laughs*)—of hawthorn berries! If it had been diamonds or sapphires! Hawthorn berries!

ERIK TROLLE: He believed you'd value a memento of a holy woman.

GUSTAV TROLLE: I never use rosaries and holy women . . .

ERIK TROLLE: I have heard that—from Rome—and that the pope never goes to church, although he's building St. Peter's . . . but you've sown dragon's teeth, and your seeds have sprouted in Germany! Have you heard of Martin Luther in Wittenberg? [42]

GUSTAV TROLLE: That fellow's not bad.

ERIK TROLLE: He doesn't believe in saints and rosaries, either . . .

GUSTAV TROLLE: He's a fine man.

ERIK TROLLE: In *your* opinion! But if he touches the peddling of indulgences?

GUSTAV TROLLE: Then the devil will take him!

ERIK TROLLE: Apollyon! [43] Apostate! It's damnable that I sent you to Rome, the great Babylonian . . .

GUSTAV TROLLE: Like father, like son! If we should let Sture come in now just to cut this conversation short . . .

ERIK TROLLE: Do! But, Gustav, be conciliatory; think of your country and remember that you're Swedish.

GUSTAV TROLLE: I? I am a citizen of Rome, as Paul said.

STEN STURE (*enters, unannounced, gentle but firm*): I'm a couple of minutes late for this meeting and beg your forgiveness.

(ERIK TROLLE *wants to leave.*)

STEN STURE: Stay, Lord Erik; you'll be a valued witness.

GUSTAV TROLLE: The meeting's between us two.

STEN STURE: I never negotiate matters of state without witnesses.

GUSTAV TROLLE: Is it a matter of state that you have had a son?

STEN STURE: No, and to avoid dealing with that matter I sent you a letter, which I see you have added to the agenda just as you've tabled my innocent gift.

GUSTAV TROLLE: Will you leave us, father?

STEN STURE: Then I won't speak!

GUSTAV TROLLE (*thinks this over; then*): My father may stay—he belongs to the council—but on the condition that he does not add one word to this conversation.

STEN STURE AND ERIK TROLLE: Agreed! (*Pause*)

(ERIK TROLLE *sits down to the side at the right;* STEN STURE *and* GUSTAV TROLLE *directly opposite each other at the table. Pause*)

GUSTAV TROLLE: Will you begin?

STEN STURE: Gladly. (*Pause*) You've had my messenger, Gustav Vasa, fired at. What was the reason for that?

GUSTAV TROLLE: Because he wanted to force his way past my guards into Stäke, my fortified castle.

STEN STURE: Didn't you know that I've confiscated the fief of Stäke to the crown?

GUSTAV TROLLE: The fief, yes, but not the castle.

STEN STURE: Did I forget the castle? Forgive me, then, since you're right. But why did you shoot at a friend?

GUSTAV TROLLE: I have no friends . . .

STEN STURE: What sort of talk is this? I was your friend when I recommended your appointment as archbishop and paid the fees.

GUSTAV TROLLE: Because I was the most learned and the worthiest, you put it then, but now you say friendship, kinship. Those are personal considerations, and you thereby admit that you wanted to win me, buy me, bribe me in a word! That's called simony and is forbidden by canonical law.

STEN STURE: You speak as harshly as to an enemy.

GUSTAV TROLLE: Yes, we are enemies!

STEN STURE: Not I.

GUSTAV TROLLE: Opponents, then.

STEN STURE: Why didn't you come to the capital when I invited you?

GUSTAV TROLLE: I didn't have time, and invitations are personal matters. (*Pause*)

STEN STURE: They say you visited King Christian on your way up here. Is that true?

GUSTAV TROLLE: That's true. So what?

STEN STURE: Do you consider that proper?

GUSTAV TROLLE: Both proper and right. Because as archbishop of Sweden I'm automatically a member of the king's council.

STEN STURE: The king's?

GUSTAV TROLLE: Yes! The king of the united kingdoms!

STEN STURE (*gets up*). Now it came out! Is Christian king in Sweden?

GUSTAV TROLLE: In the three Scandinavian kingdoms, consequently even in Sweden. Has he been deposed?

STEN STURE: Has he been elected?

GUSTAV TROLLE: On July 17, 1498, Prince Christian was elected—in Stockholm—the successor to King Hans.[44] You had just been born then, so you can't remember it.

STEN STURE: But a regent's elected when the king neglects visiting the kingdom. Now I've been elected, and I rule in the king's place.

GUSTAV TROLLE: Regents, elected by traitors, bandits, and outlaws, are rebels and nothing else.

STEN STURE: What are you saying? You pain me, Lord Gustav Trolle, but we must not part as enemies, for, if we do, innocent blood will be spilled. Give me your hand!

Ivar Nilsson as Gustav Vasa

Bror Olsson as Archbishop Trolle

GUSTAV TROLLE: No! Not to a traitor!

STEN STURE: Must the misfortune come, then? I had believed we'd meet in peace, and at the reception of an innocent child into the Christian congregation . . . my first-born son's . . .

GUSTAV TROLLE: Your feelings are absolutely foreign to me and, moreover, are beside the point. But you yourself are a child, who could use a godfather to take charge of your upbringing . . . a big child . . .

STEN STURE: If I am, may I always be!

GUSTAV TROLLE: Woe to the kingdom whose ruler is a child!

STEN STURE: I wonder. I wonder. (*Pause*)

GUSTAV TROLLE: Shall we cut this pointless small talk short?

STEN STURE: I'll give you my ultimatum.

GUSTAV TROLLE: Give it!

STEN STURE: Since the national council doesn't intend to approve your distinction between castle and fief as I've done to meet you halfway, Stäke Castle will be besieged if you haven't surrendered it within forty-eight hours.

GUSTAV TROLLE: Good! Then my liege lord, King Christian, will come from Denmark to relieve both the castle and the fief.

STEN STURE: That means war!

ERIK TROLLE (*rises; lifts his hands*): In the name of Christ, the Saviour!

GUSTAV TROLLE: Silence, father!

STEN STURE: The archbishop doesn't accept fiefs from Denmark but from Sweden, and, if he does, he's a traitor to the kingdom! And as such I address you as I go. (*Takes the letter and the rosary and puts them in his pockets*)

GUSTAV TROLLE: This talk should have begun in this way; then we would have understood each other at once. You're not showing your baby teeth, Lord Sten, and your friendship had its thorns just like the hawthorn under its leaves! (*He pours himself a glass of water and empties it.*)

STEN STURE: May God forgive him who has forgotten himself . . .

(*As if to himself*) That was a great temptation for me a little while ago, but I didn't yield—now I almost wish that I had yielded! Lord Gustav Trolle, you're a man of the spirit, and not a soldier . . .

GUSTAV TROLLE: Is that so?

STEN STURE: All that you said to contradict me has been pure sophistry and trickery, illusions and devices of the devil; if you had a heart as you have a head, I'd humble myself once again and say: Give me your hand!

GUSTAV TROLLE: A perjurer's hand shall be nailed to the wall and can't be shaken by a man of honor . . .

STEN STURE: You don't want to take my hand; if you were a knight, you'd get my glove . . .

GUSTAV TROLLE: I am a knight—of the Holy Sepulchre! *Ecce miles!* (*He opens his bishop's robes and stands in his knight's garb and sword.*)

STEN STURE: So! Take my glove, then! (*He throws his glove toward Trolle.*)

GUSTAV TROLLE: I'll take it! But you can fetch it within the castle walls of Stäke!

STEN STURE: I'll fetch it! (*Leaves*)

ERIK TROLLE (*to Gustav Trolle*): What have you done?

GUSTAV TROLLE: Be calm, father; this was only the last buckle in the harness; Christian is armed for war, and Norrby[45] has the fleet ready in the sound.

ERIK TROLLE: What good will that do if Sture yields to the temptation he was talking about?

GUSTAV TROLLE: What temptation? What did he mean? Is it something I don't know?

ERIK TROLLE: You don't seem to know that the papal legate has the mission from His Holiness—to offer Sture the royal crown.

GUSTAV TROLLE (*beside himself with fury*): Sture get the crown? Not Trolle? By the devil, that's why he acted humble! Sture, king—that hypocrite! Did you hear him? Ba, ba, ba, like a sheep, this wolf. Now he felt it was time to unmask and to challenge me at the same time, in the cathedral, my cathedral, where Jöns Bengtsson Oxenstjerna [46] once brought both helmet and armor; but if he gets to be king, I'll be regent . . .

ERIK TROLLE: He'll never become king.

GUSTAV TROLLE: No, I'll prevent it.

ERIK TROLLE: You can't!

GUSTAV TROLLE: No?

ERIK TROLLE: Sture alone can! He has already said no!

GUSTAV TROLLE: In order to be begged . . .

ERIK TROLLE: You misjudge Sture.

GUSTAV TROLLE: Say no to a crown! He's not born of woman; he's a monster, who should be shown at the market fairs; just offer it to him, on a pillow, kneeling. I know the Stures, and I hated them in my mother's womb as they have hated the Trolles. I hate him —hate, do you hear?

ERIK TROLLE: My son, I've hated like that, too, but I don't any more; there are people who are better than we have ever dreamed, and, if I taught you anything else when you were a youngster, I say: forgive me.

GUSTAV TROLLE: Come with me to Stäke!

ERIK TROLLE: I'll never go with you again!

GUSTAV TROLLE: Go to Vadstena Cloister, then; there's a house for old men . . .

ERIK TROLLE: Yes, that's fitting for me, and there I'll pray—for you.

GUSTAV TROLLE: Go ahead and pray—I command still! But, imagine, if he accepts the crown?

ERIK TROLLE: Then you'll have to bend low!

GUSTAV TROLLE: When did you ever see me do that?

ERIK TROLLE: Really—never. Your mother had a hard hand, but she never could control you.

GUSTAV TROLLE: Neither could you, father. Neither with good nor with evil.

ERIK TROLLE: Good didn't do because you're evil, depraved, born to be ruined!

GUSTAV TROLLE: Fathered by you!

ERIK TROLLE: By me. Oh, that you had never been born!

GUSTAV TROLLE: Control your tongue!

(ERIK TROLLE *bows his head.*)

GUSTAV TROLLE: You were regent a bit ago, but you couldn't stay in the saddle. Bite the grass, then; I can sit on the high horse. (*Goes to the window and taps on the pane.* ERIK TROLLE, *crushed, goes to the back.*)

CURTAIN

ACT IV

A forested area before Stäke Castle. LARS *and* GÖRAN SPARRE.

GÖRAN: This work at Stäke took a long time.

LARS: Are you tired? Take good care of yourself, then.

GÖRAN: Standing guard here while Gustav Vasa leads the storming of the castle. He'll get all the honor, I suppose.

LARS: If you're dissatisfied, don't do what Erik Lejonhuvud [47] did.

GÖRAN: You mean desert . . .

LARS: Yes! Then I'd kill you!

GÖRAN: Your own brother?

LARS: You'd no longer be my brother! But Stäke'll soon be taken, and then . . .

GÖRAN: The worst is left, because then King Christian himself will come . . .

LARS: Quiet! Someone's stealing about here . . . Hide! (*They hide behind trees.*)

(GUSTAV TROLLE, *disguised as a pilgrim, comes in with his* CHANCELLOR—*from the left.*)

GUSTAV TROLLE: That road's clear, you say?

CHANCELLOR: That road's absolutely safe; I've looked it over myself. There isn't a footprint . . .

GUSTAV TROLLE: Straight ahead, then? You go back and save my papers—you know where they are.

(*Great noise and shouting off stage*)

GUSTAV TROLLE: What was that?

CHANCELLOR: It was Stäke that fell!

GUSTAV TROLLE: Damnation! (*Goes out to the right*)

(CHANCELLOR *waves and turns back; goes out to the left with a gesture of contempt.* GÖRAN *and* LARS *come forward.*)

LARS: Stäke has fallen!

GÖRAN: But that pilgrim! I think we'll follow him.

LARS: What do we have to do with him? We'll have other things to do now.

(*Shouts of victory off stage*)

GÖRAN: Young Sture has better luck with Stäke than the old fellow [48] had when Archbishop Jakob Ulvsson defended it. But, when you have Gustav Vasa with his caul, there's nothing to the art of besieging.

LARS: Stop saying your secret thoughts aloud, Göran. Choke them in your throat; crush them in your heart . . .

GÖRAN: If you tramp down seeds, they sprout better. Poor advice!

LARS: Now we'll leave our post and go hail the victor, without grudge or envy.

GÖRAN: But that pilgrim! And his guide, who lied to him!

LARS: Come along before the gates are closed.

(*They disappear at the back; the stage stands empty; there are shouts, beating of drums, sounding of horns, and shots.*)

STEN STURE (*enters*): Halt! Who's there? (*Pause*) No one. (*Takes off his helmet and wipes his forehead*)

GUSTAV VASA (*comes in, wet, his clothes in tatters, bareheaded, bloody, dark*): Stop! With whom?

STEN STURE: With God and St. George!

GUSTAV VASA: Oh, God in Heaven! (*Embraces* STEN STURE; STURE *kisses him on both cheeks.*)

STEN STURE: Gustav! Kinsman! Friend! If I were king, I'd dub you knight right now!

GUSTAV VASA: Become king, then! Now! The Lord has anointed you with the oil of victory, little David. Why, good things by the basketful are being offered you. Stretch out your hand; take and eat.

STEN STURE: But why don't you spare yourself? How you look! Isn't your life worth more than that?

GUSTAV VASA: No, life has become a burden for me . . .

STEN STURE: Since . . .

GUSTAV VASA: You don't tell that sort of thing, when you're doing everything to forget . . .

STEN STURE: Poor Anna Bielke. If she had an idea of the sorrow she has spread, she wouldn't want to live.

GUSTAV VASA: Is this the time to talk about things like that?—Trolle has fled!

STEN STURE: He won't get far!

GUSTAV VASA: If he goes by water . . .

STEN STURE: Then we'll follow him!

GUSTAV VASA: They think he's on the island; I'll *swim* after him . . .

STEN STURE: Don't go into that cold water—you'd die!

GUSTAV VASA: Better than live!

STEN STURE: Nonsense!

    (*Two* SOLDIERS *come in from the right with* GUSTAV TROLLE, *who has a rope around his neck.*)

SOLDIER I: Hang him on the lowest branch!

STEN STURE: Who's there?

SOLDIER II: A spy in disguise!

STEN STURE: Let me see him.

GUSTAV VASA: It's—Gustav Trolle! Hang him . . .

STEN STURE: Stop!

GUSTAV VASA: Otherwise I'll drown him!

STEN STURE: A knight doesn't murder a defenseless man who hasn't any weapon in his hand.

GUSTAV VASA: You, knight, the last of the knights! Would you cross swords with an infamous traitor? The snake has bitten you three times. Throw 'im in the fire!

STEN STURE: Lord Gustav Trolle, if I now spare your life, don't misuse God's gift; and, if I do good to you, do not avenge my good deed.

GUSTAV VASA: Yes, Sten Sture, if you're too good for this world, don't forfeit heaven by an evil deed when you set free the dragon no St. George can slay.

STEN STURE: Take the prisoner away and have him kept at Västerås Castle. Go!

GUSTAV VASA: You'll regret this, and we'll pay for it. Sture, Sture! —Now I'll take to the water. Or I'll catch on fire! (GUSTAV TROLLE *is taken away by the* SOLDIERS.) There comes Bishop Heming Gad.

STEN STURE: See, he did come back—And Trolle will come back, too, and then as my friend for life.

GUSTAV VASA: And the Lord said to Joshua: See I have given thee a charge: "Be strong and of good courage!" [49]

STEN STURE (*smiles*): Am I not strong?

(GUSTAV VASA *smiles.*)

STEN STURE: Are you trying to make me change? When I do what's right?

GUSTAV VASA: The greatest right in the greatest wrong. I thank God I'm not a knight.

(STEN STURE *looks questioningly at him.*)

GUSTAV VASA: For then I'd never have stormed Stäke . . . out of fear of injuring an enemy.

STEN STURE: Bishop Heming!

GUSTAV VASA: *Electus,* elected, but not confirmed. [50]

STEN STURE: Bishop Heming with important news.

HEMING GAD: Important, indeed. But not good news. King Christian has assembled thirty thousand men, Saxons, Scotchmen, Frenchmen, and is coming with the fleet himself. It's the last struggle, Sweden's last struggle; if I'll live to see the day, I don't know, but now we'll see suffering and agony.

STEN STURE: So: another start! Isn't there any end to this strife?

HEMING GAD: No end. Only starting and starting all over.

STEN STURE: Well, then. We'll start again!

CURTAIN

ACT V

SCENE I

The rampart outside the Blockhouse, whose upper part can be seen to the left.

To the right six GIRLS *are sitting, mending the cloth for a banner with three crowns on it.*

Farthest out on the rampart MÄTTA STURE *is walking back and forth. Below the rampart mounted cannons can be seen. A* SENTINEL *stands on the rampart, where a white flag has been hoisted.*

GIRL I (*to the* SENTINEL): Is there any immediate danger?

SENTINEL: No danger as long as the white flag is up. The Danish ships are anchored opposite Kungshamn.

GIRL I: Can they fire at us?

SENTINEL: Not at this distance. What are you girls sewing?

GIRL I: We're mending the Brännkyrka banner Lord Gustav Vasa carried [51]...

SENTINEL: Bless you, girls—we need new banners ...

GIRL I: Won't there be peace now that the white flag is up?

SENTINEL: Peace? Well, that's what they say. Can you see the large ship over there? With the Danish flag on the mainmast?

GIRL I: Yes, of course, we can.

SENTINEL: King Christian is lurking on board that one!

(GIRLS *all get up in order to see.*)

GIRL 1: Is he going to fire at us?

SENTINEL: He hasn't anything to fire with, poor devil.

(GUSTAV VASA *enters, followed by a* MARKSMAN; *goes up to* MÄTTA STURE, *falls to one knee, and says something softly.* MÄTTA STURE *goes out to the right.*)

GUSTAV VASA: What are you girls doing?

GIRL 1: We're mending your banner, Lord Gustav, the cavalry banner from Brännkyrka!

GUSTAV VASA: That's good of you, and it'll soon be put to use again. Can you sing St. George's ballad?

GIRL 1: Who doesn't know that?

GUSTAV VASA: Sing it; then the Danes will be afraid of you!

GIRL 1: May we sing?

GUSTAV VASA: Yes, so it's heard to Brunkesberg, where the Danes heard it the first time.

GIRLS (*sing*):
Listen, George, to what I have to say:
You shall do a deed of might:
Fare to Cappadocia the Great
With the dragon there to fight!

That city is both long and broad;
There lives a pagan king.
Before the city the dragon lies,
For the city a harmful thing.
(*A shot is heard.*)

GUSTAV VASA: The Dane answered you!

(GIRLS *frightened*)

GUSTAV VASA: No danger, girls. That was only a polite salute to the ladies! Come, marksman, I'll teach you about the cannons. Look carefully at these. First we have Sharfmesser, which shoots hundred-pound bullets—its name in Italian is Matsicana or Big

Moses; here you have the Basilisk or the Frog—it's not for playing hide-and-go-seek with; and that's the Singer or the Nightingale—that one can sing the "Ballad of St. George," because it
was along at Vädla [52] and Duvnäs; and then we have the Monks,
the Falcons or Falconettes. Down there are the stone throwers.
When you've loaded, you set the direction with that handle, but
don't stand in back of it or you'll get the recoil on the small of
your legs. *Ein, zwei, drei*—the fire to the powder, and it goes off.
But if you turn around I'll make the sign of the cross with Master
Erik right between your eyes! Do you understand?

MARKSMAN: Yes, Your Grace.

GUSTAV VASA: Since we've loaded, you'll light up, and grab the opportunity. Don't be afraid, girls, the Danes can't shoot at us, but
we can put the larding-pin to them; that's Peder Månsson's first
law of battle! (*He takes out a spyglass and looks out on the water
for a long while.*)

STEN STURE (*enters from the right*): What do you see? What's happening on the Danish fleet?

GUSTAV VASA: If I only could tell! They're doing something that I
don't understand . . . I think they're drowning the crew . . .

STEN STURE: Let me see. (*Takes the spyglass*) They're lowering dead
people into the water. So it's true they're starving to death.

GUSTAV VASA: What did they come up here for? They knew this
place had been stripped.

STEN STURE: But it's terrible!

GUSTAV VASA: Think so? Maybe you want to feed them?

STEN STURE: I can't bear this!

GUSTAV VASA: Well, so we're back to that. You weren't so soft at
Duvnäs!

STEN STURE: In battle, life for life, but I can't fight with corpses.

GUSTAV VASA: Let them negotiate, then. (*A shot*) That was a blank!
A distress signal, then. Let's see them put out a boat to negotiate
soon.

(LEJONHUVUD *enters.*)

STEN STURE: Whom do I see? Erik Lejonhuvud? Do you dare to show up, you who stayed away from Stäke?

LEJONHUVUD: I went on a spying party.

STEN STURE: Can I believe you?

GUSTAV VASA: No, you can't!

STEN STURE: Do you know anything? Where's Gustav Trolle?

LEJONHUVUD: He has escaped from Västerås and is hiding out on Ekholm.

STEN STURE: Trolle escaped? What's happening on the Danish fleet?

LEJONHUVUD: They're starving to death, and there's a mutiny!

STEN STURE: Mutiny? Then I forgive you. Do you know anything about King Christian?

LEJONHUVUD: The king's sick with grief. Dyveke [53] is dead.

STEN STURE: Poor king!

GUSTAV VASA: Pity the devil, but not the Dane!

STEN STURE: Erik Lejonhuvud, go to my wife and ask her if the Blockhouse has food for more than its own needs . . .

GUSTAV VASA: Sten Sture, think of what you're doing. To supply the enemy with provisions is treason and is punishable with death!

STEN STURE: Gustav Vasa, you're no knight.

GUSTAV VASA: No, I'm a yeoman, and yeomen are badly needed here . . .

STEN STURE: You're a merchant, too . . .

GUSTAV VASA: Would to God we had more, and the government would have gains instead of losses.

STEN STURE: Go, Erik Lejonhuvud, go on my errand. Then be my man. I can depend on you?

GUSTAV VASA: You never can tell, said Erik Lejonhuvud!

(LEJONHUVUD *exits to the right.*)

STEN STURE: So Dyveke is dead. Who's that coming—so dark and cloudy?

GUSTAV VASA (*to the* GIRLS): Go in, girls; a hunter's coming.

(GIRLS *go.*)

GUSTAV VASA: I think it's Gustav Trolle's chancellor. You'd better tie up that fellow's hands—most likely he has a dagger under his cloak.

(CHANCELLOR *enters, embarrassed.*)

GUSTAV VASA: It's like an inn; they come and go, out and in, and look for barn and room for their wagons, too.

STEN STURE: You've become boastful, Gustav. Can't you carry good luck?

GUSTAV VASA: Forgive me, Sten, but I've had so little of that wine that it goes to my head.

STEN STURE: Sleep it off, then! Don't be angry with me because I said so.

GUSTAV VASA: You! Sten, no one can be angry with you, but I wish I could. Be merciful to the chancellor, now—he looks pretty bad because of his bad conscience!

STEN STURE (*to the* CHANCELLOR): We have met before.

CHANCELLOR: In Uppsala Cathedral, Your Grace.

STEN STURE: That's right. What do you wish?

CHANCELLOR: My errand's not of the kind that can make my visit welcome.

STEN STURE: A quick thrust hurts least.

CHANCELLOR: Yes, but the innocent messenger generally gets the counter blow.

STEN STURE: That depends on whether he shows malicious joy.

CHANCELLOR: It's about the delivery of a papal decree from His Holiness Leo X, which declares Regent Sten Sture excommunicated.[54]

STEN STURE: Excommunicated? Why?

CHANCELLOR: Because of Stäke Castle.

STEN STURE: Excommunicated, cursed by God and men, shut out of the church, and not permitted an honorable burial. What do you think, Gustav?

GUSTAV VASA: Doesn't matter about the pope, but for the people it's no recommendation to be excommunicated. That's Trolle's thanks

for your letting him keep his life. And supplying the money for
his letter of appointment.

CHANCELLOR: King Christian has stolen that money.[55]

(STEN STURE *amazed*.)

CHANCELLOR: He stole most of the indulgence money the legate sent
from Sweden, too.

STEN STURE: Who are you?

CHANCELLOR: Well, frankly, I'm not the person I seem to be.

GUSTAV VASA: Yes, you certainly seem to be . . .

CHANCELLOR: I'm not Trolle's man, although I go his errands . . .
(*Speaks softly*) I was the one who tricked him into his enemies'
hands at Stäke—and now I've come to offer you my services.

STEN STURE: Me? No, my friend, the one who has betrayed his lord
will get no place with me.

CHANCELLOR: Then I'll have to go elsewhere.

STEN STURE: Go!

GUSTAV VASA (*to* STEN STURE): Don't let a dangerous enemy go!

STEN STURE: You may go! (*Then to* GUSTAV VASA) And, you, see to
it that food is sent to the starving Danes, now, at once! Then
ask Kristina to come out.

(GUSTAV VASA *hesitates*.)

STEN STURE: What are you waiting for? (*Goes out on the rampart*)

(GUSTAV VASA *and the* CHANCELLOR *exit*.)

STEN STURE (*alone on the rampart, sends the* MARKSMAN *away, takes
the spyglass, and looks out on the water with it. Then he comes
downstage, where he meets his stepmother*): Mother! Are you
uneasy? Memories of those gone and dear—everything has passed
away from you.

(MÄTTA STURE *nods in a friendly way and pats* STEN STURE *on
the cheek*.)

STEN STURE: You taught me only what is good, for you yourself
were good.

(MÄTTA STURE *shakes her head in denial; covers her eyes and
exits*. STEN STURE *sits down at the girls' table; sighs*.)

KRISTINA STURE (*enters*): Is it bad?

STEN STURE: It's getting dark. The day's pretty far gone . . . Sit down, dear.

KRISTINA: Sten, I'd already sent food to the starving Danes . . .

STEN STURE: I knew it! (*Pause*) In the final analysis, it's only you and I. Out-and-out disloyalty, dissension, greed; every one of them's for sale, and there's no lack of buyers.

KRISTINA: Not all, not all! Why, you have your friends in there . . .

STEN STURE: Are all of them there?

KRISTINA: They're all in there, and Gustav Vasa's on your side.

STEN STURE: Yes, *he* has the heavy hand that should take hold of this.

KRISTINA: But that isn't what's oppressing you; there's something else . . .

STEN STURE: Yes! (*Pause*) That there can be a being in this world like Gustav Trolle! In whom you can't find one human trait.

KRISTINA: God save him.

STEN STURE: He has robbed me of my faith in people. Even King Christian at least shows signs of his high birth—he has grieved over Dyveke's death until he's ill.

KRISTINA: Is Dyveke dead?

STEN STURE: Yes, she's dead. But Trolle, whose life I spared, has thanked me—his benefactor—by having me excommunicated . . .

KRISTINA: Excommunicated? You! Then there isn't any point to going on living. (*Pause*)

STEN STURE: Our dear little child can't be baptized . . . and, if I should die, I can't be buried in hallowed ground.

KRISTINA: You're not going to die!

STEN STURE: We're all going to die. And I've been warned.

KRISTINA (*stands up*): I'll tell you something cheerful. Johan Natt-och-Dag and Anna Bielke have defended Kalmar Castle against the Danish fleet, and their praises are being sung all over the country.

STEN STURE: I knew that Johan was a soldier even if he didn't speak up in public. God bless them.

SENTINEL (*on the rampart*): Boat, hallo! Negotiator!

STEN STURE (*gets up*): The Danes are ready to negotiate! Sentinel, go down and get the letter.

(SENTINEL *disappears.*)

KRISTINA: Now you'll be happy, Sten.

STEN STURE: I don't know if I can be happy any more; it's as if a veil had been dropped over my life.

KRISTINA: Shall I call Gustav? He's cheerful.

STEN STURE: No, just you and I; be my councillor of councillors as always; I'll soon be on my way again, away from home and hearth . . .

KRISTINA: Are you ill, Sten dear?

STEN STURE: No, but I'm troubled unto death.

KRISTINA: Why? Why, everything has gone well, and now they're ready to negotiate!

STEN STURE: All that's happening is foreign to me; if it's good or evil, I don't know . . . Am I standing here, or am I somewhere else?—What does the sentinel want? A letter—that's it. From . . .

KRISTINA: The Danish king . . .

(SENTINEL *enters with a letter.*)

STEN STURE: Let me have the letter from—the Danish king.

(SENTINEL *goes.*)

STEN STURE (*reads the letter. Pause.*) He asks for a conference with me.

KRISTINA: Here?

STEN STURE: Out on his ship!

KRISTINA: Does he offer safe-conduct?

STEN STURE: We are Christian knights.

KRISTINA: You are, but the king isn't!

STEN STURE: If the country will get an honorable peace through such a little thing as humbling myself, then I'll have to do it.

Read his letter; he writes beautifully—and he thanks my dear wife, who saved Danish men from starving to death. Read it.

KRISTINA (*reads*): This has really been written by a person with a heart . . . He must have loved his Dyveke . . .

STEN STURE: Of course he did. And he's really grateful. I'll go!

KRISTINA: Go in the name of the Lord; you never walk the paths of unrighteousness. And, when you obey the dictates of your heart, you don't need any councillors.

STEN STURE (*shouts*): Gustav Vasa! (*Pause*) Gustav Vasa!

GUSTAV VASA (*comes on stage*): You called?

STEN STURE: King Christian wants to parley, and I'm going to row out to his ship!

GUSTAV VASA: If you do, you'll have a mutiny here!

STEN STURE: Are you deserting me, Swedes? Your Sten Sture?

GUSTAV VASA: The lords have already decided in there, and this is it: If you go to Christian and put yourself in his power, the council will meet and elect a new regent, considering you as good as dead.

STEN STURE: That's your decision! since you don't know the king. Read his letter . . .

GUSTAV VASA: No, we have read so many Danish letters, we'll soon be able to write the like ourselves.

STEN STURE: Heming Gad can!

GUSTAV VASA: He kept your father's death a secret—that was wise.

STEN STURE: But writing a false letter—that was ugly.[56]

GUSTAV VASA: But we've reached another decision, too.

STEN STURE: Is it honorable?

GUSTAV VASA: Listen. Six of us, your best men, will go out there to negotiate with the Danes.

STEN STURE: But, if he keeps you, I'll be alone, the army without commanders, the council without councillors, the country without leadership.

GUSTAV VASA: But the country will still have its head; let's say its heart and conscience.

STEN STURE: Are you singing the siren's song, Vasa?

KRISTINA: Sten! Listen to them; they talk both well and sensibly. (*Pause*)

STEN STURE: Which six are you?

GUSTAV VASA: I, Heming Gad, Lars and Göran Sparre, Ryning, and Färla.[57]

STEN STURE: Should I stoop to this?

GUSTAV VASA: Sten, you're not alone as we are; you have both wife and child.

STEN STURE: And you have a tongue . . . Now you have me! (*Looks questioningly at* KRISTINA)

KRISTINA: No, don't look at me. You must make up your own mind.

STEN STURE (*thinks; reads Christian's letter again*): Yes, if this isn't sincere, I'll never believe in a human being again. (*Struggles with himself*) God help me and all of us!

GUSTAV VASA: Amen. Your word?

STEN STURE: My word.

GUSTAV VASA (*embraces Sten Sture*): Farewell. But without leavetaking. Stay here. (*Goes; comes back*) Sten! (*It becomes cloudy; the darkness increases.*)

STEN STURE (*moved*): What is it?

GUSTAV VASA: I don't know! —But someone whispering to me in the wind, pulling at my coat . . .

STEN STURE: The wind's increasing . . .

GUSTAV VASA: What direction?

STEN STURE: Northerly.

GUSTAV VASA: Then we can sail. Without farewells, then! (*Goes*)

STEN STURE: Without farewells!

(*Pause.* KRISTINA *at the girls' table;* STEN STURE *beside her*)

KRISTINA: You do have friends, Sten! Think of old Heming Gad— eighty years old and out sailing in an open boat!

STEN STURE: Yes, Heming Gad has been tested, but . . . he talks too

much and doesn't listen enough . . . and it sounds as if someone
else were talking through him.

KRISTINA: Gustav Vasa's the best one. He speaks right from his
heart . . .

STEN STURE: Sometimes from his hot head—all Vasas are hot-
headed . . .

(SENTINEL *appears on the rampart; looks out on the water.*)

(LEJONHUVUD *enters.*)

STEN STURE: Erik, don't come. We want to be alone.

(LEJONHUVUD *points out on the water.*)

STEN STURE: I don't want to see.

(LEJONHUVUD *goes out again.*)

STEN STURE: My last man. My only one . . .

KRISTINA: But not the best.

STEN STURE: He's so weak . . . and easily led, but otherwise not bad.

KRISTINA: Otherwise!

STEN STURE: If we get peace, all this disloyalty will end, and there'll
be only one party in the kingdom . . .

KRISTINA: That will never be until they get a native king.

STEN STURE: Oh, you little rascal, do you want a crown, perhaps?

KRISTINA: No. But look at the boat!

STEN STURE: What now?

SENTINEL: There's some sort of trouble in the boat.

KRISTINA (*gets up*): They're fighting! Gustav has drawn his sword!

SENTINEL: Treachery!

STEN STURE (*gets up; takes the spyglass*): The Danish ships are
hoisting their sails . . .

SENTINEL: The lords are overpowered! The boat's tipping, and a
Danish one's picking them up!

KRISTINA: It was treachery!

STEN STURE (*throws his spyglass away*): I don't want to see anything more of this world and its madness . . . (*falls down by the
table*).

KRISTINA: Sten!

STEN STURE: My God, my God, why hast Thou forsaken me?
(*Pause*)

(MÄTTA STURE, *without seeing the* STURES, *goes to the table by the rampart as if she were going to meet someone, greets an invisible person who seems to have been expecting her, stretches out her hand, invites him to sit down, and then sits down herself.*[58])

KRISTINA: I wonder what she's seeing now, poor mother.

STEN STURE: She has her visions, which we must overlook, poor soul. Let her be.

MÄTTA STURE (*to the invisible person*): You did well to come, for the hour has come. Yes, it has! And what has happened is all my doing, all of it! Don't deny it! I won't bear it! You will listen to me! I was born a Dane, I am the kinswoman of Torben Oxe, the one who has just been executed, accused of having murdered Christian's Dyveke.[59] I have been married three times, the last time to Svante Sture. First with a Norwegian from Bergen; the second time with Knut Alfsson, who was beheaded! Didn't you know that? Why he was beheaded? Because he was loyal to his king, not disloyal, you see! Then I vowed . . . and I *took* Svante Sture! I know that! But he did not die of poison! They say that I murdered the first one, too! Oh, you knew that! Now I am so that I have to harm people, even though I do not want to. It has to be, against my better will, and I hate myself, when it's over, but I don't regret it. I have always admired good people, because they could do what I couldn't: love! You don't believe that! When I had to bring up an angelic child with blue eyes and blond hair, I loved that child more than my own children, and I took care that from me he never heard or saw anything but good! That was Sten Sture. I, the bride of hate and vengeance, I taught him to love, to believe good, and to forgive! What I couldn't become myself, he was to become! But, just the same, I was forced to harm him! I'm the one who has done it all, because I could never cease to be Danish! Why, you ask? I don't know! The powers of a shadowy destiny, perhaps. (*Pause*) What's going to happen now, you ask? (*Gets up*) I know; I have seen it in dreams and visions. I have seen Christian come with wheels and gallows—it's the day of judgment over the Swedes and the Goths,[60] who could never keep peace among themselves—always traitors and deserters—as soon as the Folkungs [61] disagreed, they fled to Norway and Denmark to set the enemy in arms against their own countrymen. Now let them enjoy it! After that? I see it in the clouds, in the water, in my dreams—Sten Sture will never get any crown but the crown of thorns. He won't live the year out—for he has had his measure of suffering and drunk all the bitterness of life. The time of wolves is at hand, evil death, and sudden death.[62] Alas! The twilight of the gods, the dusk of the powers, the fire of Surt! What more I see? (*Shades her eyes and stares out over the water*) Yes! A man with a caul and a cross on his chest will come! Who? (*Strains herself*) No! Yes! It is Gustav Vasa, with his Brännkyrka banner and Dalesmen in hosts— war of arrows, war of clubs, war of axes—and he'll get the keys to Stockholm—on a midsummer day—and then he'll get the crown! And his family will keep it for centuries—but not in direct succession—there are bends in the road! (*Pause*)

Then they will unite,[63]
then they will be reconciled,
then they will love,
light and dark!
Hail to the one who saw this,
hail to the one who knows it,
hail him who hears it!

Do you yet understand or not? (*Pause*) Now we shall never meet again! Give me your hand!—You do not want to take mine!—You're right!

Poor I
who fare on the dark billows

and never more shall become
what I have been! (Pause)

KRISTINA: Did you hear?

STEN STURE: No, I was deep in my own thoughts . . . (*They can
hear someone nailing a coffin together.*) What was that?

KRISTINA: They're nailing a coffin together in the Blockhouse!

STEN STURE: Mine, I suspect! And then they'll break my escutcheon,
and put a wreath on the lid . . . but no one will dare to say a
prayer over the excommunicated one . . .

KRISTINA: I will—if need be—but it won't be like that, Sten darling . . .

STEN STURE: Alone! How alone we are under the stars, you and I,
in the whole, wide, wide world, you and I. (*Embrace. Drums
beat.* STEN STURE *becomes suddenly attentive; tears himself away
from* KRISTINA.)

CURTAIN

SCENE 2

Stockholm Castle. The same room as in Act II, scene 1.
The right door is covered with black drapes. Within stands
STEN STURE's *coffin. He is still unburied, since he was excommu-
nicated and no one wants to perform the burial rites.*

LADY MÄTTA STURE, *his stepmother, sits at this door, dressed in
black with a black cloth over her head and shoulders.*

ANNA BIELKE *brought in by the* CASTELLAN.

CASTELLAN: Lady Kristina will soon be here . . . Yes, there Lord
Sten Sture's coffin still stands, because no one has wanted to perform the burial service.

(ANNA BIELKE *tries to convey her thoughts by means of facial
expressions; whispers.*)

CASTELLAN: Lord Sten was mortally wounded down in Västergöt-land and died on the ice of Lake Mälare; Erik Lejonhuvud betrayed us and showed the Danes the way across Tiveden Forest; King Christian is at Södermalm, and Gustav Trolle at Brunkeberg.

(ANNA BIELKE *as above*)

CASTELLAN: Lady Kristina doesn't want to surrender the castle, but Magnus Gren says we don't have any more powder or lead ... There she comes!

KRISTINA (*enters, dressed in mourning*): Anna! [64] (*Embrace*)

ANNA BIELKE: Alone, deserted, my Johan is dead as you know. He fell on the wall next to the big cannon that he called ...

KRISTINA: Anna Bielke, of course!

ANNA BIELKE: Yes, that's what he called it ... and my names were his last words. Dear Johan!

KRISTINA: Anna dear, we've had our heavy sorrows, but the heaviest remains. The castle can't defend itself any longer.

ANNA BIELKE: It must! Let me greet dear Sten first. (*She goes into the room where the coffin stands, greeting in passing* LADY MÄTTA, *who does not see her.*)

(KRISTINA *stands waiting for* ANNA BIELKE; *the stage is silent.*)

ANNA BIELKE (*comes out to her*): Sten is lying smiling like the sleeping child he was all his life ... how hopeful he looks ... as if he knew that it would end well.

KRISTINA: But first through blood and tears ...

ANNA BIELKE: How can you say that?

KRISTINA: Someone has said it ...

ANNA BIELKE: Lady Mätta's visions. Don't believe in them!

KRISTINA: We always used to believe the best; now I believe the worst ... Did you know Christian has crucified our brave Måns Jönsson? [65]

ANNA BIELKE: Crucified! Good God in Heaven!

KRISTINA: And he has given me the choice—to be burned, drowned, or buried alive! But he has even ... he has proposed to me! [66]

ANNA BIELKE: Why, he's the wild beast of the Apocalypse! [67] An insane wild animal!

KRISTINA: The last cup must be drained. There's Magnus Gren!

MAGNUS GREN: The castle can't hold out, Lady Kristina!

KRISTINA: I won't surrender it!

MAGNUS GREN: Then they'll take it!

KRISTINA: Can it be taken?

MAGNUS GREN: Yes . . . in a trice!

KRISTINA: Then let it be taken; I won't surrender!

MAGNUS GREN: Then we'll be crucified like Måns Jönsson! Do you want that?

KRISTINA (*struggles with herself*): Has Heming Gad really returned with King Christian?

MAGNUS GREN: That's true, and they say he's like a turned-over hand.

KRISTINA: I don't believe it! I don't believe it!

MAGNUS GREN: Talk with him!

KRISTINA: Let him come! If Heming Gad has betrayed us, then . . . Stockholm Castle will fall, too. Let him come!

MAGNUS GREN: Fine. He shall come. (*Goes*)

KRISTINA: What do you believe, Anna?

ANNA BIELKE: Everything! Erik Lejonhuvud betrayed the Swedish army; Göran Sparre has gone over to the enemy . . .

KRISTINA: Göran?

ANNA BIELKE: Bishop Mathias of Strängnäs is preaching for the success of the Danes; Bishop Otto of Västerås, Bishop Vincentius of Skara, the common people are all on Christian's side . . .

KRISTINA: The common people?

ANNA BIELKE: Yes, they're tired of civil war, and besides Christian has a reputation for being friendly to the people [68] . . .

KRISTINA: Is he?

ANNA BIELKE: Not at all! He hates the lords, and that's why he plays up to the despised farmers, but he hates the farmers, too, just as he hates all of humanity.

KRISTINA: Come and sit down while we wait for Heming Gad. (*They sit down.*)

ANNA BIELKE: Do you remember last time when we met in this room?

KRISTINA: Do I remember? We were expecting Gustav Trolle to be our guest, and I had carried out the birds, so that he could sleep in the morning.

ANNA BIELKE: And Johan was along helping . . . Gustav Vasa sat here at the table . . .

KRISTINA: Where is Gustav Vasa now?

ANNA BIELKE: Last time I heard he was a prisoner at Brahe's in Kallö [69] . . .

KRISTINA: He loved you, Anna.

ANNA BIELKE: Me? No! . . .

KRISTINA: Yes, and he took it very much to heart . . .

ANNA BIELKE: I never noticed that.

CASTELLAN (*enters*): Bishop Heming Gad.

KRISTINA: Let him come! Stay, Anna.

ANNA BIELKE: And Lady Mätta?

KRISTINA: She doesn't hear, doesn't see, she only mourns for her Sten. Sh-h! Now! Lord God, help me!

(HEMING GAD *enters. Pause*)

HEMING GAD: Lady Kristina! That we should meet again so . . .

KRISTINA: So?

HEMING GAD: Under circumstances at once so sad and so happy.

KRISTINA: Happy?

HEMING GAD: Yes, when I can come with the palms of peace in the midst of the pine boughs of sorrow . . . I must say . . .

KRISTINA: I must say . . .

HEMING GAD: King Christian, our gracious lord and king . . .

KRISTINA: When did he become that?

HEMING GAD: From the hour when he in July, 1498, became heir apparent to the crown of Sweden . . .

KRISTINA: Is the crown inherited? Isn't the king elected?

HEMING GAD: It used to be so, but now Christian II has even been elected king of Sweden . . .

KRISTINA: Has he been elected king at Mora meadow,[70] according to the law of the land, by the councillors and the bishops of Sweden? No! He has been elected by Danes and half-Swedish beasts . . . so the election is illegal.

HEMING GAD: And he offers eternal peace, reconciliation, forgetting everything . . . You, Lady Kristina, used to love peace as the highest good, and you had a forgiving spirit, you and the good Lord Sten . . . of blessed memory . . . Will you permit me to perform a precious duty, to see him who so sadly and too soon has passed away?

KRISTINA (*places herself in the door to the room in which the coffin is standing*): No, that I will not permit . . .

HEMING GAD: Excuse me, I understand your grief, and this door . . .

KRISTINA: It's closed to you, but the other one, that one over there, is open to you, way out into the entrance, down the stairs, all the way down into the gutter!

HEMING GAD (*revealing himself frankly*): Lady Kristina!

KRISTINA: Heming Gad!

HEMING GAD: Stockholm Castle . . .

KRISTINA: Will never be surrendered . . .

HEMING GAD: Because it has been surrendered! Magnus Gren has handed over the keys!

KRISTINA: Then I thank God that I didn't have to bear that shame!

HEMING GAD: What do you say to that?

KRISTINA: Nothing! But I shall go to Sten Sture and tell him how fortunate he was to die before he saw Heming Gad as a traitor! (*Goes into the other room*)

HEMING GAD: Lady Anna, will you listen to me?

(ANNA BIELKE *turns her back to him.*)

HEMING GAD (*goes up to* MÄTTA STURE): Lady Mätta, will you listen to me?

MÄTTA STURE (*gets up and makes a gesture of rejection as if she were cursing him*): At Raseborg Castle in Finland stand gallows that are waiting for you! [71]

HEMING GAD: Gallows?

MÄTTA STURE: Go, damned soul, into the fire of hell!

(HEMING GAD, *struck, then bewildered and half blind, he tries to get out quickly but bumps into furniture and walls before he succeeds in getting out. Silence*)

(KRISTINA *comes on stage, throws herself into* ANNA BIELKE's *arms, and sobs aloud.*)

ANNA BIELKE (*whispers words of comfort to her and caresses her cheeks*): Kersti, Kersti, dear . . . there, there.

KRISTINA: He's sleeping in there, the good man, but no one dares say a prayer over him! And now they're coming to take him . . . King Christian has threatened to burn his coffin at the stake, like a criminal! He—excommunicated! And no friend left, only strange faces, traitors, and Heming Gad, Bishop Heming Gad, the friend of the Stures for eighty years! Oh God, if I could say one good word in his defense! Help me, Anna! Speak of his imprisonment, want, and hunger, his eighty years, say that he lost his mind!

ANNA BIELKE: Say nothing! Eternal silence suits best a deed, the very mention of which is shame!

MAGNUS GREN (*enters*): Lady Kristina! Don't be angry with me. They *took* the keys . . . I am innocent!

KRISTINA: God bless you, Magnus, for that! (*They shake each other's hands firmly.*)

MAGNUS GREN (*kisses her hand*): Lady Kristina . . .

KRISTINA: We have not surrendered! Hear that, Sten . . . we have not surrendered!

ANNA BIELKE: Child!

MAGNUS GREN: Lady Kristina! Now you may be happy . . . dry your tears—([KRISTINA] *takes her handkerchief and dries her eyes*) I have something to tell you!

(KRISTINA *interested*)

MAGNUS GREN: I've found a man—a Swede—who'll conduct Lord
   Sten's burial!

KRISTINA: Have you found a man in this country?

MAGNUS GREN: See, now she smiled! She hasn't done that for a long
   time, poor lady. Yes, the son of a smith from Örebro has just
   come back from Germany. He's . . . what was his name? Yes,
   Olof Pederson, that is Olaus Petri,[72] I think. He's a bit of a
   heretic as people usually are, and, when he heard that Lord Sten's
   not yet buried, he swore in his young beard that even if the Dane
   and the devil should intervene he'd still perform the last rites for
   Sten Sture. And so he went to the Gray Friars on their island—
   they're a little on the outs with the pope, too—and there he got a
   grave!

KRISTINA: Olaus Petri, a new face!

MAGNUS GREN: New times, new faces, when we old ones pass on. At
   any rate, I've approached the builders' guild, and they've arrived
   to carry our dear Lord Sten to his last resting place. Things are
   working out pretty well.

KRISTINA: You're kind, Magnus, and, if I can only secure the peace
   of the grave for Sten, we'll manage. Are the builders here?

MAGNUS GREN: Yes, I'm treating them to food and drink out there,
   for it must be honorable when Sture's to be buried.

KRISTINA: Hurry then, Magnus!

   (MAGNUS GREN *goes nodding and speaking to himself.*)

KRISTINA (*at the door with the black drapes*): You and I, for the
   last time! (*Kneels.* ANNA BIELKE *beside her*)

KRISTINA: Let us each say a prayer.

MÄTTA STURE: "And another angel came out from the altar, which
   had power over fire; and cried with a loud cry to him that had
   the sharp sickle, saying, Thrust in thy sharp sickle, and gather
   the clusters of the vine of the earth, for her grapes are fully ripe.
   And the angel thrust in his sickle into the earth, and cast it into
   the great winepress of the wrath of God. And the winepress was

trodden without the city, and blood came out of the winepress, even unto the horse bridles." [73]

ANNA BIELKE: "And God shall wipe away all tears from their eyes; and there shall be no more death, neither sorrow, nor crying, neither shall there be any more pain: for the former things are passed away." [74]

KRISTINA: "For love is strong as death; jealousy is cruel as the grave; the coals thereof are coals of fire, which hath a most vehement flame. Many waters cannot quench love; neither can the floods drown it: if a man would give all the substance of his house for love, it would utterly be condemned." [75]

ALL: Amen! (*Pause*)

(MAGNUS GREN *enters.* BUILDERS' GUILD *with their banner and axes wreathed with pine twigs.* KRISTINA *greets them. They bow.* KRISTINA *talks softly with their* ALDERMAN *who thereupon goes into the coffin room with his hammer.* MAGNUS GREN *and* KRISTINA *go downstage.*)

MAGNUS GREN: Now, dear lady, there will soon be sunshine for you, it will dry up after the rain, and then everything will become green. Listen! Gustav Vasa has fled from the Danes—has gone to Lübeck, where he has got help . . . returned to his country . . . and now he's in Dalarna.

KRISTINA: In Dalarna! Then there's hope!

MAGNUS GREN: Where love is, is faith, and hope builds on faith!

KRISTINA: And God shall dry all tears . . . for the past is past!

(*Powerful hammer blows can be heard as the coffin is nailed down.* ALL *look at each other with emotion.* MÄTTA STURE *lifts her hands to the sky.* KRISTINA *and* ANNA BIELKE *embrace.*)

MAGNUS GREN: For the past is past!

CURTAIN

Notes on

'The Last of the Knights'

BETWEEN 1397 AND 1523 Sweden was nominally united from time to time with Denmark and Norway under the supremacy of the ruler of Denmark. Except for relatively brief periods, however, Swedish adherence to the union was uneasy and uncertain. In fact, in 1434 the Dalesmen's leader, Engelbrekt, led a successful revolt against the Danish exploiters of Sweden which not only secured independence until his assassination by Bengt Stensson Natt-och-Dag, the father of Johan Natt-och-Dag in Strindberg's play, in 1436 but which awakened the spirit of Swedish nationalism, a spirit that was to remain alive throughout the whole so-called union period.

After Engelbrekt's death, the Swedes divided into the two parties, the nationalists and the unionists, represented in the play by Sten Sture and the Trolles, respectively. The nationalists consisted mainly of commoners, but fortunately there were enough members of the great aristocratic families to provide leadership for the party during the union period. Karl Knutsson, a member of the Bonde family, managed to be elected king of a free Sweden for three periods, 1448–1457, 1464–1465, and 1467–1470. On his death in 1470, Sten Sture the Elder was elected regent (or admin-

83

istrator). A year later, the Danish king tried to conquer Sweden, but in the Battle of Brunkeberg in October, 1471, the Danes were so thoroughly defeated that no further attempt was made to bring Sweden by force into the union again until King Hans ascended the Danish throne in 1481.

The unionists consisted mainly of the great lords and their personal followers and, unfortunately for the church, many of the highest prelates in the country. The lords favored the union for many reasons, the most important of which were (1) the conviction that if the king lived in Copenhagen the lords themselves would have the real power, (2) the conviction that the nationalist cause represented a democratic trend that would rob the lords of power, and (3) the custom of intermarriage between members of many of the aristocratic families of the various Scandinavian countries. In the play, the Trolles, for example, represent all these reasons; among other things, the Trolles are partly Danish and partly Swedish. Throughout the whole period the lords intrigued and brought pressure on both regents and kings to forward the aristocrats' selfish interests.

Between 1482 and 1497, King Hans worked hard to secure Sweden for himself, but not until 1497 did he succeed in entering Stockholm and being crowned. The lords eventually acknowledged Hans's son Christian as heir apparent to the throne, thus laying the foundation of Christian II's claim to the Swedish throne. During his stay in Stockholm, King Hans knighted many Swedes, among them the very young Sten Sture the Younger, the "last" of the knights. In 1503, Sten Sture the Elder died and was succeeded as regent by Svante Sture, a relative who had assumed the popular Sture name. Svante Sture's regency proved a continuation of the struggle between the Danish king and the nationalist Swedes.

Upon the death of Svante Sture in 1512, the lords hastened to elect Erik Trolle, a pro-Danish unionist, regent, but within a few months the nationalists, supported by overwhelming public opinion, forced through the election of nineteen-year-old Sten Sture the Younger, the son of Svante Sture.

Strindberg's account of Sten Sture the Younger's regency is in keeping with the sources: Sture did try to unite the Swedes and to secure peace and prosperity for the country, but he found himself opposed by the young archbishop, Gustav Trolle, and many of the other lords at every turn. Three times, at the archbishop's request, Christian II of Denmark invaded Sweden. In 1517, the Swedes defeated him at Vädla, now a part of Stockholm. In 1518, the Swedish forces defeated Christian's at the battle of Brännkyrka—Gustav Vasa may have been the Swedish flagbearer. Before Christian sailed away that time, he had managed to secure six important hostages. In 1520, the Danes invaded Sweden from both land and sea; Sten Sture was wounded and shortly afterward died. His widow, Lady Kristina Gyllenstierna Sture, defended Stockholm Castle for over half a year, but in the fall she had to surrender. Christian II was at last master of Sweden.

THE CHARACTERS

Sten Sture the Younger (*ca.* 1492–1520), the last of the knights—SB, II, 625, says that on a document signed by Erik Trolle as regent in January, 1512, the last cosigner among the knights was Sten Sture. The son of Svante Sture (regent, 1503–1512), knighted by King Hans about the turn of the century, he became the knightly hero indicated in the quotation on page 3 and, by moving swiftly in cooperation with advisers and particularly his father's commandants of the fortified castles throughout the realm, forced through his own election as regent in July, 1512. A gifted ruler, great folk leader, and military man of great ability, Sten made appreciable progress both in uniting the Swedes and in governing them well until he consented to the election of Gustav Trolle as archbishop. The major facts of the period were much as Strindberg has given them: Trolle's refusal to recognize Sture as the legal ruler; the archbishop's intriguing with dissident lords at his court at Uppsala and Stäke; his traitorous correspondence with the Danish king; his rejection of every conciliatory move of the regent; the siege of Stäke; the regent's presentation at the meeting of Arboga of his measures against Trolle; the defeat of the Danes at Vädla in 1517; the arrest and deposal of the archbishop; the excommunication of Sture (Christian II was assigned the task of executing the papal decree); the defeat of Christian at Brännkyrka in 1518; the treacherous kidnaping of the Swedish hostages; and the death of Sten Sture in February, 1520. One of the ugly details of the bloodbath was the removal of the bodies of Sten Sture and an infant son from their coffin on Christian's orders and their being burned as heretics along with the Stockholm victims of Christian's bloodbath. Descendants of Sten

Sture, including the young Svante of *The Regent,* played important roles in the reigns of both Gustav I and Erik XIV. See particularly Strindberg's *Erik XIV.*

Lady Kristina Gyllenstierna Sture (1494–1559), the beautiful daughter of Nils Eriksson Gyllenstierna, and the half-sister of Cecilia of Eka (Gustav Vasa's mother), not only belonged to one of the great aristocratic families but was related to many of the others. Married at seventeen to young Sten Sture, she was, according to the records and traditions, the perfect wife for the last of the knights—SB (II, 624) says, for example, "Kristina was idealistic and noble by temperament, capable of great sacrifices for the welfare of her country and . . . was a worthy wife for Lord Sten." While Strindberg's presentation follows his sources' account of Lady Kristina, it should perhaps be emphasized that her heroic defense of Stockholm Castle against the Danes after her husband's death is the fact that has made her one of the heroines of the Swedish people. Even after the surrender of the castle in the fall of 1520, Kristina was one of the very few who dared to protest against the barbaric brutality of Christian II. She was imprisoned in Copenhagen but released in 1524. Strindberg's suggestion that Sören Norrby, the Danish naval hero and later Baltic pirate, sued for her hand is probably true. She married Johan Turesson Tre Rosor, a Swedish lord, in the late 1520's.

Archbishop Gustav Trolle (1488–1535), the son of Lord Erik and Lady Ingeborg Tott Trolle, is the subject of many stories which suggest he was extremely intractable and obstinate, brilliant, and ambitious. A unionist perhaps largely because he saw in the union his greatest opportunities to acquire possessions, prestige, and, above all, power, Gustav Trolle—an apt scholar in Rome—was chosen archbishop in 1514 largely because of the intrigues of his aging predecessor, Archbishop Jacob Ulvsson, and other members, lay as well as clerical, of the unionist party and because of the naive optimism of Regent Sten Sture. His qualifications for the high position included brilliance and learning but certainly neither the faith nor the humility usually associated with the Christian ministry. What Strindberg has to say about his behavior as archbishop in both *The Last of the Knights* and *The Regent* in no way exaggerates the source accounts of his hatred of Sten Sture, their meetings, his treachery and deception, his treasonous correspondence with Christian of Denmark, his defense of Stäke, his use of military force and ambitions as a military man, his being deposed at a national meeting in 1518 on the basis of treason, his imprisonment, the destruction of Stäke, his resumption of the position of archbishop in 1520 upon Christian's arrival in Sweden, and his major role in the Stockholm bloodbath (see pp. 163-164). Finally in 1521, when the war for independence from the union under Gustav Vasa promised to succeed and Christian II was in serious trouble throughout all Scandinavia, Gustav Trolle fled to Germany, where he fought as a volunteer in the Lübeck forces until he died as the result of wounds received in the Battle of Öxnebjerg (1535). None of the sources expresses any admiration for this Renaissance prelate. Fryxell (II, 185) says, for example, "Gustav Trolle became proud and ambitious, hard and revengeful, tenacious and uncompromising." He has been called the Judas Iscariot of Sweden.

Heming Gad or *Gadd* (*ca.* 1439–1520), a native of Småland, was Sten Sture the Elder's representative in Rome for over twenty years and there became a favorite of Pope Alexander VI, who made him chamberlain. Shortly after Gad's return to Sweden, Bishop Henrik of Linköping died in 1500; already cathedral dean there, Gad was elected bishop by the cathedral chapter, but the election was never confirmed. A close friend and supporter of the Stures, Gad served them not only as an adviser but as their commander in the sieges of both Stockholm and Kalmar castles. Fryxell (II, 181) says that Gad "was learned, fluent, courageous, intrepid, and quick-witted as well as highly experienced in everything. During his youth he had often been in Rome, where his great learning and cleverness brought him into great favor with the Pope." As much at home on the battlefield as in the church, Heming Gad had the gift of arousing the enthusiasm and loyalty of the commoners; he is remembered for many things, among them his skill in diplomacy and intrigue, his genuine patriotism, his gift for moving oratory, his earthy language, his sense of humor, and his bitter hatred of the Danes. His relationship with Sten Sture the Younger was apparently much as Strindberg says. The sudden change in his attitude toward the union after he had been treacherously carried off to Denmark by Christian II has never been satisfactorily explained. Perhaps, as Strindberg suggests, old age and a sincere conviction that the Swedes could never withstand Christian may have caused Gad's defection. His execution at Raseborg in Finland shortly after the bloodbath—on Christian II's orders—was an undeserved end to the brilliant and long career of one of the ablest and most colorful men of his day.

Johan Månsson Natt-och-Dag (died 1520), the son of Engelbrekt's murderer, was not, as Strindberg says, ostracized by his contemporaries because of his father's crime. He did, however, take part in the nationalists' efforts for independence, was commandant at Kalmar Castle, and died there defending it against the Danes. He was married twice, the second time to *Anna Bielke,* who defended the castle after his death. Two of his sons by his first wife played heroic roles in the struggle for independence. About Johan's father, SB (II, 456–457) says: "It is said that Magnus [Måns] Bengtsson completely changed his whole attitude. In the first heat of repentance over his crime he wanted to commit suicide and to kill the Danes who were his advisers."

Burgomaster Nils Brems and the merchants *Cord König* and *Herman Israel* of Lübeck were the three pro-Swedish Lübeckers who befriended and protected Gustav Vasa after he managed to escape from imprisonment as a hostage in Denmark in 1519. They were in large part responsible for preventing the Hanseatic city's council from handing over Gustav to Christian II as the latter had demanded. The three men were particularly active in helping Sweden in the war for independence; their major motive was, as Strindberg says, commercial benefit. Herman Israel is also an important character in *Master Olof* and *Gustav Vasa.*

Magnus Gren belonged to an old aristocratic family. He is known primarily for the support he gave Lady Kristina in the siege of Stockholm Castle by Christian II and Archbishop Trolle.

Mätta (or *Märta*) *Ivarsdotter Dyre Sture* was by birth apparently a Danish or Dano-Norwegian noblewoman. She married in turn Anders von Bergen, Knut Alfsson, and Svante Sture, the first two Norwegians and the third the widowed father of Sten Sture the Younger. Knut Alfsson, first married to a granddaughter of Charles VIII of Sweden, had estates both in Sweden and Norway, had tried to secure Norway's independence from the union, and was for many years a close associate of Svante Sture. After Alfsson's murder, his widow fled to Sweden and soon afterward became engaged to Svante Sture. Whether she poisoned Sten Sture the Elder to hasten her fiancé's election as regent, as some of the sources say, is not known, but Strindberg's sources provided him with many conflicting details about her person and her activities. How many of the details Strindberg selected and adapted for his purposes are accurate is uncertain, but it is certain that she made her presence felt and that the Swedish nationalists did not love her.

Lars Siggesson Sparre (died 1554) was one of Gustav Vasa's most loyal supporters throughout his lifetime. Among other services he rendered the great king was the crushing of the Dacke rebellion in the 1540's (see Strindberg's *Gustav Vasa*). He was also a member of the national council.

Erik Trolle (*ca.* 1460–*ca.* 1529) belonged to an old and powerful aristocratic family. At the time of Svante Sture's death, Erik Trolle, says SB (II, 621), was "an old, learned, experienced, and soft-spoken man, who most likely would have preferred to live in peace on his estates." The pro-union lords and prelates elected him regent in January, 1512, but the independence party which controlled the fortified castles throughout the kingdom forced through the election of Sten Sture the Younger in July of that year. Lord Erik's role in Sten Sture's regency was apparently pretty much as Strindberg defines it. During Gustav Vasa's reign, Trolle tried to stir up a rebellion against the king among the Dalesmen; when that failed he fled to Denmark, where he had relatives and estates.

Erik Abrahamsson Lejonhuvud (*Leijonhufvud*) (died 1520) was a descendant of the illegitimate son of Princess Judith of Denmark and King Valdemar of Sweden (see *Earl Birger of Bjälbo* in this volume). As Strindberg says, the man's career was one of fluctuating loyalties. His last treacherous act—guiding the Danish forces through Tiveden Forest so as to encircle the Swedish forces under Sten Sture's command—ironically did not benefit him: he was the first lord executed in the Stockholm bloodbath.

For a note on *Gustav Vasa,* see pp. 164-165. For information about the other characters not mentioned above, see the notes on the following pages.

LIST OF CHARACTERS

1. Even the Swedish lords did not have official family names until *Riddarhuset* (the House of Lords) was opened in 1626 by Gustav II Adolf. Before that time most of the aristocrats were identified by the names of the father and the clan, for example, *Gustav Eriksson Vasa.* Gustav

was the son of Erik Johansson of the clan of Vasa. To simplify the identification of the characters, I have eliminated the patronymics whenever possible. Specifically, these are the changes: Kristina Gyllenstjerna > Kristina Sture; Gustav Eriksson (Vasa) > Gustav Vasa; Johan Månsson Natt och Dag > Johan Natt-och-Dag; Lars Siggesson Sparre > Lars Sparre; Göran Siggesson Sparre > Göran Sparre; Erik Abrahamsson Lejonhuvud > Erik Lejonhuvud; and Mätta Ivarsdotter Dyre > Mätta Sture. Since Strindberg makes a point of the Swedes' unwillingness to address Lady Mätta by the popular and even idolized name of Sture, I have called her Lady Mätta rather than Lady Sture.

ACT I

2. The reference is apparently to the meeting at Arboga in 1471 when Sten Sture the Elder was elected regent. "Olaus Petri says that a shipload of German ale was distributed among the farmers, and for that reason they cast their votes as he who gave them the ale demanded" (SB, II, 419).

3. The Danish flag had then as now a white cross on a field of red. Strindberg says in *Svenska folket i helg och sökn* (Chicago, n.d.; first published in Stockholm, 1882) that the present Swedish flag (a yellow cross on a field of blue) is first mentioned in the accounts of John III and his reign (1568–1592) (chap. vii, pp. 309-310). Strindberg believed that in 1511, the year of Sten Sture the Younger's election, blue was considered the Swedish color, and that the Swedes frequently used a standard having three golden crowns on a field of blue. The Trolles belonged to the Unionist (hence pro-Danish and peace party); the Stures to the Independence or Nationalist Party.

4. In 1497 King Hans of Denmark-Norway succeeded in gaining the Swedish crown by right of conquest. According to Strindberg's sources, Lejonhuvud's record was of shifting his allegiance from party to party as either the unionists or the nationalists seemed to gain advantage in the struggle for the control of Sweden.

5. In Sweden only the king had the right to knight anyone. During King Hans's brief reign in Sweden (1497–1501), a great many Swedes were knighted, but in the long period between 1501 and 1520, when Christian II was crowned king, no one received the coveted rank. Note,

for example, Gustav Vasa's urging Sten Sture to accept the Swedish crown.

6. The accounts of the whole so-called union period (1397–1523) testify to the fluctuating loyalties of many of the aristocratic families. Both the Vasas and the Oxenstjernas had been primarily unionists, and hence from the nationalists' point of view pro-Danish, up until the sixteenth century.

7. *Lejonhuvud* means "Lion's head." *Fårskallen,* Strindberg's term, is here translated "Muttonhead."

8. Johan Natt-och-Dag (literally, Night-and-Day) was the son of the lord who murdered the great Swedish folk leader Engelbrekt in April, 1436. Hence, the ostracism which Strindberg has emphasized to a degree not supported by historical sources.

9. In the original, Gustav Vasa's question and Johan's reply are in Danish.

10. Erik of Pomerania, Queen Margaret of Denmark's nephew, was elected king of Sweden in 1396; in her presence, he was crowned king (the first of the union kings) at Kalmar in 1397.

11. Engelbrekt Engelbrektsson, a nobleman, led the successful revolt against the oppressive union forces between 1434 and 1436. Among his many achievements was the assembly of the first *riksdag* (parliament) with representatives of all four classes—lords, clergy, burghers, and farmers—at Arboga in 1436. For Strindberg's interpretation of this hero, see his play *Engelbrekt* (1901).

12. Both of these Dalesmen played important parts in Gustav Vasa's liberation of Sweden from the union in 1520–1523; both are included among the characters in Strindberg's *Gustav Vasa* (1899).

13. Rydboholm and Lindholm (where Gustav Vasa was perhaps born) in Uppland, and Rävsnäs in Södermanland, were Vasa estates.

14. See note 8.

15. Upon King Hans's death in 1513, he was succeeded in Denmark and Norway by his son Christian II. While in Bergen, Christian met Dyveke, the beautiful daughter of Sigbrit, a Dutchwoman. The daughter became his mistress and the mother one of his major advisers. See Karen Larsen's *A History of Norway* (New York: American-Scandinavian Foundation, 1948) for a fairly detailed account of the king's behavior in

Norway. Christian married Elizabeth of Austria, the sister of Emperor Charles V.

16. The Dalesmen provided Gustav Vasa with his key support in his war for independence (1520–1523). All of the places mentioned are prominent in the Gustav Vasa story largely because of engagements with the Danish forces that took place there.

17. Kalmar Castle, frequently called the key to Sweden, was controlled in 1502 by Erik Lejonhuvud, Swedish by birth but frequently disloyal to the nationalist cause (see note 4). At the head of an army, Heming Gad had besieged both Stockholm and Kalmar castles, but, according to Strindberg's sources, Kalmar Castle did not come into the nationalists' control until the fall of 1510.

18. Zechariah 13:7.

19. I Samuel 16:7, 12.

20. Psalms 128:1, 3, 4, 5.

21. According to Strindberg's sources, Sten Sture did make this unfortunate statement.

22. Heming Gad spent the last twenty years of the fifteenth century in Rome, primarily as a representative of the nationalists. Apparently a favorite of Pope Alexander VI, Gad had had ample opportunity to observe the immorality of high-ranking church officials in Rome.

23. Strindberg probably had Ture Turesson Bielke, the half-brother of Lady Anna's father, in mind. SB (II, 344) says: "Incidentally, it was during this battle [between King Christian I and the Swedish commoners at Stockholm in 1463] that Ture Turesson earned his nickname 'butcher of the commoners.' He is supposed to have been the one who, in the church on Helgeandsholmen [now Riddarholmen], without mercy cut down the farmers who had taken refuge there."

24. Johan Natt-och-Dag was commander of the strategic Kalmar Castle in 1511, according to SB (II, 604), and died there as its heroic defender in 1520. Strindberg has adapted the facts about both Johan and his second wife, Anna Bielke. See note 8. For the allusion to Johan's fear that he has killed a man, see the reference to Jeppe Bagge, note 34.

ACT II

25. Svante Sture, regent with some interruptions from 1503 to his death in 1512, married in 1504 Mätta or Märta Dyre, the Danish-born

widow of Knut Alfsson, the leader of the Norwegian independence movement. See pp. 88-89.

26. Göksholm was the Natt-och-Dag family castle on the southern shore of Lake Hjälmare. See note 24.

27. In October, 1514, Gustav Trolle was elected archbishop of Sweden, largely through the efforts of retiring Archbishop Jacob Ulvsson and other unionists. Hoping to secure the new archbishop's friendship and support, Sten Sture acquiesced to the election—the pope had given him the right to veto—and prepared to receive Trolle with honor and festivity upon his return from Rome in the fall of 1515. The archbishop disregarded the regent's invitation, however, and proceeded directly to Uppsala and then to his fortified castle, Stäke.

28. When Sten Sture the Elder, regent with interruptions from 1471 to 1503, died, one of the current rumors was that Mätta Dyre Ulvsson, then fiancée of Svante Sture, had poisoned the old regent (see SB, II, 551 and 664). During her last husband's regency (1503–1512), Lady Mätta was rumored to be in treasonous correspondence with her native countrymen, the Danes. See note 25.

29. See note 21.

30. Quoted by Strindberg from a speech that Heming Gad was supposed by some of Strindberg's sources to have made.

31. The archbishop's fortified castle on Lake Mälare, northwest of Stockholm.

32. The *pallium* or band of white woolen cloth conferred on an archbishop by the pope as a symbol of pastoral power. Sten Sture not only secured the pope's confirmation but sent the pope the customary sum of money for it.

33. Archbishop Trolle was in Rome at the time of his election; on his way home, he conferred with King Christian of Denmark-Norway in Lübeck (SB, II, 641).

34. I have been unable to find any information about Jeppe Bagge.

35. Alexander Borgia (1431–1503) was Pope Alexander VI from 1492 to 1503. He was known not only for his brilliance but also for his licentiousness and cruelty.

36. Johannes Angelus Arcimboldus, the pope's legate, came to Sweden to investigate the archbishop's complaints against the regent and to sell

pardons. In 1518, after Trolle had been removed as archbishop, Sten Sture apparently entertained the idea of making Arcimboldus archbishop.

37. The leading German bankers of the period.

38. On more occasions than one, Christian appropriated money raised by the church in Sweden by simply taking it from captured vessels and messengers.

39. Karl Knutsson, of the powerful Bonde family or clan, was king of Sweden three times during the so-called union period (1448–1457, 1464–1465, 1467–1470). An admirable man, King Karl (Charles VIII) was unfortunately the object of envy of the other great families, most conspicuously the Oxenstjernas, the most prominent of whom was the militant archbishop Jöns Bengtsson Oxenstjerna. See note 46.

ACT III

40. All these emphasize the charge that the church, or at least many of its highest-ranking leaders, no longer placed the major emphasis on spiritual matters but on worldly pleasures and power.

41. St. Birgitta (*ca.* 1303–1373), Sweden's most widely known saint, was the founder of the Order of the Saviour (the Brigittine Order). She was canonized in 1391. She is a character in Strindberg's play *The Saga of the Folkungs* (1899).

42. Martin Luther's questioning of one church doctrine and practice after the other began, of course, in 1517.

43. Apollyon is the Hebrew Abaddon (Revelations 9:11), the angel of the bottomless pit, i.e., Satan.

44. Strindberg's date should be 1499. See Ingvar Andersson's *Sveriges historia* (Stockholm, 1950), p. 134: "In 1499, Christian, the son of King Hans, was elected heir to the Swedish throne."

45. Sören Norrby (died 1530), a Danish nobleman and military man, commanded the Danish fleet which attacked Sweden in 1517 and again in 1520. Rumors had it that, after the Stockholm bloodbath (1520), Norrby was a suitor for the hand of the widowed Lady Kristina Sture.

46. Archbishop Jöns Bengtsson Oxenstjerna (died 1467), one of Charles VIII's bitterest enemies, in 1457 took off his episcopal garb in the Cathedral of Uppsala and put on helmet and armor to lead an army against the king. For a time, that archbishop succeeded in his goal of

being both archbishop and regent. His predecessor's example obviously intrigued Gustav Trolle. See notes 6 and 39.

ACT IV

47. See note 4.

48. In July, 1497, Sten Sture the Elder had besieged Stäke Castle unsuccessfully.

49. Deuteronomy 31:23.

50. Heming Gad (*ca.* 1439–1520) was elected bishop of Linköping in 1500, but his election was never confirmed.

ACT V

51. According to tradition, Gustav Vasa was the flag bearer at the Swedish victory of Brännkyrka in July, 1518. The folk ballad about St. George (*Sankt Göran*) was sung by the Swedish forces as they went into battle. The patron saint of chivalry, St. George was a native of Cappadocia, became an outstanding soldier, and was martyred. Note that the Swedish battle cry was "With God and St. George." The battle of Brunkeberg, north of Stockholm, in which Strindberg says the Swedes let the Danes hear the ballad first, was the Swedish victory over the Danes in October, 1471. The battle led to almost twenty-five years of nonintervention by the Danes. Incidentally, the ballad is, from a literary point of view, one of the unhappiest of Swedish ballads.

52. Little is known about the battle of Vädla (Duvnäs) in August, 1518, except that Gustav Vasa participated in it and that the Danes were routed.

53. The Dutch (Norwegian only by residence) mistress of Christian II died suddenly. The king suspected that she had been poisoned by Torben Oxe, a Danish rival for her affections, according to tradition. Oxe was shortly thereafter executed. See note 15.

54. Gustav Trolle and Christian II were primarily responsible for Sten Sture's excommunication in 1519.

55. See notes 36 and 38. SB (II, 666) says that Christian's seizure of all the money Arcimboldus had collected in Sweden proved very useful to the king in his preparation for war against the Swedes.

56. When Sten Sture (not Svante Sture, as Strindberg says) died in 1503, a letter was written in the dead man's name to gain time to secure Svante Sture's succession. Whether Heming Gad wrote it or not is uncertain.

57. The six hostages that Christian II carried off to Denmark. Except for the powerful Heming Gad, all were very young men and members of leading aristocratic families.

58. Strindberg has made use of legendary hints that Mätta Sture did have visions and that she suffered from pangs of conscience. Nevertheless, this speech is perhaps the most amazing in any of his plays about Swedish history: The prophecy that ends with "there are bends in the road" is hardly in keeping with Strindberg's usual realistic standards. See notes 25 and 28.

59. See note 53.

60. To this day southern Sweden is called *Götaland* (the land of the Goths) and central Sweden, *Svealand* (the land of the Swedes). The union of the two Scandinavian tribal kingdoms in perhaps the sixth or seventh century to form Sweden is one of the subjects of the Anglo-Saxon epic, *Beowulf*. Hence, the title of the Swedish king, "King of the Swedes, the Goths, etc."

61. See Strindberg's *Saga of the Folkungs* (1899) and the notes on *Earl Birger of Bjälbo* in this volume.

62. Details in this scene are highly reminiscent of *Ragnarok,* the twilight of the pagan Scandinavian gods. See Peter Andreas Munch's *Norse Mythology* (New York: American-Scandinavian Foundation, 1927), pp. 108-112. Surt, the black one, is the fire giant who stands watch at the borders of Muspelheim.

63. See H. A. Bellows' translation of the "Voluspa" in *The Poetic Edda* (New York: American-Scandinavian Foundation, 1923).

64. Lady Anna defended Kalmar Castle heroically for a time after the death of her husband.

65. Måns Jönsson, the commandant at Västerås Castle, was—on Christian II's order—hanged on the gallows on the Great Square and cruelly and unmercifully tortured and quartered, two days after the king's entrance into the capital, says Fryxell (II, 211). He was one of those to whom the king had promised amnesty.

66. These are details from the many legends about Lady Kristina.

67. For the beast of the Apocalypse, see Revelations 13 ff.

68. Christian II attempted to break the power of the great lords and council of Denmark by improving the conditions of the Danish farmers and helping the burghers develop Danish commerce.

69. While in Denmark, Gustav Vasa was in the keeping of distant relatives at Kallö in Jutland.

70. The traditional place in Uppland for the election of Swedish kings in the days before Sweden became a hereditary monarchy.

71. Heming Gad gained nothing by his conversion to Christian's unionist point of view while a prisoner in Denmark. On the king's orders, he was executed at Raseborg shortly after the bloodbath of Stockholm.

72. Olaus Petri, Sweden's Lutheran reformer. See Strindberg's *Master Olof* (1872).

73. Revelations 14:18-20.

74. Revelations 21:4.

75. Song of Solomon 8:6-7.

Introduction to The Regent

No OTHER royal Swedish figure attracted Strindberg as much as Gustav I Vasa (reigned 1523–1560). He appears in four plays: *Master Olof* (1872), *Gustav Vasa* (1899), *The Last of the Knights* (1908), and *The Regent* (1908), in the first and third as an important secondary character, in the other two as the central character. In each of the plays Gustav Vasa is presented at a critical point in his career as the founder of modern Sweden. In *The Last of the Knights* he is a very young man who learns about the harsh realities of life in a kingdom sadly torn by domestic dissension and by the attempts of foreign kings to exploit it for their own gain; in that play, Gustav Vasa receives the training and discipline necessary to a leader with a great mission. In *The Regent,* Gustav is a heroic but realistic leader who lets nothing stand in the way of the realization of his major objective—the complete independence of his country from a highly unsatisfactory union. In *Master Olof,* Gustav is a young king confronted with serious problems stemming in large measure from more than a century of internal disorder and foreign attempts at exploitation. In *Gustav Vasa,* the mature king has, in spite of personal and family as well as national and international difficulties, more than laid the foundations for an independent and powerful kingdom. In all four of the plays, there is a remarkably consistent interpretation of Gustav Vasa, even though the earliest, *Master Olof,* was written when Strindberg was a young man of twenty-three, and the last, *The Regent,* when Strindberg was fifty-nine.

The Regent was designed as a companion play to *The Last of the Knights:*

> The same settings as in *The Last of the Knights,* but in reverse order. This contrapuntal form which I have borrowed from music and used in *To Damascus I* has the effect of awakening in the theatergoer memories of the various places in which earlier actions took place, and thereby the drama has the effect of happening much later in life with a great deal behind it; accumulated impressions arise; there are echoes from better times; the hard reality of maturity dominates; the defeated are counted; crushed hopes are recalled; and the drama *The Last of the Knights* serves as the saga of youth in contrast to the heavy struggle of *The Regent.*

This little note prefixed to the play suggests that in both content and form the two plays are closely related. Note the reverse order of the same settings:

THE LAST OF THE KNIGHTS	THE REGENT
Act I The Rathskeller in Stockholm's Town Hall	*Act I* The same room in Stockholm Castle (*The Last of the Knights,* II and V)
Act II Scene 1: A room in Stockholm Castle Scene 2: The Lübeck office	*Act II* Outside the Blockhouse
Act III The sacristy in Uppsala Cathedral	*Act III* Scene 1: Before Stäke Castle Scene 2: The sacristy in Uppsala Cathedral

THE LAST OF THE KNIGHTS	THE REGENT
Act IV	*Act IV*
Before Stäke Castle	The Lübeck office
Act V	*Act V*
Scene 1: Outside the Blockhouse	Scene 1: The room in Stockholm
Scene 2: The same room in Stockholm Castle (Act II, Scene 1)	Castle
	Scene 2: The Rathskeller in Stockholm's Town Hall

The effect is what Strindberg says it is: *The Regent* does recall memories of the action in *The Last of the Knights;* with the qualifications implicit in passing of time and increase in age, *The Regent* serves as an illustration of the Strindbergian idea, *"Allt går igen,"* "Everything repeats itself." While *The Last of the Knights* gives one the impression of youngsters' idealistic, usually cheerful, and occasionally playful struggle for a goal, *The Regent* is the drama of the thoroughly realistic struggle of matured people for what is essentially the same goal.

If one takes the two plays together, they are a highly interesting study of the two extremes of human conduct as contrasted with the middle way of human behavior. Sten Sture, the last of the knights, represents the code of chivalry, with its dedication to idealism; he is crippled, however, by the childlike innocence, impulsiveness, and unthinking behavior which result from the sincere application of that code. Sture's and Vasa's leading opponent, Archbishop Gustav Trolle, in spite of his profession and office, represents the natural egotism of a man who from necessity gives lip service to honor but coldly and calculatingly plays for the highest stakes he can win. Between these two extremes is Gustav Vasa, the representative of the middle way.

In *The Regent,* Gustav Vasa is the leader who knows the world in which he has to function as a world of imperfection, hypocrisy, and compromise. It is not a pretty world, but it is not so ugly that Gustav Vasa feels—as Strindberg's Sten Sture does toward the end of his life—any particular desire to withdraw from it. Gustav Vasa knows that there is work to be done, and he believes that with due regard for the nature of man and of society he can get it done. He avoids the unrealistic excesses of the chivalric code represented by his beloved Sten Sture, with its frequent crippling unawareness of the nature of reality, and of the egotistic code of Archbishop Trolle, a code that he senses is evil and destructive. Gustav Vasa chooses the only code of conduct which will do for him in a very real and imperfect society: devotion to duty, resolution to do what is necessary even if it is unpleasant, thinking problems through, and basing his actions on practical considerations, even stooping to scheming and agreeing to compromise when there is no other way out.

Note how effectively Strindberg has contrasted the Machiavellian conduct of the archbishop, who is dedicated to the goal of acquiring the highest power in his country, worldly as well as spiritual, and Vasa's sane, careful working toward an idealistic—but attainable —goal. Strindberg significantly points up the immaturity and fundamental cowardice of Trolle's behavior in the scenes in which the archbishop appears. For example:

ERIK TROLLE: There is—mercy!

GUSTAV TROLLE: For me?

ERIK TROLLE: You were once condemned to death—in the forest of Stäke; then a knight came along, one of the fair ones, and he granted you mercy!

GUSTAV TROLLE: That was Sture!

ERIK TROLLE: And he was only a human being . . . This will teach you, head of the Church of Sweden! what every child knows! You learned people and Pharisees—flee! Through that door! Gustav Vasa is here—and the hand of the Lord is with him!

GUSTAV TROLLE: That door is locked!

ERIK TROLLE: It is not locked!

GUSTAV TROLLE: It is!

ERIK TROLLE (*opens the door to the secret passage*): You see, you of little faith, the door *is* open!

GUSTAV TROLLE (*amazed*): Come with me, father!

ERIK TROLLE: Are you afraid of the dark?

GUSTAV TROLLE: Yes, I am afraid, very much afraid!

ERIK TROLLE: I will go with my child who's afraid of the dark! (*He weeps.*) My big, old, lost child!

This is part of effective and sustained contrast, and, far from incidentally, an effective commentary on the comedy and tragedy of human life.

It is the Machiavellian antagonist who appears first in this thoroughly Strindbergian realistic play. The archbishop now is in nominal control of Sweden; the goal of his ambition, the high stakes for which he has worked and intrigued, are tantalizingly close to his grasp. By revealing the archbishop's attitude to his new rival for power, and by presenting the archbishop in the presence of his underlings—his father, the women held as hostages, Gustav Vasa's child sister, Bishop Brask (whom he tried to have executed at the bloodbath), and young Svante Sture—Strindberg quickly introduces the Machiavellian prince of the church. He is a tense, uneasy man, beset by inner conflicts and insecurity, frightened and terror-stricken because he can rely on no one but himself, with no tranquillity of conscience, yet capable of treating a little girl in a playful and not unfriendly manner.

The characterization of Archbishop Trolle in Act I is further developed in Act III by means of what might well be called the Strindbergian dissection of a soul—not a little reminiscent of *The Father, Lady Julie,* and, particularly, *Creditors.* Note this excerpt from the highly dramatic scene between the caretaker's wife and the archbishop:

CARETAKER'S WIFE (*hisses*): It's the enemy, the evil one, who's fetching you! You took the life of my youngest son, and you have ruined my daughter! You have butchered bishops and lords, and you've had the corpses brought to the stake by the barrel! You had the noble Sture dug up, you grave robber, you corpse spoiler; half the kingdom is in mourning, in sorrow; children rise up against parents, and parents against children; I have two sons whom you made traitors; there isn't one person to rely on; I sleep with my kitchen axe under my bed for my own husband's sake— listen, how it's rustling out there in the church—do you know what that is? Look this way, and you'll see. (*She opens the door at the back; black-clad ladies and children pass by as if in pro-cession.*) There they go to the graves, the widows and the father-less—the Vasas, the Stures, Brahe, the Gyllenstjernas, Ryning, Kurck, Lejonhuvud—yes, look for your sword, you hangman, you'll get rope . . .

This, in turn, is followed by Strindbergian self-analysis of the awakened sleepwalker. He is looking at his portrait:

It is horrible! I believe it is Alexander VI Borgia; and this is I! A human being, born of woman, nursed by a woman, and doesn't resemble a human being! (*Shrinks back*) It's not possible! I have seen my spirit—I have seen myself, I must die! But it is not I; it is someone else! I am not like that! (*He takes down a mirror from the wall and observes himself in it.*) Yes, it is! This is still worse . . . Flee? Oneself? How? Throw oneself on one's own sword, like Saul, but no one wants to hold it! No one!

It is a portrayal, amazingly rich in nuances, of a man who is a strik-ing contrast to the central character, who has chosen a more prac-tical and idealistic code of conduct.

In Act II Gustav Vasa appears for the first time after the careful introduction of his leading opponent, the theme, the major conflicts, and necessary exposition. The Vasa that appears is still, as Heming Gad had described him, "gifted . . . and realistic about the evil in people," but he is no longer the faithful squire in the service of the last of the knights. He is a young but tried commander-in-chief who has no illusions about himself, the people whose leader he is, or his opponents. The still young lord is, as Herman Israel later says in Act IV:

. . . a very wise man, very wise, because in his younger years he had to learn the difficult art of living in a hard school, and Gustav

Vasa knows that the ships and the goods weren't what they should have been—there weren't any others—and he knows that the money is defective; but instead of looking a gift horse in the mouth, and wasting time by complaining, he went ahead on rotten ships and with false money, straight to his objective . . . in a straight line—

He has become a folk leader who has earned the respect not only of the imprisoned Swedish ladies, who know that he is not likely to let sentiment stand in the way of the attainment of his goal, but also of the archbishop, who knows that Gustav Vasa is an opponent who will be disposed of only when he is in his grave.

The self-reliant leader, who is not above indulging in a practical joke on occasion, is quickly revealed in Act II in the presence of his principal henchmen, young Sture, his mother, and Lady Mätta. He is obviously the object of admiration and loyalty on the part of his men (Göran Sparre's resentment and envy serve as necessary contrast to the pleasant relations between Gustav and his other men). He has the knack of dealing with the men about him; he can be tender and manly with young Sture; when he is with his mother, he reveals that he is religious in his own unorthodox fashion, that he has a strong sense of what is right and fitting, that he loves his mother but will not let that love blunt or change his purpose; and, in the conversation with the unpopular Lady Mätta, he shows that he has self-confidence, strong feelings, and a violent temper. The portrayal of Gustav Vasa at the end of Act II is of a practical yet idealistic realist who knows what should be done, who believes that he is the one chosen to do it, and who will permit nothing within his control to prevent him from doing it.

Now regent, the Gustav of Act III states plainly what his concept of his office is: "The one who manages the affairs of the kingdom when they are neglected by foreign tyrants, stairway opportunists and court sneaks, by Roman swine, defilers of men and extortionists!" and a moment later what his kind of statesmanship is: "Honest words! Honest blows! To the point!" His firm but respectful treatment of Bishop Brask; his sincere approval of Lars Sparre because "he has the unusual gift of being honorable, is a man who keeps his word, and is truthful"; his genuine concern about his mother and sisters—hostages held by the Danes as a very real threat to force him to give up his goal—and his relatively slight hesitation in choosing between his duty to his country and his duty to his mother and sisters are further developments of the leader who rejects both extremes of human conduct for the realistic middle way.

Gustav Vasa does not appear in Act IV, but Strindberg nevertheless continues the development of the characterization of the leader who has now been elected King Gustav I. The comments of the Lübeckers, the archbishop's father, and Bishop Brask represent two of the conflicts that have faced Gustav Vasa all along—the envy and scheming of the powerful lords and the intriguing and enmity of the prelates of the church. Both the lords and the princes of the church have pursued their own selfish aims with little or no consideration for the common good. Brask's objections to Gustav Vasa's election to the throne ironically rest not a little on the fact that Squire Vasa does not have the polished and suave manners of the knight:

> ISRAEL: Vasa is Vasa; he's a crude fellow—
> BRASK: Exactly! I really like him for his blunt manner, but he's godless as his father was, and, as long as there are Stures, then . . .

It is clear, moreover, that Lübeck supports Vasa because it is good business to support the man with the heavy hand who can prevent Denmark from destroying Lübeck's commercial supremacy in the Baltic.

Act V presents Gustav Vasa's triumphal entry into his capital, but his triumph is clearly imperfect and incomplete. King Gustav I knows that his is not an out-and-out victory. In Gustav Vasa's and Strindberg's world of reality, victory is never clear-cut. Gustav's day of joy is the day when Sweden is at last free from the union, but fellow Swedes are already threatening to give him trouble,

Lübeck is sure to make his reign difficult, there is much to be done before Sweden is truly united, and, worst of all for him as a human being, his mother and sisters—hostages in Denmark—have perished there. But the practical realist can make the best of a far from perfect situation: "King Christian of Denmark has fled, is deposed—and Fredrik is king! Fellow Swedes! Christian the Tyrant is no more! Let us go to the altar of the Great Church and sing *Te Deum laudamus!*"

The play is a highly effective study of the practical but idealistic realist who is at once a man of ideas and a man of action and who avoids both extremes of human conduct. His actions are motivated by the sincere conviction that Sweden and the Swedes will benefit more from independence than from union with their neighbors, the conviction that internal unity can come only through the discipline of a strong central government headed by a strong man, unhandicapped by either the gullibility and impulsiveness of the true knight or the selfish egotism of a Machiavellian prince, clerical or lay. Strindberg's Gustav Vasa is complex in his very human mixture of egotism, idealism, and practical realism; the fact that dominates the behavior of the blond young king is the conviction that he is the one chosen to do a task in a very real and human world and that he can perform that task in spite of the imperfections of himself, his fellows, and society itself.

Like *The Last of the Knights, The Regent* is a realistic historical play which has very genuine merits as a folk drama. It tells a story that Swedes have known down through the centuries as well as Americans know—or used to know—the story of George Washington and the men about him during the Revolution. By means of typically Strindbergian techniques the story becomes intensely alive and intensely dramatic. By suggestion as well as by illustration the conflicts, the action, and the personalities become so vivid that only afterthought and careful re-examination reveal that less physical action takes place on the stage than one had first thought. the sharp exchanges—between the archbishop and the women, young Sture, and

Bishop Brask; between Herman Israel and Bishop Brask and Erik Trolle; and between Olaus Petri and Israel, for example—are the sort of thing that an audience likes. Such matters as well as the effective characterization, the realistic exposition, the interest implicit in the plot, the lively tempo, and the convincing treatment of an important idea about the human conduct of a leader make *The Regent* a folk drama that cannot lightly be dismissed in a discussion of Strindberg's historical plays.

The Regent · A Play in Five Acts

Characters [1]

The play ends with Gustav Vasa's triumphal entry into Stockholm, Midsummer Day, 1523.

Settings

ACT I

A room in Stockholm Castle. The same scenery as in the second and fifth acts of The Last of the Knights. *A door to the right and one to the left; a door leading to the balcony, at the back. In the middle of the stage is the council table with five chairs, writing equipment, water decanters, candles, etc.*

The servants are Swedish-speaking but are dressed in the Danish color (red); GUSTAV TROLLE, *the archbishop, is dressed in armor and sword and has a councillor's cloak over his armor.*

GUSTAV TROLLE *is standing at the back, restless, tapping a window pane with his fingers.*

Pause.

PAGE (*enters*): The palace constable requests an audience, Your Lordship.

GUSTAV TROLLE: Hasn't Councillor Erik Trolle arrived yet?

PAGE: No, Your Grace.

GUSTAV TROLLE: When he arrives, bring him in here at once. After announcing him, of course. Let the constable come in.

(PAGE *goes out. Pause.* CONSTABLE *enters.*)

GUSTAV TROLLE: Welcome, constable. What does Lord Henrik Slagheck, the governor of the castle, have to say about the situation?

CONSTABLE (*looks about*): The commander can't be addressed.

GUSTAV TROLLE: Speak plainly—you are Swedish.

CONSTABLE: Yes, I am, Your Grace.

GUSTAV TROLLE: Why can't you speak with him?

CONSTABLE: He had a drinking bout last night with his brother, Councillor Didrik Slagheck . . .

GUSTAV TROLLE: And who else? Jens Anderssen Beldenacke?

CONSTABLE: Yes.

GUSTAV TROLLE: So the members of the government [2] are sleeping it off. Have you heard anything about the army to the north?

CONSTABLE: Yes. Gustav Eriksson Vasa . . .

GUSTAV TROLLE: His name is Gustav Eriksson of Rydboholm, for he isn't a knight, and never will be as long as I live. Go on!

CONSTABLE: After the crossing of the Dal River [3]—Your Grace remembers . . .

GUSTAV TROLLE: You don't need to remind me that I waged an uneven struggle with my incompetent troops . . . Go on!

CONSTABLE: Gustav Eriksson is now outside Uppsala . . .

GUSTAV TROLLE: Can Stockholm Castle defend itself?

CONSTABLE: Only if Severin Norrby [4] gets here with the fleet.

GUSTAV TROLLE: The imprisoned Swedish noblewomen are here under strict guard, aren't they? Who are they?

CONSTABLE: Lady Cecilia of Eka, Gustav Eriksson's mother, and his little sister Märta . . .

GUSTAV TROLLE: Those are hostages that will do . . . Go on!

CONSTABLE: Lady Kristina Sture, Lady Anna Bielke Natt-och-Dag . . .

GUSTAV TROLLE: Where are they?

CONSTABLE (*gestures toward the right door*): They're about the palace, but they're well guarded.

GUSTAV TROLLE: Let them go about freely in the castle, but you'll answer for them with your head!

CONSTABLE: What am I to do with Lady Mätta Sture? [5]

GUSTAV TROLLE: She's crazy, but harmless; let her wander about and be foolish . . .

CONSTABLE: I hear cries at the drawbridge and have to go down, begging your pardon . . .

GUSTAV TROLLE: Speak plainly. And, when my father Lord Erik
Trolle arrives, bring him here at once.

(CONSTABLE *goes. Pause.* CECILIA, GUSTAV VASA's *mother, and her
little daughter* MÄRTA *come in from the right.*)

GUSTAV TROLLE: Who's there?

CECILIA: Excuse me . . .

GUSTAV TROLLE: Who are you? Why do you come in here? What do
you want?

CECILIA: I am Cecilia of Eka . . . the widow of Erik Vasa, the executed councillor [6] . . .

GUSTAV TROLLE: And the mother of Gustav Eriksson, the traitor . . .
Take the child away, so that I may speak with you. I don't like
children's screaming . . . Take the child away!

(CECILIA *leads her little girl out through the right door and returns. Pause*)

GUSTAV TROLLE: Lady—Cecilia—Vasa . . . Your son has stirred up
the people of Dalarna, Hälsingland, and Uppland in rebellion
against their king and government; he's now encamped outside
Uppsala—sit down here and write a letter—or sign one at least—
in which you advise him to change his plans and be off to Norway; or you and your daughters will be taken to Denmark as
prisoners. Do you understand?

CECILIA (*submissively*): Lord Gustav Trolle! Since my husband
died, life hasn't meant much to me, but, for the sake of my children, I must live out the days of my misery . . .

GUSTAV TROLLE: It wouldn't be so miserable if you had brought up
your corrupted son properly . . . You didn't want to apply the
switch; now I will discipline him with scorpions! Perhaps I
should write it?

CECILIA: Yes—Lord Councillor . . . if you would.

(GUSTAV TROLLE *sits down at the table and writes.* CECILIA *remains standing, looks about the room occasionally and at the
door to the right. Pause*)

(MÄTTA STURE *enters from the right; as if half asleep, she feels and searches on the walls.*)

GUSTAV TROLLE (*writing, without turning about*): Who is it? Is it your child? Take the child away!

CECILIA: It's not my little girl—she is very obedient.

GUSTAV TROLLE (*turns*): So, it's Mätta Sture![7] Are you finding any treasures in the walls? (*When* MÄTTA STURE *does not answer, he turns to* CECILIA.) She was the one who poisoned Sten Sture the Elder and who notified the Danish Council so that the Swedish hostages were caught in their own trap. Don't look so frightened. I say it as it is. I am a little outspoken! Sometimes! (*Laughs. Writes. Pauses*) Not always . . . (*Writes*) That would be careless . . . (*Writes. Pauses*) Well, now we have the little note ready. Please read it before you sign it—I make it a rule always to read what I sign . . . (*Laughs*)

(CECILIA *remains standing; reads; then she makes a gesture and sits down.* CHILD *enters and tries to conceal herself behind her mother's skirts.* GUSTAV TROLLE *looks at the* CHILD *without anger; the* CHILD *looks with fear at* GUSTAV TROLLE.)

CECILIA (*uneasy*): Forgive an innocent little child!

GUSTAV TROLLE: Yes, I forgive it—just so it doesn't scream. (*To the* CHILD) Boo!

(CHILD *smiles with superiority.*)

GUSTAV TROLLE: Has mother written to big brother now?

(CHILD *conceals her head playfully in her mother's skirt.* CECILIA *gets up and gives* GUSTAV TROLLE *the letter.*)

GUSTAV TROLLE: Yes, yes, so there! Now Gustav Eriksson will know what he has to go by—and you, too, Lady Cecilia. Farewell! And be careful! The walls have ears even if they don't have treasures as that crazy fool thinks! (*Nods in a friendly way to the* CHILD, *who, holding her mother's hand, curtseys and goes out with her mother. Pause*)

(GUSTAV TROLLE *at the table; lights a candle and seals the en-*

velope; his lips move as if he were speaking. Then he rings. PAGE
enters.)

GUSTAV TROLLE: Have an ensign and two runners deliver this letter
to Gustav Eriksson's camp outside Uppsala! Without delay!

(PAGE *goes out.*)

GUSTAV TROLLE (*extinguishes the candle and straightens the things on
the table; then he speaks to* MÄTTA STURE, *who does not answer*):
You're still here haunting us, Lady Svante Sture; I suppose there
aren't many Stures left at this stage; the last one lay in his coffin
in there, I've heard; was buried by the Franciscans; but was dug
up and burned at the stake in Södermalm with the other traitors
. . . That's how it can go, and a great deal happens that one
doesn't expect.

MÄTTA STURE (*comes up to him and picks at his shoulder*): Yes,
that one doesn't expect.

GUSTAV TROLLE (*unmoved*): Now we need only see to it that we get
the Vasas in their graves; then everything will be calm in the
country.

PAGE (*enters*): Lord Erik Trolle, National Councillor.

GUSTAV TROLLE (*without getting up*): He may come in.

(PAGE *goes out. Pause*)

(HANS BRASK *enters from the left door, where the* PAGE *went
out.*)

GUSTAV TROLLE (*shrinks back in horror, trembles, stammers*): Hans
Brask?

HANS BRASK: Bishop. Hans. Brask!

GUSTAV TROLLE (*bewildered*): I don't understand!

HANS BRASK: You don't need to, Gustav! You used to call me
"father," so I took the fatherly liberty of coming in before Erik
Trolle. (TROLLE *shrinks back when* HANS BRASK *approaches him.*)
Are you shrinking? You thought I was dead, because you got me
sentenced to death! [8] That was in this room! There that blood-
hound Christian stood, and there stood the executioners. There

you stood! As the prosecutor! So I was sentenced. For twelve hours I suffered the agonies of death!

(GUSTAV TROLLE *moves his lips but can't find any words.*)

HANS BRASK: But then I became so well prepared for death that I am ready for it every moment, and this gave me courage to live, courage to speak, courage to meet you! Why did you want the axe at my throat? Because I slapped you in the face once when you were a boy. That was a blow that you had coming! My business?—I come from the graves of your victims, from Bishop Vincentius of Skara and Bishop Mattias of Strängnäs, from the ninety-eight martyrs you had beheaded, and I come for my own sake to keep a vow I swore on the day of the bloodbath: that, if I got out of it with my life, I would seek you out, dead or alive, as you had Sten Sture sought out in his grave, and I would place the mark of the slave on your face. (HANS BRASK *strikes* GUSTAV TROLLE, *who accepts the blow.*) That burned, eh? Like the executioner's red-hot iron! Now you are brought to shame! That was all of my business! (*Stands quiet for a while staring at* GUSTAV TROLLE) Now I shall go, but not so fast that you can say I have fled. (*Walks slowly and with dignity to the door at the left; then turns*) Within a year from this day I shall summon you before the judgment seat of the Almighty God, whether you are struck down by death, sickness, or misfortunes! You, the most evil of men! You son of a revenger, you slave, you thief, you liar! May you be damned! (*Goes*)

(GUSTAV TROLLE, *shaken, has retreated backward until he has reached the wall, where he stands like a baited cat at bay. Pause*)

PAGE (*enters*): Lord Erik Trolle.

(ERIK TROLLE, GUSTAV'S *father, enters.*)

GUSTAV TROLLE (*pulls himself together and "takes it out" on his father*): It's a long time since I saw you, people generally say; but time levels everything, and that we'd meet again could be taken for granted; you became sensible rather late; you look pretty worn out, old man.

ERIK TROLLE: You're as red as a rose, at least on one cheek! But you're not anxious to turn the other one!

GUSTAV TROLLE (*strikes back*): Apropos turning, you've turned your windmill according to the wind!

ERIK TROLLE: Windmills turn, unfortunately, only with contrary winds! But I want to ask you: How and on what basis have I become a member of the royal council?

GUSTAV TROLLE: On my recommendation! Sit down; take your place at the council table. There are only four of us.

ERIK TROLLE: Is this the council table? Is this the government of Sweden?

GUSTAV TROLLE: The government! We four! The two absentees are sleeping off their drunkenness. So it is you and I. That's a game that has been well played!

ERIK TROLLE (*sits down hesitantly at the table*): So the council of the Swedish realm sits here—besides you and me—Didrik Slagheck, formerly a shoemaker, now bishop of Skara; and here to the right Jens Anderssen Beldenacke, formerly a barber, just named archbishop of Denmark. Does this seem to you a government worthy of our country and of our pitiable people?

GUSTAV TROLLE: To every man his due!

ERIK TROLLE: Gustav! I was a supporter of the union, but never a supporter of the Danes. When the union was dissolved because of the Danish king's neglect of Sweden, I became a supporter of Sture. But now there isn't any Sture left. I'll never become a supporter of a Vasa!

GUSTAV TROLLE: That's your stand, but this is mine. I am a Dane, the Trolles were born Danes, but you must not believe that I am King Christian's man—not at all! Do you think I want to serve that scoundrel? You smile scornfully, but I'll tell you the story of the bloodbath in a few words. (*Drinks a glass of water*) In this room I was the prosecutor, but I demanded no man's life, but only compensation—among other things, the reconstruction of Stäke. Then Slagheck came and threatened *me* with the exe-

cutioner if I didn't demand their heads. Well! I was forced to do
it! Like Hans Brask! Now you know! (*Pause.* GUSTAV TROLLE
straightens up things on the table.)

ERIK TROLLE: Who—was in here before me?

GUSTAV TROLLE: Here? No one. The page. Lady Sture. (*Pause*)

ERIK TROLLE: Will the present state of affairs in the country last
long, do you think?

GUSTAV TROLLE: No. When Severin Norrby has arrived with reinforcements, Gustav Eriksson will be defeated. When Vasa is
defeated, then—well, you have been regent; I can become regent!

ERIK TROLLE: You will never be elected!

GUSTAV TROLLE: I'll elect myself!

ERIK TROLLE: It seems to me you have changed. You're uneasy and
tense. Something has happened.

GUSTAV TROLLE (*pretends to misunderstand him*): Yes, a great deal
has happened in Denmark that you don't know.[9] Christian has
appointed Mother Sigbrit, the procuress, lord high steward!
Christian has abolished serfdom in order to ruin the lords and to
become absolute monarch. Dissatisfied with this, the Danes have
slowly risen in rebellion and are trying to get Fredrik, Christian's
uncle, as king. That's the water in which I'm fishing!

ERIK TROLLE: That was a precious bit of information for me.

GUSTAV TROLLE: How so?

ERIK TROLLE: Well! Christian was the only man I feared, and only
out of fear of him did I sit down at this table. Now, since he isn't
dangerous any more, I won't sit here any longer, but rise, get up
—and go. Yes! I don't sit at table with Danish swine and Swedish traitors!

GUSTAV TROLLE: Watch out! The Danes aren't done with Christian,
and Fredrik isn't to be played with!

ERIK TROLLE: You were born a Swede; your mother, Ingeborg
Tott,[10] was a Swede; and that's why I call you a villain! You
took your mother's life, and you have dishonored your father!
May you be rewarded as you deserve! Only with justice, without

mercy, without grace! (*Goes to the door but turns*) Never shall I work for the Vasas! But I won't oppose the Vasas. I shall stay out of it, and, no matter what weapons I'm forced to bear, I'll never bear them against my own country! (*Goes. Pause*)

(GUSTAV TROLLE *stands as if thunderstruck; then he throws off his cloak; sits down, uneasy, at the table to write a brief message; then he rings.*)

PAGE (*enters*): The constable.

(PAGE *goes.* GUSTAV TROLLE *gets up, goes to the window, and taps on a pane.* CONSTABLE *enters.*)

GUSTAV TROLLE: It's getting cloudy. We'll get a storm.

CONSTABLE: How can Your Grace say that? The sky's perfectly clear.

GUSTAV TROLLE: I felt—as if—Where is the army?

CONSTABLE: At Rotebro,[11] Your Grace.

GUSTAV TROLLE: But that's not what I was going to ask . . . Is there any news from up north?

CONSTABLE: Yes, rumor has it that all the people of Hälsingland, Gästrikland, and Uppland have joined the rebels.

GUSTAV TROLLE: And you haven't told me that! Order them to get their horses saddled and to get ready to go with me to Rotebro. Can the burghers of Stockholm be relied on?

CONSTABLE: No, Your Grace, and the castle garrison—well! If the Danish fleet doesn't arrive soon—

GUSTAV TROLLE: Not even the garrison, then! Call Lady Anna Natt-och-Dag. Have the other ladies taken to the Blockhouse—have them put on the Danish ships when they arrive.

(CONSTABLE *goes out at the right.* GUSTAV TROLLE *loosens his armor; seems to find it difficult to breathe; rings.* PAGE *enters.*)

GUSTAV TROLLE: What is your name and whom do you serve?

PAGE (*frightened*): I serve—here in the castle.

GUSTAV TROLLE: And your name?

PAGE: Svante . . .

GUSTAV TROLLE: Go on.

PAGE: Stensson.

GUSTAV TROLLE: Go on.

PAGE (*courageously; takes one step forward*): Sture!

GUSTAV TROLLE (*shrinks back in horror*): Satan! I could feel there was a Sture in the room!

PAGE: I am Sten Sture's son! Yes! I am! And I am neither ashamed nor afraid!

(GUSTAV TROLLE *shrinks back and looks sick.*)

PAGE: Your Grace! Are you afraid of me?

GUSTAV TROLLE: Never before . . . but I believe I am ill. This room— the eighth of November [12]—(*sits down*) Give me water!

(PAGE *delays.*)

GUSTAV TROLLE: I have a bone to pick with you, because you let Bishop Brask in; he's the only person I fear—why, I don't know.

PAGE: I know!

GUSTAV TROLLE: Tell me!

PAGE: Because Bishop Brask is a good man!

GUSTAV TROLLE: Listen to the little devil! Don't you know that I have your mother in there in a cage?

PAGE: I know. But you can take only her life!

GUSTAV TROLLE: Only? Give me water!

PAGE: I can't—I don't want to! Yes, do with me as King Christian did with the young Ribbings [13]—in Jönköping—

GUSTAV TROLLE (*ill*): What did he do? I have forgotten.

PAGE: One of the boys was five, the other eight (*with tears in his eyes*)—and when the younger one saw the older one's clothes get blood-stained—he asked the executioner: "Sir, don't get spots on my clothes, for mother will scold me."

GUSTAV TROLLE: Did he say that?

PAGE: And then the executioner was overcome with pity—and threw his sword away! (*Angry*) But you never had any pity, Lord Gustav! The executioner did, but not you!

GUSTAV TROLLE (*his teeth are chattering*): How does it happen that you're alive? There must be a mistake!

PAGE: If God is with me, what can people do? But if you want to take my life, take it! Since father died, life doesn't mean much.

GUSTAV TROLLE: I believe they've deserted me . . .

(ANNA NATT-OCH-DAG *comes in, behind the* CONSTABLE.)

GUSTAV TROLLE (*straightens up*): There! Lady Anna Natt-och-Dag. We have met before.

ANNA: In this room, Your Grace!

GUSTAV TROLLE: Don't speak of it. Now I want to do you a favor. As the widow of Natt-och-Dag, the son of the noble Måns Bengts-son,[14] who freed the united kingdoms from the rebel whose name no friend of the union ever mentions . . .

ANNA (*always gently*): Yes, I'll say the name Engelbrekt and reject the favor, which my husband himself would have rejected . . . when it was offered on such conditions!

GUSTAV TROLLE (*to the* CONSTABLE): Lady Natt-och-Dag goes with the others! Help me out of here! I am ill! But I must get to Rote-bro. (*To* LADY ANNA) Do you believe that Gustav Eriksson will lower the flag of revolt if his mother writes to him saying that it means her freedom?

ANNA: Gustav Eriksson Vasa will never lower a flag before he himself has been struck down!

GUSTAV TROLLE (*to the* CONSTABLE): Help me out, down to the court-yard—then arrest all the ladies—and take them to the Block-house. And now! Trolle—or Vasa!

ANNA (*half-aloud*): Vasa!

KRISTINA (*enters; gently*): Has Trolle gone?

(PAGE, *her son,* SVANTE STURE, *runs into her arms.*)

ANNA: He has gone—but we're to be held as hostages for Gustav Eriksson!

KRISTINA: Try to escape, Anna. Gustav will sacrifice his mother, his sisters, all of us, for his country, but I'm afraid he'd give up if you were involved.

ANNA: If he sacrifices his country for a woman's love, I never want to see him again!

(MÄTTA STURE *comes in from the right. Pause*)

MÄTTA STURE: Kristina Gyllenstjerna! Sture! Listen to me! (*Pause*)

KRISTINA: Not with pleasure, however.

MÄTTA STURE: With or without—(*pause*) I've hated your people and your country! But I loved Sten, your husband, as my own son! For his sake—nothing else matters to me—I'll let you try to escape. You thought I was seeking treasures here, but I was looking for a door, a secret door to the entrance on the water—I have found it, but not in this room: there (*indicates the right door*)—Hurry! Quickly: But let me take the child . . .

KRISTINA: I won't leave the child . . .

MÄTTA STURE: Go quickly! The guards are coming! I'll answer for the child!

KRISTINA: I don't understand you . . .

MÄTTA STURE: You don't need to. Go!

ANNA: Kristina! We'll obey Lady Mätta; she senses what we don't; I believe her . . . because of her love for Sten, the only star in her darkness . . .

MÄTTA STURE (*shoves* KRISTINA GYLLENSTJERNA STURE *to the door to the right*): Go, in the name of the merciful Jesus! They're here! (*She takes the* PAGE *and places herself in front of him so that he cannot be seen. Guards appear at the door to the right*).

MÄTTA STURE: It was too late! (*To the guards, recovering her presence of mind*) Conduct the wives of the Swedish lords to the Blockhouse! (*She pats the* PAGE's *head, so that the audience will understand that she is acting.*) Quickly, guardsmen!

(*Guards look about but conduct the ladies out.*)

MÄTTA STURE (*takes the* PAGE *in her arms and caresses him*): It was too late. But it's not too late!

CURTAIN

ACT II

The terrace of the Blockhouse with a quay; a lookout tower to the left; cannons can be seen; to the right a table with benches (same scenery as in The Last of the Knights, *Act V, scene 1).*

A red-clad Danish WATCHMAN *stands on the lookout tower; a Danish soldier is walking back and forth as a* SENTINEL.

LARS SPARRE *and* GÖRAN, *his brother, can be seen in the left wing.*

LARS SPARRE (*half-aloud*): Göran, you take the watchman, and I'll take the sentinel. And, when I call out the Swedish password, our men will rush up and storm the Blockhouse.

GÖRAN: But we mustn't frighten the imprisoned women and children.

LARS: They aren't so easily frightened. I think you're beginning to get scared!

GÖRAN: I'm very tired!

LARS: Mustn't be tired!

GÖRAN: Shall I kill the watchman over on the lookout?

LARS: Throw him into the water when you've cut him down.

(GÖRAN *remains silent.*)

LARS: I believe you're hesitating. Just remember what I've promised you if you desert!

GÖRAN: You won't kill me!

LARS: When you see that those two begin talking with each other, we'll rush them; that's called a surprise attack.

GÖRAN: Can you depend on Gustav Eriksson's coming in the boat?

LARS: He'll come by water with relief forces. Can we depend on Gustav Eriksson Vasa? You ought to get it, you! (*Pause*) Do you remember the day when we were captured in a boat right here and taken as prisoners to Christian's fleet? [15]

GÖRAN: Do I remember? And what we had to put up with in Denmark!

LARS: They're beginning to talk! Watch for your chance!

(*The* WATCHMAN *on the lookout bends over the railing and speaks to the* SENTINEL.)

LARS: Know what? We'll both get the sentinel first, and then the watchman together. In two turns.

GÖRAN: That's more like the art of war!

(*They steal forward, jump the* SENTINEL, *cut him down, and shove his body into the water; then they shout, "God and St. George!" From the stage to the right can be heard the same cry from a large number of men, and then the clash of weapons. Then the brothers climb up on the lookout tower, engage the* WATCHMAN *in sword play, cut him down, and throw him into the water.*)

LARS (*waves the plumes of his helmet toward the water*): *Alls todt!* Clear for landing! The water's fine! Come here! Gustav Vasa! Arvid Vestgöte! [16] Peder Fredag! Lars Björnram! All of you this way!

GÖRAN: There's the boat at the headland! Yes, that Gustav! He thinks he'll get Stockholm Castle, because we've taken the Blockhouse! And how'll he thank us for that?

LARS: Wait a minute, and you may greet him.

GÖRAN: I don't want to! I can't stand him! That yokel! I'll join the others on shore . . .

LARS: Don't go. The boat's capsizing! Their . . .

GÖRAN: Well, they can swim! (*Goes to the right*)

LARS: Göran!

GÖRAN: I'm tired of this adventure! In half an hour, believe me, the Danes will have retaken the Blockhouse—and we'll be on the gallows! Good-bye!

LARS: Göran! Siggeson Sparre! Consider what you're doing! Now they're swimming!

GÖRAN: Swim to hell! For all of me! (*Goes. Pause*)

LARS (*down from the lookout, hauls up one after the other on the quay—last of all,* GUSTAV VASA): Better strokes, Lars Björnram! Can't you swim? Even strokes! Chin up, or you'll sink! There!

(BJÖRNRAM *climbs up, shakes himself, and goes to the right.*)

LARS: There we have Peder Fredag. Up with you!

(FREDAG *climbs up, shakes himself, and goes to the right.*)

LARS: Get in there and fight, and you'll get warm! Arvid Vestgöte! Good day to you! Here's my hand! Where's Gustav?

FREDAG: That fellow'll always manage, with his caul. No, let him alone, he can't stand having anyone help him! (*Goes to the right*)

LARS: But he's sinking now, by Satan!

FREDAG: He's just diving to frighten us! He's full of practical jokes!

LARS: Over here, Gustav! The Blockhouse has been taken! No danger! One stroke more! There! Let's have your fist! Now! Bless you for coming!

(*To the stage director! The quay is so high that neither the boat nor the swimming can be seen, since these two matters always turn out badly on the stage.*)

GUSTAV VASA (*climbs up; embraces* LARS SPARRE): Yes, Lord Eternal God of Heaven! Now I'm here again, just as on that day of horrors! [17] (*Emotionally*) The dear Sten—Sture—and Kristina! (*Holds his hand over his eyes as if in silent prayer*)

LARS: Go in and change your clothes now, Gustav.

GUSTAV VASA: That's not necessary. (*Empties the water from his helmet and wrings out the plumage*) Are the imprisoned ladies here?

LARS: All of them! And they have the others for company! Lady Mätta . . . and . . .

GUSTAV VASA (*sits down at the table*): My mother is here? And my sisters? I don't want to talk with my mother now—one at a time. Why, she wrote a letter to me—and wanted me to give up everything! It's useless to talk, of course . . . Lars, go and see to it that sentries are properly stationed, so that I can breathe for a

moment; we can't hold this place very long, for Norrby is at
Sikla Island! Go on; I'll sit here and get dry. There comes that
damned woman! Lady Mätta! who's allowed to be at large! It's a
good thing I lost my sword, or I'd have her head! She betrayed
us . . .

LARS: That she has regretted and made up for. She has hated the
Danes since Sten died. Don't make any mistake about that,
Gustav!

GUSTAV VASA: Go and see to the guard. I haven't slept for seventy-
two hours, and I haven't eaten for twenty-four! Go! I'll scratch
away at Lady Mätta. Don't let anyone come here without my
permission.

(LARS *goes. Pause*)

(MÄTTA STURE *comes in holding* SVANTE, *the* PAGE, *by the hand.*
GUSTAV VASA *gets up in anger, threateningly. They fix each other's
glances for a moment.* PAGE *comes up to* GUSTAV; *falls to one knee.*
GUSTAV VASA *sinks down on the bench, observing the boy. Pause.*
PAGE *rises, steps forward, places his head on* GUSTAV's *lap.*)

GUSTAV VASA (*gently*): Who are you, my child, who place your head
on my lap? Do you believe I wanted to hurt you? I? (*He lifts
the boy's head and looks into his eyes.*) By God! I believe! It is
Sten—Sten Sture! (*He rises, takes the boy into his arms, kisses
him on the cheeks.*) What's your name?

PAGE: Svante Stensson Sture!

GUSTAV VASA: And your brothers and sisters? Yes—they're dead. But
you shall live—become *my* man—and you shall have a little
sword and serve your country. Lady Mätta! For the sake of this
child—we'll call off our quarrel—I thank you for this precious
gift—but I cannot shake your hand! That would be asking for
too much . . .

MÄTTA STURE: Gustav! Vasas have not loved Stures before this—you
were the first! . . .

GUSTAV VASA (*puts the boy down on the ground*): You'll get wet,
my friend . . . Go up on the lookout and stand watch; I don't

see any watchman there. You'll have my dart so that you're not without weapons. (*Gives him a dagger*) And sing out if you see any enemy; you're starting your service!

(PAGE *goes up on the lookout simply and modestly without strutting or swaggering.*)

GUSTAV VASA: One word, Lady Mätta—no one wants to call you Sture! Tell me if the rumor's true that . . . I dread the answer so that I hardly dare ask . . . (*Pause*) Is it possible that Kristina Sture—had become so smitten with Severin Norrby that—that she at least has not rejected his proposal? Say that it's false; say that!

MÄTTA STURE: There is such a rumor. But I don't know if it's unfounded or not.

GUSTAV VASA: If it's true, I never want to see her again! Fate! How outrageously cruel you can be! Lady Mätta, ask my mother to come out here—alone, without my sisters.

MÄTTA STURE (*smiles*): Do you send me on errands?

GUSTAV VASA: Forgive me, but I'm used to commanding . . .

MÄTTA STURE: But I've been almost a queen . . .

GUSTAV VASA: What does that matter? I can become king!

MÄTTA STURE (*looks at him for a time, then goes willingly*): Yes! (*Pause*)

GUSTAV VASA (*to the* PAGE): What do you see out on the water, young Sture?

PAGE: Only trading ships, without cannons . . .

GUSTAV VASA (*by the cannons*): Here are my weapons, lad, my friends that live! Do you see my Scharfmesser, the Singer, and the large Moses on the mountain—that one can prophesy? Do you know how to swim, boy?

PAGE (*with dignity and politeness*): Of course I can swim, Your Grace!

GUSTAV VASA: And dive headfirst?

PAGE (*politely*): I could do that when I was six, Your Grace!

GUSTAV VASA: You're a fine young man, but you should say kinsman,

or father, because I intend to be your father! Go aside a little
now, and don't listen to the conversation.

PAGE: I never listen, kinsman!

GUSTAV VASA: You've been reared at the Sture court—you as well as
I! [18] (*Pause*)

CECILIA (GUSTAV VASA's *mother, enters*): Gustav!

GUSTAV VASA: Dear mother! (*Embrace*) Here you see me; after father's death . . .

CECILIA: He died a hero's honorable death—you don't know that—
Christian wanted to reprieve him, but your father said "No,
thanks!" and so it happened! But where have you been?

GUSTAV VASA (*quickly*): That's a long story,[19] and time is short; it
was hardest at Kallö in Denmark; it wasn't bad in Lübeck; in
Kalmar and Småland they threw rocks after me as they do at
dogs; Dalarna hemmed and hawed mostly because the Danes
wage a war of lies with false letters and false rumors. Can you
imagine the Dalesmen had been persuaded that the bloodbath
never had taken place! They didn't believe what I said . . .

CECILIA: Did you get my letter?

GUSTAV VASA: Yes, and here's the answer! I like a personal reply!

CECILIA: You'll end badly, Gustav!

GUSTAV VASA: I! No, I always end well . . .

CECILIA: Has any astrologist told your fortune?

GUSTAV VASA: I tell my own fortune every day; when I've said my
evening prayer . . .

CECILIA: You haven't forgotten it?

GUSTAV VASA: How you talk!

CECILIA: Why have you rebelled, then?

GUSTAV VASA: One, two, three, four, five—I'll not count to one hundred, but I want to talk about something else. Sit down. (*He
dusts the bench with the sleeve of his coat.*)

    (CECILIA *sits down.*)

GUSTAV VASA: Without circumlocution, is it true that Kristina Sture,
Sten Sture's widow, is in love with Severin Norrby?

CECILIA: Yes, that's true!

GUSTAV VASA (*beside himself, tightens his belt, takes off his helmet, and shakes the plumage*): Sture's wife goes over to the enemy! Is all hell loose?

CECILIA: My dear Gustav, today enemies, tomorrow friends; you know Lady Mätta; you knew Heming Gad, Erik Lejonhuvud—you're surely not in love with Kristina?

GUSTAV VASA: I'm not listening to you, mother!

CECILIA: I don't believe that, either, but why did you get so angry?

GUSTAV VASA: Severin Norrby, a Dane!

CECILIA: Dear, the Vasas have Danish blood, too! Krister Nilsson Vasa had two Danish wives, and we're related to the Billes, Rönnows, Krummedikes . . .

GUSTAV VASA (*strikes the table with his fist*): Stop!—Would you like to see our good Kristina Sture marry the enemy, who's at anchor over there by Sikla Island?

CECILIA: Norrby is a knight.

GUSTAV VASA: A plundering knight, a sea pirate [20] . . . Has he bewitched her?

CECILIA: Well, you don't know a woman's heart, and you don't know that love is invincible . . .

GUSTAV VASA: I conquered mine.

CECILIA: For Anna Bielke!

GUSTAV VASA: Where did Kristina meet Norrby?

CECILIA: That I'll tell you! At the bloodbath, when all the rest were crawling like dogs before Christian, there was only one Dane, one single person, who dared to say what many of them thought. That was Norrby! He turned his back to the king, left saying that the whole thing was swinish! Kristina saw that—and—yes—so love springs up when a woman sees a courageous and noble deed!

GUSTAV VASA (*thoughtfully*): Is Norrby like that? (*Gets up*) He may be an angel from heaven or St. George himself, but the

devil take me if my Sten Sture's son's going to have a Danish
enemy for a stepfather!

CECILIA: Stepfather? I hadn't thought of that!

GUSTAV VASA (*to the* PAGE): Boy! What do you see on the water?

PAGE: Nothing new, kinsman!

CECILIA (*gets up*): I hadn't thought that far . . .

GUSTAV VASA (*to the* PAGE): What do you see on shore?

PAGE: Trouble at the posts! Lord Lars Sparre has drawn his sword!
They're attacking . . .

GUSTAV VASA (*to* CECILIA): Good-bye, briefly, mother!

CECILIA (*on her knees*): Gustav! Give this up!

GUSTAV VASA: Go away quickly. I'm afraid we're caught off guard!
Out of the way! (*Goes to the right side and looks over the situation.* CECILIA *gets up, wants to seize* GUSTAV VASA *by his arm, but
he shoves her gently out to the right.*)

GUSTAV VASA (*feels for his missing sword*): Without weapons! (*To
the* PAGE) Sture! Will you follow me?

PAGE: In life and death, kinsman!

GUSTAV VASA: Get set, then, but don't take off your clothes; we
haven't any to change into and have to get to Uppsala tonight.
Do you see my boat at the headland? *I* have several boats!

PAGE: Two boats on the headland!

LARS SPARRE (*comes in, in despair*): We've been betrayed—

GUSTAV VASA: Hell!

LARS: Göran, my own brother, has gone over to them, and Norrby's
here . . .

GUSTAV VASA: Göran! Norrby! (*To the* PAGE) Sture, look at me, and
get set. (*To* LARS SPARRE) Then the only thing left to do—is to
go the same way we came.

LARS: But the ladies! Your mother!

GUSTAV VASA: My father and my mother forsake me, but the Lord is
with me! Sture! Look at me! But if you turn around—there
comes Kristina Sture! Sture, look at me! (GUSTAV VASA *is now*

standing on the edge of the quay.) One, two, three! (*Jumps into the water*)

PAGE (*jumps from the lookout tower into the water as he cries*): With God and St. George!

LARS: With Sture and Vasa! (*Jumps into the lake*)

KRISTINA STURE (*rushes in*): My son!

ANNA BIELKE NATT-OCH-DAG (*enters*): Where are they, Kristina? What's happening?

KRISTINA: Anna! Why, I saw them here! Svante was along! Where —are—they?

ANNA (*looks out on the water*): There!

KRISTINA: In the water? My child! Do you see them?

ANNA: Don't you see? The little blond head like a water lily on the waves—

KRISTINA (*waves her handkerchief*): Who's swimming by his side?

ANNA: Why, that's Gustav!

KRISTINA: He *took* my child . . . *he* took my child!

ANNA: Don't you understand why?

KRISTINA: Did he believe . . . ? Did Gustav believe . . . ?

ANNA: He believed—he wanted to save your son from a Danish stepfather——

KRISTINA: He believed that Sten Sture's wife wanted to outrage the memory of Sture! Gustav! Gladly take my son, then, as a hostage!

ANNA (*looks to the right*): We're prisoners! The soldiers are coming.

KRISTINA: Are we prisoners again? See, now they're landing! He's waving to me! Svante, dear little child! (*Waves toward the water*) God bless you, Gustav, who saved my child; God bless you —even if you thought so badly of Kristina Sture!

(*Danish soldiers march in from the right.*)

CURTAIN

ACT III

Scene 1

The forest at Stäke. The same scenery as in the fourth act of
The Last of the Knights; *but this time the highway and an ale
shop are to the right. Tables and benches outside the shop.*
The TAVERN KEEPER *at a table.*
GUSTAV TROLLE'S *former* CHANCELLOR, *who is now a soldier, en-
ters. He is wearing a Danish uniform.*

KEEPER: *Wer da?*

CHANCELLOR: Only good friends—friends and enemies! Isn't it a
public highway?

KEEPER: Yes, indeed it is! And that's where Stäke Castle stood, the
one that was all torn down—they say Gustav Trolle haunts the
place, though he's still alive with a little bit of life in him; he
can't sleep nights since Brask pronounced the minor ban over
him, and all of Sweden's commoners, merchants, and nobility
are praying about him. What would a soldier like to drink at
this time of day? We have a great deal of beer and a little liquor,
fiery liqueur—

CHANCELLOR (*sits down at the table*): I want a lot of liquor and
very little beer!

KEEPER: That's a little involved for me—I don't think fast—here
we have some liquor. And you ought to look at that pine—it's
called the Trolle pine—they almost hanged Gustav Trolle from it
once back in Sten Sture's day, but Sture spared his life!

CHANCELLOR: Is that the pine? Too bad they didn't let the tree ful-
fill its great destiny, because you could say that the bloodbath
has grown from its roots . . .

KEEPER: You must have gone to the Latin school, for you speak in such a learned way that I can't keep up with you . . .

CHANCELLOR (*has been drinking*): I admit it with shame—I have studied at Uppsala, and I have seen better days, though they really were worse. Have you seen any Swedes on the road?

KEEPER: Swedes and Danes—I can't tell 'em apart—but they all come from Västerås, since the castle was taken and Gustav Vasa became regent . . .

CHANCELLOR: Is he regent? Legally elected?

KEEPER: Legally elected in Vadstena. They wanted to make him king right away, but he said absolutely not! They're afraid of the crown in this country, ever since Karl Knutsson was lord of Fogelvik [21] . . .

CHANCELLOR: So it's Vasa, then! *Certe quidem.* But why didn't they keep on with the Stures?

KEEPER: Is any of 'em alive?

CHANCELLOR: Why, there's a young Sture, Svante, who's Gustav Vasa's page . . .

KEEPER: Really! Really! More people are coming. (*Pause*)

GÖRAN SPARRE (*enters, disguised as a monk, sits down carefully at the table*): Beer!

KEEPER: That was to the point. (*Serves* SPARRE *beer*)

GÖRAN: Is it good?

KEEPER: Taste it.

(CHANCELLOR *stares sharply at* GÖRAN SPARRE. GÖRAN *drinks.*)

CHANCELLOR: *Bonum vinum laetificat cor hominis.*

GÖRAN: *Ja wohl, ja wohl!*

CHANCELLOR: *Primum vivere deinde philosophare* . . .

GÖRAN: *Sehr schön! Aber* . . .

CHANCELLOR: Don't you know Latin, monk?

GÖRAN: *Gewiss!*

CHANCELLOR: No, you don't, so you're not a monk!

GÖRAN: *Doch!*

CHANCELLOR: And no German, either, for they don't say *dosch* but *doch!*

GÖRAN: What difference does it make what one is? What one seems to be matters more . . .

CHANCELLOR: Yes, you look it, Göran Sparre!

GÖRAN: Who are you, that you know me?

CHANCELLOR: *Wer da?* A good friend, so far as that goes!

GÖRAN: Now I know! You were Gustav Trolle's chancellor in a way—I remember you from the Blockhouse—and from—that pine!

CHANCELLOR: Don't talk about rope in a hanged man's house! Then I won't talk about Kungshamn's hostages [22]—

GÖRAN: Don't touch me and mine, and I won't touch you and yours! . . .

CHANCELLOR: Said the viper! To whom are we drinking?

GÖRAN: King Christian!

CHANCELLOR: All right. *Cum grano salis.* All right, I'll drink with anybody at all except the executioner!

GÖRAN: God, no! (*They drink and soon appear affected. Pause*)

GÖRAN: Is the highway safe here? I keep hearing so many things—and there are a lot of tracks on the ground—

CHANCELLOR: Here in the middle of the forest there's no danger—Isn't that right, keeper?

KEEPER: No danger. Look at the hoof prints here. Why, they're only farm horses—why, that's easy to tell!

GÖRAN (*gets up and looks at the tracks*): They weren't shod in the military fashion—and the mark looks like a bird track in a rabbit thicket—or like an eye without a hook—they were only small Uppland horses—but—they were shod—because here can be seen . . .

(CHANCELLOR *winks at the* KEEPER, *who winks back at him.*)

GÖRAN: . . . the marks of horseshoe nails—and here a cavalryman has gone; he stayed on the grass to conceal the track—but you can't fool me!

CHANCELLOR: Come on, sit down. The bushes are rustling, and you might be taken for a spy!

GÖRAN (*cockily*): The devil! No! (*Sits down and drinks*)

CHANCELLOR: Tell us, now—when drinking a man should tell the news from the outside world. How was it in Denmark?

GÖRAN: It wasn't so bad, that is for us; for Gustav Vasa at Kallö it was worse. The rest of us hostages, my brother and I and Heming Gad, were treated like guests in Copenhagen. We dined with King Christian . . .

(LARS SPARRE *enters; signals to the* KEEPER *and the* CHANCELLOR; *sits down at a distant table and pretends to write.*)

GÖRAN: Did someone come?

CHANCELLOR: Only the forester who's making his rounds.

GÖRAN: Well, King Christian, he was a man all day; and I'll tell you—in confidence—do you know why Heming Gad, *electus,* as we called him, do you know why he went over to Christian?

CHANCELLOR: No! Tell us!

GÖRAN: Well, Heming Gad went over to the Danish party, because —the Danish party's right! Yes! King Christian was right! Because he was the elected heir-apparent—

CHANCELLOR (*in order to tease* GÖRAN): What the hell is that? Elected heir-apparent?

GÖRAN: Both elected and heir-apparent! That's good enough! (*Strikes the table with his fist.* CHANCELLOR *wants to speak but is interrupted by* GÖRAN SPARRE's *bluster.*)

GÖRAN: And Gustav Vasa—Vasa versus an Oldenburg! [23] Ha ha! And the strangest thing of all is that Christian had the right of inheritance all the same. You don't know that! Because he was descended from St. Erik!

CHANCELLOR (*laughs*): So are the Stures.

GÖRAN: The Stures, you said! You shouldn't talk about the Stures, because I know—I know a lot, a lot!

CHANCELLOR: The hell you do—why, anyone can see you're drunk!

GÖRAN: Mind your manners! But I'll tell you—confidentially—that

young Sture had better watch out for Gustav Vasa—yes! He's
the Rydboholmer's page—I call 'im Rydboholmer, because he'll
never be anything else! But the Rydboholmer fooled the page to
jump into the water to drown him, you can be sure, and the boy's
mother stood on shore by the Blockhouse looking on! That was
a nice story!

LARS (*comes up*): Now we'll stop, Göran!

GÖRAN (*crushed*): Is it Lars, my own brother—

LARS: It's I, who used to call you brother! But I swore in this forest that, if you deserted, you'd never be called my mother's child
again, and I'd kill you, have you killed! The cock has crowed
three times, and I've forgiven you. Now you have consumed all
grace, and your life's over. But you may sleep until you're sober,
and a priest will prepare you, afterward. But you must be rooted
out from this earth, like every other traitor to his country!

GÖRAN (*sober*): Let me get away!

LARS: You can't! The forest is full of people who want to kill you,
because you were on the side of the enemy, and set fire to Västerås!

GÖRAN: Then . . .

(LARS *strikes his hands together; turns away. Soldiers enter and
take* GÖRAN SPARRE *prisoner.* KEEPER *and* CHANCELLOR *turn away
with horror.*)

LARS: God be merciful to his soul!

CURTAIN

SCENE 2

*The sacristy of Uppsala Cathedral. The same scenery as in Act
III of* The Last of the Knights.

Door at the back, another to the right. To the left on the wall

are portraits of the archbishops, among them one covered by a
green cloth.

A SOLDIER *at the right door.*

CHANCELLOR (*formerly in* GUSTAV TROLLE's *service, now a soldier, enters from the back*): What are you up to?

SOLDIER: Sacristies generally are like rat traps, but this one has a
hiding place—a secret passage—look—up to the archbishop's
palace!

CHANCELLOR: That's news! Otherwise everything's the same here—
but they've added portraits—on the wall—all the arch—

SOLDIER: Why arch?

CHANCELLOR: You tell me! But Gustav Trolle certainly was an
arch—

SOLDIER: Listen to the sounds here in the passage—Bengt Bjugg's [24]
sitting in the archbishop's palace carousing—

CHANCELLOR: Where is the arch—then?

SOLDIER: Gustav Trolle was almost killed by Peter Hansson,[25] who
threw his sword at him—I think he got a scratch, but got over it,
and he's marching back . . .

CHANCELLOR: Why should the bishop be out fighting? He ought to
sit here fencing with his pen; it was a lot better when he and I
wrote false letters together. He taught me the art, the swine, but,
when I began to write on my own, he drove me out—

SOLDIER: They say Brask is in Uppsala, and the regent isn't far
away—I think there'll be a tussle here before evening—

CHANCELLOR: When the thieves are fighting, the farmer gets his cow
back!

SOLDIER (*takes the water decanter and drinks out of it*): Is it true
that Lars Sparre had his own brother killed?

CHANCELLOR: A bit of truth in that! But Göran was killed by the
people at Kolsund. His brother did sentence him to death, though.

SOLDIER: That's how it goes in war—and Lars was named Lord
High Chamberlain because of that exploit—don't you hear something out there in the church?

CHANCELLOR: Yes, I think I do!

SOLDIER: See who it is. Björnram's Swedish forces are just at Danmark's [26] parish church—

CHANCELLOR (*looks out into the church*): It's the caretaker's old woman—and the archbishop—Gustav Trolle!

SOLDIER: Then we'll take shelter in here in the passage.

CHANCELLOR: Perhaps we'd better. He asks so many questions, you see—and wants to know everything—and you have to answer yes or no at once—and that's not always so easy—

SOLDIER: If a person minds his *p*'s and *q*'s, it goes.

CHANCELLOR: How about you—who don't answer at all?

SOLDIER: That's the art of war—not to take up anything! I never take up anything in battle—

CHANCELLOR: You're a hell of a soldier! What do you do, then?

SOLDIER: I take cover and wait for the outcome of the battle—

CHANCELLOR: Back of a bush—

SOLDIER: To get the pleasure of sharing in the victor's triumphal entry—

CHANCELLOR: And excel at plundering—

SOLDIER:—rather than bite the grass and be struck from the rolls as a dead man! (*Goes in through the right door*)

CHANCELLOR (*follows him*): I'll be your disciple and follow you!

(*Pause*)

(GUSTAV TROLLE *enters, followed by the church* CARETAKER'S WIFE; *he is wearing his armor, has an arm in a bandage, and a bandage on his forehead; he staggers to the table and sits down.*)

GUSTAV TROLLE: Replace the bandage on my forehead, old woman; my head hurts!

CARETAKER'S WIFE: Crazy cats get their skins scratched. (*Takes off his helmet*) When they get beat up, they run home! (*During the next speeches she first takes his sword, then his cuirass from him without any apparent purpose.*)

GUSTAV TROLLE: Loosen the bandage, but do it carefully—

CARETAKER'S WIFE (*loosens the bandage*): You certainly have a fore-

head, I must say, like a bull, and a blow like that—I can put two
of my fingers in the hole—

GUSTAV TROLLE: You're hurting me, woman—

CARETAKER'S WIFE: The one who hurts, gets hurt—

GUSTAV TROLLE: Watch out, then! What a lot of pictures they've put
on the walls! Take the bandage off my arm now. There should
be a soldier at the secret passage, but there isn't any. Only rascals! Rascals, all of them! No one obeys; all give orders!

CARETAKER'S WIFE: Yes, things are going downhill, little man.

GUSTAV TROLLE: That's a damnable way you have of addressing the
archbishop of the kingdom of Sweden!

CARETAKER'S WIFE: Yes, that's our way; we old women have seen all
of you fellows in the raw, and I have tall sons, who are soldiers,
and then respect disappears—my old man isn't so big-mouthed—
when he's in the mood—

GUSTAV TROLLE: Do you know why priests may not get married?

CARETAKER'S WIFE: No, I don't know that, but I can figure it out on
my fingers . . .

GUSTAV TROLLE: You're hurting me, woman, and that seems to give
you pleasure!

CARETAKER'S WIFE: Are you soft? What are you going out to fight
for, then? You should've got married, and had children; then
you'd have been a human being, and you'd have had peace of
mind and been able to sleep nights . . .

GUSTAV TROLLE: I've heard the contrary! (*Pause*) Who has told you
I can't sleep at night?

CARETAKER'S WIFE: Your old Katrina said so, the one who has to sit
up nights to keep watch with candles, right in front of you.

GUSTAV TROLLE: She lies . . .

CARETAKER'S WIFE: Oh, no! The whole town knows you scream in
your sleep—because you have nightmares! And that's your bad
conscience—because of the bloodbath. Yes, it is! You're fainting,
I do believe.

GUSTAV TROLLE (*faints*): Help! I'm sinking! Why, the chair's sinking, and the floor, too! Do you have any water?

CARETAKER'S WIFE (*takes the water decanter*): The water's gone.

GUSTAV TROLLE: I'm burning up!

CARETAKER'S WIFE (*revealing herself*): Yes, burn!

GUSTAV TROLLE: People are coming! Where's my sword? They're enemies!

CARETAKER'S WIFE (*hisses*): It's the enemy, the evil one, who's fetching you! You took the life of my youngest son, and you have ruined my daughter! You have butchered bishops and lords, and you've had the corpses brought to the stake by the barrel! You had the noble Sture dug up, you grave robber, you corpse spoiler; half the kingdom is in mourning, in sorrow; children rise up against parents, and parents against children; I have two sons whom you made traitors; there isn't one person to rely on; I sleep with my kitchen axe under my bed for my own husband's sake—listen, how it's rustling out there in the church—do you know what that is? Look this way, and you'll see. (*She opens the door at the back; black-clad ladies and children pass by as if in procession.*) There they go to the graves, the widows and the fatherless—the Vasas, the Stures, Brahe, the Gyllenstjernas, Ryning, Kurck, Lejonhuvud [27]—yes, look for your sword, you hangman; you'll get rope . . .

(GUSTAV TROLLE *finally succeeds in getting up out of the chair, goes to the secret passage, but the door is closed.*)

CARETAKER'S WIFE: It was shut!

GUSTAV TROLLE: And you have disarmed me, Satan—otherwise, I'd have your head . . . Help me get my armor on . . .

CARETAKER'S WIFE: Go out in the church and pray for help—then you'll see! You don't dare go out—you're afraid of their black veils—sit where you're sitting—you're not sitting in the lake, not in the lake, where there is any water! (*Goes to the back*)

GUSTAV TROLLE: Don't go!

(CARETAKER'S WIFE *nods three times and shuts the door at the back when she exits.*)

(*Pause*)

GUSTAV TROLLE (*looks about, notices the portraits, goes up and examines some of them; then he lifts the green cloth, shrinks back in horror, and snatches the cloth away; his own portrait becomes visible*): Is that I? Is this I? Do I look that horrible? The devil himself has painted it!

VOICE: In his image!

GUSTAV TROLLE: Is someone here? (*Pause*) It is horrible! I believe it is Alexander VI Borgia; [28] and this is I! A human being, born of woman, nursed by a woman, and doesn't resemble a human being! (*Shrinks back*) It's not possible! I have seen my spirit—I have seen myself, I must die! But it is not I; it is someone else! I am not like that! (*He takes down a mirror from the wall and observes himself in it.*) Yes, it is! This is still worse . . . Flee? Oneself? How? Throw oneself on one's own sword, like Saul, but no one wants to hold it! No one!

(*Organ music out in the church. Pause.* GUSTAV TROLLE, *in despair, goes to a prayer stool; stops there, struggling with himself.*)

ERIK TROLLE (*his father, comes in slowly from the back*): Is that you, Gustav? Flee! The enemy's upon you! Flee!

GUSTAV TROLLE: Flee! I can't!

ERIK TROLLE: Let me look at you! (*Stares*)

GUSTAV TROLLE: What do you see?

ERIK TROLLE: Have you awakened at last?

GUSTAV TROLLE: Yes, so that I can never sleep again!

ERIK TROLLE: That is sleeplessness, you see. And nightmares!

GUSTAV TROLLE: Father! Help me!

ERIK TROLLE: No one can, but One, the only One! Every time I eased your burden, you struck me. (*Pause*)

GUSTAV TROLLE (*shows his father the portrait*): Father! Do I look like that?

ERIK TROLLE: Good God! Is that my child? (*Weeps*) My child!
Now, God, I am thoroughly punished for the sins of my fathers!

GUSTAV TROLLE: I am damned!

ERIK TROLLE: Condemned! Yes!

GUSTAV TROLLE: To death!

ERIK TROLLE: Yes!

GUSTAV TROLLE: The end?

ERIK TROLLE: No! Until the sentence is executed, there is still hope—

GUSTAV TROLLE: What? What hope?

ERIK TROLLE: There is—mercy!

GUSTAV TROLLE: For me?

ERIK TROLLE: You were once condemned to death—in the forest of
Stäke; then a knight came along, one of the fair ones, and he
granted you mercy!

GUSTAV TROLLE: That was Sture!

ERIK TROLLE: And he was only a human being . . . This will teach
you, head of the Church of Sweden! what every child knows!
You learned people and Pharisees—flee! Through that door!
Gustav Vasa is here—and the hand of the Lord is with him!

GUSTAV TROLLE: That door is locked!

ERIK TROLLE: It is not locked!

GUSTAV TROLLE: It is!

ERIK TROLLE (*opens the door to the secret passage*): You see, you of
little faith, the door *is* open!

GUSTAV TROLLE (*amazed*): Come with me, father.

ERIK TROLLE: Are you afraid of the dark?

GUSTAV TROLLE: Yes, I am afraid, very much afraid!

ERIK TROLLE: I will go with my child who's afraid of the dark. (*He
weeps.*) My big, old, lost child! (*They leave by the door to the
right.*)

(*Pause*)

GUSTAV VASA (*comes in at the back*): Is anyone here? No one?
Come on, Lars.

(LARS SPARRE *enters.*)

GUSTAV VASA: They said Trolle was here. There's a suit of armor—and there—a helmet—and a sword! He has laid down his arms! Fine! We did this like men, Lasse!

LARS: Now you're happy, Gustav.

GUSTAV VASA: Now we can be satisfied, too! All that remains is a little talk with Bishop Brask—right here—he's not easy to deal with; even Gustav Trolle was as afraid of him as of the devil—look here, what's this? (*Points at the portrait*) It's horrible—look at it! (*Turns the portrait*) Better have its back showing.

LARS: Well, since we're now at home here, and it's to go anyway, I'll do this! (*Takes down the portrait and throws it in the fire*)

GUSTAV VASA: His name will be exterminated from the earth along with his portrait—

PAGE (*young* SVANTE STURE *comes in with a portfolio*): Bishop Brask is coming!

GUSTAV VASA: Then we'd better be serious! Svante, guard that door from the inside—you won't listen, for you are a Sture! Go, Lars, when the bishop has come. Now the axe is at the root—and now I'll cut down the old tree: the home of the heathens! (*Pause*)

(HANS BRASK *comes in at the back, observes* GUSTAV VASA *sharply to see how the latter feels toward him; with a look asks* LARS SPARRE *to leave.*)

GUSTAV VASA: Am I the one to welcome you, or you me, bishop?

BRASK: Here in the cathedral perhaps I am the host and you the guest.

GUSTAV VASA: Then we'll sit down at the same time—then you'll have been courteous to your guest without having lost any of your dignity. (*He sits down.*)

BRASK: You don't need your witness—I know Lars Sparre—

GUSTAV VASA: I know him better. He's no great light in learning and arguing but he has the unusual gift of being honorable, is a man who keeps his word, and is truthful. That's why he's the best of my men. Go, Lars, but not too far.

(LARS SPARRE *leaves.*)

BRASK: Lord—Gustav Eriksson—

GUSTAV VASA: Say regent!

BRASK: What's that?

GUSTAV VASA (*lashes out*): The one who manages the affairs of the kingdom when they are neglected by foreign tyrants, stairway opportunists, and court sneaks, by Roman swine, defilers of men, and extortionists!

BRASK: What sort of talk is that?

GUSTAV VASA: That was Swedish, in the Uppland dialect!

BRASK: The Holy Father . . .

GUSTAV VASA: Who's he?

BRASK (*nonplussed*): The Holy Father in Rome . . .

GUSTAV VASA: To hell with Rome; now I want to talk about Munke-boda![29] You, Lord Bishop, received King Christian as a guest of honor when he came directly from the bloodbath. He spent Christmas with you, and, because you received the enemy of the nation as a friend, you have forfeited your palace, your fortified palace.

BRASK: You'll never get it.

GUSTAV VASA: Then I'll take it!

BRASK: With what?

GUSTAV VASA: With this! (*He throws his sword on the table.*)

BRASK (*touches the sword and examines it*): This!

GUSTAV VASA: There are twenty thousand like it, and one man with each. That is the sword of justice, and power, the secular power . . . and of authority!

BRASK: Who is the authority here?

GUSTAV VASA: I am! Elected by the people with the grace of God and for my services in saving the fatherland from foreign rabble . . .

BRASK (*quickly*): Listen, my young friend, you speak entirely too loftily for your age, and with firm regard for the nature and sanctity of the place—I want to tell you only this, that the bishop's

palace is fortified and that Bengt Bjugg has both powder and
lead—

GUSTAV VASA: But Lars Björnram has both arrows and balls with
which to set fire to it, and, at the very moment this talk takes the
wrong turn, the bishop's palace will be going up in flames and
will burn with both man and mouse!

BRASK: Then this talk shall take the right turn immediately! Here
is a letter!

GUSTAV VASA: Whom is it from?

BRASK: Read it!

GUSTAV VASA: Oh, no! I want to know whom it's from before I stick
my nose into the filth!

BRASK (*hesitantly*): It's from King Christian II in Denmark.

GUSTAV VASA (*throws the letter on the floor*): The devil!

BRASK: Is that your kind of statesmanship?

GUSTAV VASA: It's mine: Honest words! Honest blows! To the point!
Get to the point now, or the bishop's palace will be ablaze at all
four corners!

BRASK: You happen to be sitting on the chair of the archbishop of
the kingdom of Sweden . . .

GUSTAV VASA (*gets up*): Yes, I am—but I don't want to sit where
Gustav Trolle has been sitting—

BRASK: But where King Christian has sat, you want to sit—on the
throne—

GUSTAV VASA: I'll make a new one when I get there; they have already offered me both the crown and the throne . . . What's in
the letter? Quickly?

BRASK: It says this: That, if you touch the archbishop's palace in
Uppsala, your mother and sisters, who are imprisoned in the Blue
Tower of Copenhagen, will be broken upon the wheel!

GUSTAV VASA (*crushed*): The devil! (*Paces the floor with his sword
in his hand, hacking at chairs and table*)

BRASK (*triumphs*): Yes! One ought to read one's letters and answer
them, too!

GUSTAV VASA: I'll soon answer—orally! (*At the prayer stool by the crucifix, but remains standing*) Coriolanus! [30]

BRASK: Yes, Coriolanus! He was a humane person who had a heart for his mother—

GUSTAV VASA: Quiet! Be quiet! Christian had our brave Jöns Magnusson crucified. In Vadstena King Christian (*emphasizes*)—had Sven Hök and Peder Smed cut into pieces alive when he came from Bishop Brask's Christmas celebration! [31] (*Pause*) Lars Sparre had his own brother killed as a traitor to his country! Brutus!

LARS SPARRE (*enters*): I was called.

GUSTAV VASA (*slowly*): I spoke your name, but I did not call you. Still—since you came, my honest friend, come and advise me.

LARS: A doubting mind seeks advice. Do you doubt? *You?*

GUSTAV VASA: Yes—it concerns both my mother and my sisters!

LARS (*hesitantly*): Mother and sisters? Don't make me advise you!

GUSTAV VASA: Do you doubt? *You?*

LARS: Mother and sisters? (*Pause*)

GUSTAV VASA: God help us!

LARS: Mother and sisters? That's different all the same from brother!

GUSTAV VASA (*in anguish*): Help me, Jesus Christ, Saviour of the world, help me!

LARS: Mother—and sisters!

GUSTAV VASA: Little sister! Märta!

LARS: Look at the old man—I believe he's weeping.

GUSTAV VASA: Yes, I think so. Are there any human feelings in a bishop?

BRASK: Yes, there are, even though my stern calling has denied me the privilege of the pleasant ties which bind human hearts to life.

GUSTAV VASA: Go on, man!

BRASK: Gustav! I used to call you that! I am and have been just as good a patriot as you; although I sought our strength in the union, I have hated the tyrant just as you have; but in this matter there is no way out except for the rebel to lay down his weapons!

GUSTAV VASA: No! No! No!

BRASK: Christian is your legally elected king, to whom God has given the country as punishment for our meanness, our envy, our disloyalty to each other; and the bloodbath was a judgment over the hundred-year treachery here at home . . .

GUSTAV VASA: No! No! No! (*Beside himself*) Lars Sparre, go out and set fire to the bishop's palace! God help me! Amen!

(LARS *tarries. Pause*)

GUSTAV VASA: Are you going? Or . . .

LARS: Or what?

GUSTAV VASA (*furious*): That you know: Disobedience in war is death!

LARS: Help us, bishop!

BRASK: Mother and sisters!

GUSTAV VASA: Woman, what have I to do with you? said the crucified One.

BRASK: God alone can help in this!

GUSTAV VASA: Help us, God in Heaven! (*Pause*)

PAGE (*enters through the door of the secret passage*): Excuse me, kinsman, but there's smoke in the passage; I'm choking so I can't stay there!

GUSTAV VASA: What sort of passage is that?

PAGE: I think it goes to the archbishop's palace.

LARS (*at the window*): The palace is on fire!

GUSTAV VASA: Lord God, that was your help! Now, Father Brask, as I used to call you, I'll trouble you as a trustworthy, honorable friend, or enemy; answer the king's letter and say that I am innocent of the deed!

BRASK: I will, for your mother's and sisters' sake.

(*Glow of fire in the window*)

GUSTAV VASA (*offers the* BISHOP *his hand*): Why can't we be friends?

BRASK: Perhaps we are—more than you believe.—Who's the boy?

GUSTAV VASA: He's a young Sture!

BRASK: Are there Stures living?

GUSTAV VASA: Yes, praise God, he came like an answer to the prayer! Stay here, Bishop Brask, and no harm will come to you. Sture will keep watch over you—

LARS: The whole city is in flames!

GUSTAV VASA: Then I won't have to take Uppsala! Now only Stockholm is left!

BRASK: Now you're happy, Gösta! And I, too!

GUSTAV VASA: You, too?

(BRASK *nods affirmatively in a friendly fashion; beckons to the boy to come up to him, and places one hand on his head.*)

CURTAIN

ACT IV

The Lübeckers' office. The same scenery as in The Last of the Knights, *Act II, scene 2.*

TWO CLERKS *present.*

CLERK II: What's going to happen here? Surely not the election of a king?

CLERK I: Just about it. They talked in this office once about Sten Sture and a crown, but he said no!

CLERK II: That's what Vasa, too, said in Vadstena, but he was just prancing for the harness!

CLERK I: But they're busy in Strängnäs [32] just about now electing a king.

CLERK II: But nothing'll be settled before we're along, Israel said. This time it's Lübeck that'll give Sweden a king. Herman

Plönjes, alias Polonius, and Bernt Bomhower have gone up to Strängnäs, and now it'll be Vasa anyhow.

CLERK I: You heard what I said—Gustav Vasa will never accept the crown—the night courier says he's already said no. He doesn't dare as long as there are Stures and a Sture party.

CLERK II: You mean Sture's widow, Kristina, who's in the Blue Tower of Copenhagen—and is going to marry Severin Norrby, who thinks he'll be king in Sweden—

CLERK I: That's a lie, all of it—Kristina'll never marry Norrby! I'll bet with you!

CLERK II (*looks out of the window*): Now the big shots are coming! Old Erik Trolle and Bishop Brask.

CLERK I: Is old Trolle still alive?

CLERK II: Yes-s, he's alive, all right, and Gustav Trolle, too! *He's* in Stockholm Castle and has become a bit cockier, though he felt weak for a while . . . Open the door!

(CLERK I *opens the door at the back*. ERIK TROLLE *and* HANS BRASK *enter*.)

BRASK (*to* ERIK TROLLE): Is this—where the election of king actually takes place? They've certainly fooled us. Why, that's being held in Strängnäs!

ERIK TROLLE: But it takes place here!

BRASK: That's why I wanted to be along, when the fate of the country is decided. (*To* CLERK I) Isn't Herman Israel here? Isn't he in Stockholm?

CLERK I: The councillor will soon be here.

BRASK (*to* ERIK TROLLE): Then we can be calm, for without Lübeckers nothing will happen in Strängnäs!

ERIK TROLLE: Well, can we be calm with these Lübeckers who never do anything but scheme?

BRASK: In this case, where their own interests are at stake, we can be calm. You have the same errand as I?

ERIK TROLLE: Yes! When I left the union party, I became pro-Sture, but I'll never go along with the Vasas!

BRASK: Then we do have the same errand! Sture the Elder gave the kingdom twenty-five years of peace [33]—Svante was a man of honor, and Sten Sture the Younger a Christian knight—so when there is a young Sture—he shall have it!

ERIK TROLLE: Exactly my idea! We'll have a Sture!

(CLERKS *grimace at each other*.)

BRASK: I know little Svante—he's a good child, like his father—

HERMAN ISRAEL (*comes in, rubbing his hands*): Welcome, noble lords.

BRASK: We're happy to see you, Herman Israel; your presence here is a sort of guarantee that nothing injurious is happening over in Strängnäs.

ISRAEL (*lies*): Nothing injurious is happening, and, until Lübeck goes along, nothing can be decided. (*Pause*)

BRASK (*sits down*): Well, is Lübeck working definitely for Vasa?

ISRAEL (*dodges the question*): Definitely? Nothing can be decided like this in a trice. Vasa is Vasa; he's a crude fellow—

BRASK: Exactly! I really like him for his blunt manner, but he's godless as his father was, and, as long as there are Stures, then . . .

ISRAEL: Why, Vasa has rejected the crown, so there'll never be talk of that!

BRASK: Has he seriously—rejected it?

ISRAEL: Seriously!

BRASK: And then he's in debt to Lübeck over his ears . . .

ISRAEL: Exactly, yes. He owes us ten barrels of money for ships alone—

ERIK TROLLE (*uneasy, to* BRASK): Don't talk so much!

BRASK: Why, we can talk frankly here (*The* CLERKS *grimace at each other*.)—why, all have taken oaths—

ISRAEL: You can talk frankly here—our walls have no ears—and in business, trade, and politics frankness is the first virtue.

BRASK: I wonder! And I wanted to talk about trade—

ISRAEL (*winks at* CLERK I, *who goes out*): You understood trade well, Bishop Brask, and they say you fit out ships yourself! [34]

BRASK: That's right! And that's why I understand that the ten ships you sent to Söderköping to relieve the regent were rotten way down to the kelson, that the cannons were rusty, that the cordage was rotten, and all the goods were spoiled . . .

ISRAEL: Really? If that's the case, we'll exchange them at once.

BRASK: When it is too late! And the Lübeck coins that have flooded the country are as good as counterfeit! That Gustav Vasa didn't understand, because he understands only military matters.

ISRAEL: Lord Bishop, the regent is a very wise man, very wise, because in his younger years he had to learn the difficult art of living in a hard school, and Gustav Vasa knows that the ships and the goods weren't what they should have been—there weren't any others—and he knows that the money is defective; but instead of looking a gift horse in the mouth, and wasting time by complaining, he went ahead on rotten ships and with false money, straight to his objective . . . in a straight line—

(BRASK *looks at* ERIK TROLLE.)

ISRAEL (*smoothly*): And, while you are sitting here talking nonsense, he has accepted the royal crown in Strängnäs! What did you say?

BRASK (*gets up*): What are you saying?

ERIK TROLLE: He's making fools of us!

ISRAEL: Sit down, gentlemen!

BRASK: No, we won't sit here like fools any longer! Your frankness shall be answered, Herman Israel. Erik Trolle will go to Dalarna and get the friends of Sture to take up arms!

ISRAEL: Gustav Vasa has already had Peder the Chancellor [35] there; and the Sture party is done for since Severin Norrby's name started to be mixed into the Sture case.

BRASK (*to* ERIK TROLLE): What did we come here for?

ISRAEL: I wonder! Bishops should attend to their diocese and not come to countinghouses and warehouses. That's how it is when you meddle in matters that you don't understand! (*Signal outside*)

BRASK: Come to Munkeboda, and we'll speak with powder and lead . . .

ISRAEL: Lübeck's art of war has always consisted of avoiding fortified places . . . They fall of themselves in time, Lord Bishop, with time and patience—

BRASK: Patience?

ISRAEL: Admittedly, the patience can end, and now mine has ended! (*Rings*)

(CLERK I *enters.*)

ISRAEL: Bring in the courier from Strängnäs! (*Pause*)

BRASK: Is this a play you're putting on?

ISRAEL: It's a comedy! The curtain's going up! (*Pause*)

ERIK TROLLE: And we were fooled! We deserve it! (*Pause*)

(PAGE, *young* SVANTE STURE *as a courier, comes in with a bag.*)

BRASK: Sture!

(PAGE *gives the bag to* HERMAN ISRAEL, *who opens it and reads a letter. Pause*)

ISRAEL: Yes! Gustav I, King of the Swedes and the Goths, proclaims—

BRASK: Has he been elected?

ISRAEL: In the presence of Ture Jönsson Ros, the Lord High Steward Lars Siggeson Sparre, the Lord High Constable, etc., etc.—

BRASK: But Lübeck wasn't permitted to participate!

ISRAEL: Also present at the election of the king were: Bernt Bomhower and Herman Plönjes, councillors from Lübeck. (*Pause*)

BRASK: Well! They have deceived us—and we—have drawn the shortest straw. What do you say to this, Sture?

ISRAEL: Be ashamed, Bishop Brask, to appeal to a child and to involve a minor in intrigues . . .

BRASK: We can hear the truth from the mouths of children . . .

ISRAEL: Well! Let young Sture speak, then. (*Pause*)

PAGE (*modestly and with dignity*): Since you, my good lords, permit me to speak in your well-informed circle, I use, with your permission, your good will. You see that my lord and king has

honored me by having me deliver the news of his election to the
city of Stockholm and the council of the free Hanseatic city of
Lübeck. For you, Bishop Brask, is that not assurance that in spite
of my youth and my Sture name I have pledged my faith and
allegiance to Vasa? He is my lord; I am his man!

BRASK (*crushed*): Fine, Sture! I have nothing to add—my time is
over. My broom is worn out—toss it on the fire! Come, Erik!
(*Goes toward the back*)

ERIK TROLLE: Vasa! The ways of the Lord—I submit!

BRASK: You submit! If I could! (*Pause*) Suppose I'll have to. (*Goes*)
(*Pause*)

CLERK (*announces*): Master Olaus Petri,[36] secretary of the Council
of Stockholm! (*Pause*)

CURTAIN

ACT V

SCENE I

A room in Stockholm Castle. The same scenery as in The Last
of the Knights, *Act II, scene 1, and Act V, scene 2, and in the first
act of* The Regent.

*The rooms look stripped: the windows have been taken out,
the furniture knocked over, the council table with its legs turned
up.*

*People are running across the stage from left to right, remov-
ing furniture.*

CONSTABLE (*enters*): Don't run in that direction; they're firing at
that side!

MAN: They're shooting from all sides! (*Exits to the right*)

CONSTABLE: Don't run in that direction; why, they're shooting!

WOMAN: Where are we to run, then?

CONSTABLE: Stand still, for heaven's sake!

WOMAN (*as she goes out to the right*): Where is a person to stand?

> (GUSTAV TROLLE *enters from the left, beside himself.* MÄTTA STURE *comes in calmly from the right.*)

GUSTAV TROLLE: Where shall I flee?

MÄTTA STURE: Whither shall I go from Thy spirit? Whither shall I flee from Thy countenance? If I took the wings of the morning and flew toward the rising of the sun, Thou wouldst follow me; if I made my bed in hell, Thou hast caught me.[37]

GUSTAV TROLLE: Where shall I flee?

MÄTTA STURE: It doesn't matter where you flee; you'll never be freed from yourself.

> (GUSTAV TROLLE *half creeps out to the right.* MÄTTA STURE *remains standing in the ruins. Pause*)

ANNA NATT-OCH-DAG (*comes in from the left*): Where shall a person flee?

MÄTTA STURE: Anna, you don't need to flee.

ANNA: I was sick in bed but had to get up . . .

MÄTTA: Stay! And the deliverer will come!

ANNA: Death, you mean?

MÄTTA (*sighs*): He'll not come that soon. Our deliverer is—Gustav!

ANNA: Johan was mine—now I haven't any.

MÄTTA: Go out into the Green Corridor—they won't hit that.

ANNA: Why don't you go yourself?

MÄTTA: They'll not take me before my time is up—I've walked in ruins all my life, the time of my misery, the days of my suffering . . .

ANNA: Why don't you enter a cloister?

MÄTTA: They won't take me. No one wants me, the executioner doesn't want me, so I wander here—that's my punishment!

ANNA: God comfort us! How you talk! If my mother were alive, she'd have prepared my death bed and arranged my hair—I'm dying, Lady Mätta.

MÄTTA: And you're sorry for yourself!

ANNA (*drags herself out to the right*): Poor Lady Mätta!

(*Pause*)

(MÄTTA *strikes fire with steel and flint and tries to set fire to something in the wall.*)

PAGE, SVANTE STURE (*enters from the left*): What are you doing, grandmother? What are you up to? Don't set fire to it! The king's here; he has taken the drawbridge—

MÄTTA: Are you here? Have you been captured?

PAGE: They caught me on the road to Strängnäs—don't set fire to it!

MÄTTA: No, my child, I won't. Is the king here? Come out! Will you take my hand?

(PAGE *goes unwillingly toward her.*)

MÄTTA: You don't want to? Go into the Green Corridor; then you'll be safe.

PAGE: Grandmother! You mustn't stand there!

MÄTTA: May I take your little hand?

(PAGE *gives her his hand.*)

MÄTTA (*kisses his hand*): A little child's hand—

(PAGE *wants to kiss her hand.*)

MÄTTA: No, you may not!

CONSTABLE: The castle has fallen! The king is coming!

VOICES (*outside*): The king is coming!

(MÄTTA *takes the* PAGE *in her arms.*)

CURTAIN

SCENE 2

Town Hall Rathskeller in Stockholm. The same scenery as in Act I of The Last of the Knights, *but the tavern is decorated with leaves, and in front of the arches hang Renaissance "fruit garlands."*

KEEPER *goes about looking at everything to see that it is in order.*

ERIK TROLLE *enters; has aged.*

KEEPER: Aren't you in the procession, councillor, when the king's making his entrance into his capital?

ERIK TROLLE: That's too much to be expected of a Trolle, I suspect; I'll welcome his arrival—because it means peace for the country.

KEEPER: The years have gone by, Your Grace, since we stood here last. That was when young Sten Sture made his entrance—and you ordered the banquet—

ERIK TROLLE: I've always been allowed to help set the tables, where others have eaten. (*Goes and sits down to the side*)

KEEPER: Have I ever been allowed to do anything but set tables— for others? I guess there's a difference between people and beasts, but sometimes there's a certain likeness; and I'm glad I get out of doing the dishes!

(MÅNS NILSSON *and* ANDERS PERSSON *enter.*)

MÅNS NILSSON (*looks about*): We've been here before. The same keeper, I believe!

KEEPER: The same one during all the changes of all times . . . Whether their names be Trolle, Sture, Vasa . . .

ANDERS PERSSON: New names and old matters—

KEEPER: But how did you take Stockholm Castle?

MÅNS NILSSON: Lady Mätta Sture was just going to set fire to the arsenal when the king took the drawbridge, and then Gustav Trolle fled from the kingdom for the last time [38] . . .

KEEPER: But without the Lübeckers they'd never have taken Stockholm—

ANDERS PERSSON: Yes, you can say that—

MÅNS NILSSON: And it's true . . . Now Gustav controls the whole kingdom except for Brask's Munkeboda. He doesn't want to take it—but he'd like to have it from Brask's own hand, for he wants to have the hand, too! (*Pause*)

ANDERS PERSSON: What's meant by a friend of the union?

KEEPER: Someone who sticks to the union—the three united kingdoms—

MÅNS NILSSON: Then Gustav Trolle was right—

KEEPER: Yes, in that way, he was right—

ANDERS PERSSON: Listen, is it midsummer eve? Is the Danish war over? Is this the time to stir in the dirty linen? Haven't we come here to forget the worst and to remember the best? Shan't we drink forgetfulness from the cup of memory?

KEEPER AND MÅNS NILSSON: Yes! Yes! Yes!

ANDERS PERSSON: Then we'll do it!

MÅNS NILSSON: All that and this, too, is fine, but we've held banquets before, without thinking about the host or the bill. Christian's alive, and, no matter how it goes, he'll always come back.

ANDERS PERSSON: Let him come, just so he doesn't come today. But I suspect he has got a lot to think about at home—and besides he has repented of the bloodbath—

MÅNS NILSSON: I've heard he's raising an army in Flanders [39] . . .

ANDERS PERSSON: Keep your mouth shut, or we'll be out in the field fighting! Old men that we are!

MÅNS NILSSON: There are still so many old charges in the cannons, that all that's needed is a spark . . .

ANDERS PERSSON: Quiet! Here comes the new broom—

MÅNS NILSSON: Is it the secretary of the council? . . .

ANDERS PERSSON: Yes, he's a hell of a man, Olaus Petri—that fellow has a mug like a man from Mora!

(OLAUS PETRI *and* HERMAN ISRAEL *enter from the back.*)

HERMAN ISRAEL: Let's have peace, Master Olof, peace for this day, at least. Do you want to disturb this banquet, and make the midsummer sun blush for shame?

OLAUS PETRI (*angry*): That won't matter in the least! Let the thunder roll, if there's sunshine afterward! You demand the city of Stockholm in lien—have you lost your mind?

HERMAN ISRAEL: Loans are to be repaid, and with interest!

OLAUS PETRI: But not with usurer's interest! If Lübeck is to own

Stockholm, while the king owns the country, then we have the Käplinge murders [40] all over again! And your help will be the country's ruin! *Zahlen, zahlen!* Do you think the Dalesmen demand pay? And they were the ones who set the country free—you damned Germans . . .

HERMAN ISRAEL: Those are the thanks!

OLAUS PETRI: First to pay with your skin and then say thanks as well! Poor goods and false money, exorbitant interest and eternal gratitude to boot . . .

ANDERS PERSSON: Freedom is the best thing. Can it be bought too dearly?

OLAUS PETRI: Yes, when you can get it for less in the next shop!

ERIK TROLLE (*gets up*): What is this? Have we come here to listen to quarrels?

OLAUS PETRI (*goes toward* TROLLE): Listen! (*Pause*) When your name is Trolle, you shouldn't even show yourself on a day like this, and at a place where Swedish men gather for a celebration quite different from Trolle's bloodbath!

ERIK TROLLE: Shall the sins of the sons be visited on their fathers?

OLAUS PETRI: Yes, by reverse inheritance—occasionally. But I feel that at your age you ought to understand that your presence is offensive . . .

ERIK TROLLE: Is that what you others think, too? (*All are silent, embarrassed.*) Well, then, I'd better be on my way. You may be right.

OLAUS PETRI: No, I *am* right, and so I insist on my point!

ERIK TROLLE: Come out with me, young man, and I'll give you something—to offer the king—because I am his friend, even if he isn't mine!—It's good news—that I want to deliver myself—but I shall let you empty the cup of victory because I can never have any more joy in this life. Come out with me—You can do me this last service, just as I do you the first.

OLAUS PETRI: But don't deceive me!

(ERIK TROLLE *looks at him sharply and goes.* OLAUS PETRI *follows him.*)

ANDERS PERSSON: Poor old man!

MÅNS NILSSON: That Master Olof isn't attractive.

HERMAN ISRAEL: He's a currycomb!

ANDERS PERSSON: He tears. People like that are needed nowadays. And the king wants him like that.

MÅNS NILSSON: Have you heard anything about the imprisoned ladies in Denmark?

HERMAN ISRAEL: Yes, reports say they're free! Kristina Sture is in Stockholm.

ANDERS PERSSON: And Severin Norrby?

HERMAN ISRAEL: I don't know.

MÅNS NILSSON: Anna Natt-och-Dag is ill . . . but she'll most likely come here anyway.

ANDERS PERSSON: The air down here is heavy. This isn't really midsummer, this.

HERMAN ISRAEL (*listening to something outside*): But it will be! Now they're at Southgate—

(*People circulate in the background.*)

KEEPER: Here come the girls with the Brännkyrka banner—then King Gösta will be happy—there are memories, though! Others than the eighth of November!

ANDERS PERSSON: Don't talk about that!

KEEPER: I almost lost my head, and Master Olof, too, because he couldn't keep still [41]—

ANDERS PERSSON: Hush!

(GIRLS, *crowned with wreaths, enter carrying the banner and singing the ballad of St. George.*)

LARS SPARRE (*enters*): Good, my friends! Listen to me! (*Pause*) Bitter news has come from Denmark. (*Pause*) Our king's noble mother and sisters—have passed away during their captivity—no one knows how.[42] Now I beg of you and urge you that no one, no matter who it may be, let anything come out about it this day, which is King Gustav's day of joy. Tomorrow or when the matter is announced—then—but, until then, promise me silence.

ALL: We promise!

LARS SPARRE: With all the greater pleasure I can announce that the noble Lady Kristina Sture has returned, unharmed and dear to all Swedish hearts, so much the more as the rumor of her union with a Dane is demonstrably unfounded.

ALL: Hail! Kristina Sture!

LARS: Here she is herself!

(KRISTINA STURE *enters.* MAYOR *and members of the council enter.*)

MAYOR: Stockholm's mayor and councillors bid Your Ladyship welcome back to the fatherland and hope that among your faithful friends you may forget the sufferings you have endured.

KRISTINA STURE: I thank you, the elders of the city, for your welcome, and I feel secure in your midst, since all dangers are at an end—all of them!

VOICE: Lady Anna Bielke Natt-och-Dag!

(ANNA *enters, gloomy, goes threateningly toward* KRISTINA.)

KRISTINA STURE (*holds out her hands to show that she is wearing no rings*): Anna Bielke, with the most beautiful of names, the sorrowful, the afflicted one, rejoice with us today; see that I approach you with clean hands, and not as you so badly thought! (*Embrace*)

CRY: The king is coming!

ALL: Long live King Gösta!

LARS: Make way for the king!

(*All draw back, and the ladies go aside.*)

(GUSTAV VASA *enters, wearing golden armor and a wreath on his helmet.*)

LARS SPARRE: Long live Gustav I Vasa, King of the Swedes and the Goths!

(*Fanfares; shouts: Long live Gustav Vasa!*)

GUSTAV VASA (*looks for* HERMAN ISRAEL): First, my thanks to the people of Sweden, and to the Dalesmen particularly! And to the free Hansa city of Lübeck for its generous support! (*Gives his hand to* HERMAN ISRAEL) Do not make me ungrateful! Stockholm's mayor and councillors, my greetings! I rely on you henceforth! (*Notices* KRISTINA STURE; *darkens*) Who is that?

(PAGE, *young* STURE, *wants to force himself up to his mother, but* GUSTAV VASA *holds him back.*)

ANNA NATT-OCH-DAG (*leads* KRISTINA *up to* GUSTAV VASA): Kristina is free! From prison and all other bonds.

GUSTAV VASA: Free? From all bonds?

KRISTINA STURE: Yes, free! From *all* bonds! All!

GUSTAV VASA (*takes young* STURE *and places him in her arms*): Then you're to have your child again! Glorious woman, I jumped into the water for you once and took your son with me! *If* I wronged you, forgive me!

KRISTINA STURE: You did wrong me a little, Gustav, but . . . but not entirely; and now I have made my sacrifice, to the memory of my husband, for Sweden, and for Gustav Vasa!

GUSTAV VASA: Give me news of my mother and sisters!

KRISTINA STURE (*embarrassed*): They sent you the message . . .

GUSTAV VASA: That . . .

KRISTINA STURE: That—you'll meet again! Eventually!

GUSTAV VASA: Do I understand you?

(KRISTINA STURE *remains silent.*)

GUSTAV VASA: God! (*Covers his eyes with his hands*) O, God in heaven; receive *my* sacrifice! My country! My mother and my sisters! (*Music in the background*)

GUSTAV VASA: My mother and my sisters! Anna Natt-och-Dag, her husband! Lars Sparre, his brother! Kristina, her husband—and her poor heart!

(OLAUS PETRI *comes in with a parchment.*)

GUSTAV VASA: Are you coming with midsummer gifts, my horseman?

OLAUS PETRI: A midsummer gift for the king!

GUSTAV VASA: Let me have it!

OLAUS PETRI: Since there's a hurry. Bishop Hans Brask hereby surrenders Munkeboda Castle and stronghold and takes his oath of allegiance and fealty to the king of Sweden!

GUSTAV VASA: God bless the old man! Then Sweden's realm is one, and the Swedes have become their own masters! (*To* OLAUS PETRI) You begin well, you, who are to have it out with the Romans!

(LARS SPARRE *comes in with a letter.*)

GUSTAV VASA: Other midsummer gifts?

LARS: The greatest, the best one!

GUSTAV VASA: From you, my faithful Lars, it is most welcome! (*Reads*) King Christian of Denmark has fled, is deposed—and Fredrik is king! [43] Fellow Swedes! Christian the Tyrant is no more! Let us go to the altar of the Great Church and sing *Te Deum laudamus!*

(*The* GIRLS *come forward with the Brännkyrka banner;* GUSTAV VASA *kisses its cloth; gives one hand to* KRISTINA STURE *and the other to* ANNA NATT-OCH-DAG.)

(*Music, etc.*)

CURTAIN

Notes on 'The Regent'

THE TIME

WHEN Sten Sture the Younger was wounded in battle with the unionist forces in 1520 and died shortly afterward, most of the nationalist defense of Sweden collapsed. Perhaps the most striking exception was his widow's heroic defense of Stockholm Castle until the fall of 1520. Christian II then made his entrance into the capital, having promised amnesty to all its heroic defenders. After his coronation as hereditary king of Sweden, he gave a series of banquets and other festivities to which he invited the leading Swedish lords and ladies as well as Swedish prelates and important Swedish burghers. During the festivities, he conferred with Archbishop Gustav Trolle and various non-Swedish advisers on the problem of dealing with the Swedes who had opposed him.

The results of the conferences became plain on November 7, 1520, when the Swedish guests were summoned to the palace, called upon to defend themselves before Trolle (the accuser and prosecutor) and the king, and imprisoned. The next day, November 8, they were tried for heresy before a so-called spiritual court on the flimsy basis of what they had done to the archbishop during the course of the preceding years (see the note on Trolle on pp. 86-87). Two hours after the prisoners, except Bishop Brask (see note 8 on p. 167), were declared guilty, Christian II the Tyrant had sent his first victims, Bishops Mattias of Strängnäs and Vincentius of Skara, and the lords, including Gustav Vasa's father, to the place of execution on the Great Square. This was the ugly massacre that has received the name Stockholm bloodbath and that, perhaps more than any other factor, rendered all thought of Sweden's willing and lasting entrance into the union impossible. About a hundred of the leading Swedes lost their lives; the Swedish ladies were imprisoned. The massacre at Stockholm was not the only one. In Finland Heming Gad was only one of those executed on Christian's orders, and, when Christian returned by land to Denmark, gallows and executions marked his route. The regency he appointed included Archbishop Trolle, the notorious Didrik Slagheck, and the Danish bishop Jens Anderssen Beldenacke; it did not bring to an end the reign of terror designed to end all Swedish opposition.

It is ironic that no other action of Christian's could conceivably have done more to arouse well-nigh unanimous and violent Swedish opposition to him and the union. It is ironic, too, that an earlier act of treachery—the taking of the six hostages to Denmark in 1518—should have provided the Swedes with the leadership with which to free themselves completely from effective interference by Danish kings in Swedish affairs. For the hostage Gustav Vasa escaped from his Danish prison, obtained help in Lübeck, returned to Sweden, and within three years had secured Swedish independence. It is the story of that heroic achievement that Strindberg has to tell in *The Regent.*

THE CHARACTERS

About *Gustav Eriksson Vasa* (*ca.* 1494-1560) it should be remembered that he belonged to a clan that had for generations been largely unionists but had swung its support to the Stures and the nationalists in the late fifteenth century; that he had been sent to the Sture court to acquire knightly skills and manners; that he had come under the influence not only of the gentle Sten Sture but also of the wily Heming Gad—perhaps the ablest propagandist against the union; that he had fought bravely with Sten Sture until Christian II had kidnaped Gustav and kept him in detention in Denmark, from which he escaped to Lübeck in 1519; that he lost his father in the bloodbath; and that he led the Dalesmen and other patriotic Swedes in the war for independence.

He was elected regent at Vadstena in 1521 and king in 1523. He made his entry into Stockholm at midsummer of that year. As Strindberg says, both his mother and his sisters died in prison in Copenhagen.

The long reign of Gustav I (1523-1560) resulted in a united and strong Sweden; of necessity, he ruled as a benevolent dictator who brought order out of chaos in almost all phases of Swedish life and laid the foundation for Sweden's greatness. See *Master Olof* and *Gustav Vasa* for Strindberg's interpretation of Gustav Vasa as king.

The late Professor Stomberg (*A History of Sweden* [New York: Macmillan, 1931], pp. 283-284) summarized the generally accepted facts about Gustav Vasa's appearance and personality:

> Vasa is described in his mature years as a stately individual of medium size, with keen, penetrating blue eyes, ruddy complexion, flaxen hair, and a long flowing beard. By nature he was jovial and delighted in the companionship of congenial souls, loved music, in which he was himself quite proficient, and wholesome frolic. People who were associated with him marvelled at his extraordinary memory; he knew the roads over which he had not travelled for thirty years and persons with whom he had once come in contact were decades later recognized by him and called by their right names when he chanced to meet them again. In his acts he was generally actuated by the highest motives of public interest, and keenly felt an overpowering sense of responsibility to God and to the Swedish nation. A quick temper which often got beyond control, a tendency to suspect everyone of evil designs, intolerance and harshness against those who dared to oppose him, and a thriftiness which often tended upon penury were the main weaknesses in his otherwise sturdy personality. In his private life he set a noble example of rectitude; in the whole list of calumnies that his enemies and traducers cited against him, there was never even a hint of licentiousness or scandal; he was a good husband and a kind, perhaps too indulgent, father.

Bishop Hans Brask (1464-1538), famous particularly as the last Catholic bishop to oppose the reformation, was a brilliant and canny churchman who in 1513 was elected and confirmed bishop of Linköping, the very position Heming Gad had been elected to some years previously. As bishop of the wealthiest diocese in Sweden, Hans Brask quickly became one of the most powerful men in the country, engaged not only in politics, clerical and nonclerical, but also in business projects of various kinds, and kept an armed force of hundreds of men as his personal army with headquarters at his fortified castle of Munkeboda. At the meeting of Arboga which deposed Archbishop Trolle, Bishop Brask signed the document drawn up but slipped a bit of paper stating, "To this I am forced and compelled" under his seal. It was this act which saved his life during the bloodbath. Not an enthusiastic supporter of Gustav Vasa, he nevertheless assisted him on occasion. After the first steps had been taken to make Sweden Lutheran, Bishop Brask fled to Danzig, where he spent his final years in a monastery. See also *Master Olof.*

Olaus Petri (1493–1552), the son of an Örebro smith, studied in Wittenberg, came under the influence of Luther, returned to Sweden in 1518, and is said to have witnessed the bloodbath. After the accession of Gustav I, Master Olof, as he is often called, became the leader of the Lutheran reformation in Sweden and promoted the first complete Swedish translation of the Bible (1526, 1541). One of the first churchmen to renounce celibacy, he married a young woman who may have broken her vows. Olaus Petri served King Gustav in various ways: he was secretary of the city of Stockholm, Gustav's chancellor, and, as preacher in the Great Church in Stockholm, led the reformation. He is the central character in Strindberg's first great historical play, *Master Olof* (1872).

For information about other characters, see pp. 86-89.

LIST OF CHARACTERS

1. See note 1 on pp. 89-90 for information about the family names.

ACT I

2. According to Strindberg's semipopular sources (SB, II, 699, and III, 32; and Fryxell, II, 220), Christian made Archbishop Trolle, his father Erik Trolle, Didrik Slagheck, and Jens Anderssen Beldenacke the temporary regency council upon the king's departure from Stockholm in December, 1520. The inclusion of Slagheck and Beldenacke was par-

ticularly insulting; neither was by birth either Swedish or aristocratic. Slagheck, a favorite and perhaps a relative of Sigbrit, the influential mother of King Christian's mistress Dyveke, had started out as a barber's apprentice and come into Christian's favor to the extent of being made a member of the "court" that tried the Swedish lords and commoners who perished in the Stockholm bloodbath. He was the successor of the then executed Bishop Vincentius as bishop of Skara and commander of Stockholm Castle, and, in 1522, archbishop of Denmark. Two months after becoming archbishop, he was burned at the stake in Copenhagen as a gesture to the Church of Rome for having had the two Swedish prelates, Bishops Vincentius of Skara and Mattias of Strängnäs, executed at the bloodbath (SB, III, 56). Slagheck's brother Henrik served as commander of Stockholm Castle. Beldenacke, another of Sigbrit's and Christian's favorites, was a Dane who, although he was already a bishop of a Danish diocese, was made successor to Bishop Mattias. Only slightly less disreputable than Didrik Slagheck, Beldenacke found it wise to leave Sweden with Archbishop Trolle in 1522.

3. With Gustav Trolle, Didrik Slagheck, and Jens Beldenacke in command, a large pro-union (largely Danish) army set out to quell the uprising of the Dalesmen in its incipient stage early in 1521. A smaller force of Dalesmen met them at Brunn Brook ferry, crossed the Dal River, and routed the government forces.

4. The commander of the Danish fleet.

5. See notes 25, 28, and 58 on pp. 92 ff.

6. Gustav Vasa's father, it should be remembered, was one of the lords executed in the Stockholm bloodbath.

7. See note 5, above. The various accounts of Danish-born Lady Mätta are contradictory; they range all the way from accusing her of murder and treason to acclaiming her for her loyalty to her husband and stepson.

8. Bishop Brask escaped execution through having the foresight to slip a piece of paper on which he had written, "To this I am compelled and forced" under his seal attached to the decrees of the council of Arboga (1517), which recorded measures taken against Archbishop Trolle.

9. See notes 15 and 53 on pp. 91 and 95, respectively.

10. According to Strindberg's sources, Lady Trolle drowned, appar-

ently as a result of her own obstinacy. Gustav, an extremely self-willed and unmanageable child, undoubtedly caused both his parents grief.

11. Rotebro is a few miles northwest of Stockholm.

12. November 8, 1520, was the day when the majority of the victims of the Stockholm bloodbath were executed.

13. Christian II's bloodbath was not restricted to Stockholm. In Jönköping in the southern province of Småland the young Ribbings were only two of many executed on the king's orders.

14. See notes 8, 11, and 24 on pp. 91 f.

ACT II

15. See *The Last of the Knights*, pp. 70-72, and note 57 on p. 96.

16. Arvid Vestgöte, Peder Fredag, and Lars Björnram were among Gustav Vasa's ablest and most daring associates in the war of independence.

17. The day when Christian II captured the hostages. See note 15.

18. As a young man, Gustav Vasa was a member of Regent Sten Sture's court, at which the knightly ideas of conduct were held up as the ideal pattern by the regent and his noble-minded wife, Lady Kristina. It is significant that Heming Gad, the brilliant old bishop-elect, was one of the dominant figures at the court. See, for example, SB (III, 8-9).

19. Strindberg summarizes briefly the story of Gustav Vasa's imprisonment in Denmark; his escape to Lübeck, where he obtained help of various kinds; his return to Sweden and the refusal of the people of Småland to help him; and his flight to Dalarna where the Dalesmen, after some consideration, granted him their support and made him their leader in the war for independence.

20. After Christian II's departure from Denmark, Sören Norrby was for several years a pirate in the Baltic; for some time, he controlled the island province of Gotland, from which base he became the terror of Baltic shipping interests.

ACT III

21. Gustav Vasa was elected regent at a meeting of the Estates in Vadstena in August, 1521, after refusing the offer of the crown. It is quite possible that the difficulties of Charles VIII (Karl Knutsson), a

lord who had been king during three different periods in the preceding century, may, as Strindberg suggests, have helped Gustav decide to reject the crown. See note 39 on p. 94.

22. See notes 15 and 17, above. For the allusion to Gustav Trolle and the pine, see *The Last of the Knights*, pp. 60-61.

23. In direct and indirect lines, the Oldenburgs have been the royal house of Denmark since the middle ages.

24. Bengt Bjugg was Archbishop Gustav Trolle's Danish bailiff in Uppsala. According to Fryxell (III, 24), the arrogant and violent Bjugg disregarded rumors of the approach of Swedish forces and arranged a large banquet and drinking bout to show his contempt for the Swedish yeomen and their leaders. At two o'clock in the morning when the Swedes marched into Uppsala, Bjugg and his forces were sleeping off their drunkenness: awakened, Bjugg and some of his men managed to escape after setting fire to the city. On the flight to Stockholm Bjugg was severely wounded by one of the pursuing Swedish archers and died shortly afterward.

25. In an engagement shortly after Bjugg's death in the summer of 1521, Archbishop Trolle was forced to flee at the head of his army. According to Strindberg's sources, a Swede, Lars Olsson (not Peter Hansson as Strindberg says), tried to kill the archbishop by throwing his sword at him. The archbishop, the story goes, bent his head down along his horse's neck; the sword may have nicked him but passed on to hit Peter Hansson, who at that moment was riding a little ahead of him.

26. The parish of Danmark in Uppland, not the country.

27. A partial list of the powerful aristocratic families that suffered losses in the Stockholm bloodbath.

28. See note 35 on p. 93.

29. Munkeboda was Bishop Brask's fortified castle near his episcopal city of Linköping. The wily bishop, who had barely escaped with his life at the bloodbath, served as King Christian's host at Munkeboda after the latter's departure from Stockholm for Denmark.

30. Coriolanus was the legendary Roman hero of the fifth century who retired from his campaign against Rome as the result of the pleas of his mother and his wife. See Shakespeare's *Coriolanus*.

31. On his journey by land from Stockholm to Denmark after the

bloodbath in 1520, Christian II continued to execute atrocities in one central and southern Swedish community after the other, as Strindberg suggests.

ACT IV

32. The meeting of the Estates was held at Strängnäs in the summer of 1523. Gustav Vasa was elected king on June 6. The Lübeckers, who had promoted his election primarily to guarantee the payment of the extended loans and to gain trade concessions, were participants in the manner Strindberg suggests in this scene.

33. Under Sten Sture the Elder, Sweden enjoyed domestic peace from 1472 to 1495.

34. Worldly Bishop Brask was an excellent businessman as well as an impressive prelate and a brilliant man. The accounts in Strindberg's sources as well as in more scholarly ones stamp him as one of the ablest and most colorful men of his time.

35. Peder the Chancellor (Peder Jakobsson) was a priest who served Gustav Vasa for propaganda purposes in Dalarna. In 1523–1524, he was bishop-elect of Västerås; leader of the first uprising in Dalarna, he was arrested and in 1527 executed.

36. Olaus Petri (1493–1552), the leading Lutheran reformer in Sweden, had studied in Wittenberg, come under the influence of Luther, and, after his return to Sweden in 1518, become more and more imbued with Lutheran protestantism. A witness to the atrocities in the bloodbath in 1520, Olaus Petri became Gustav Vasa's trusted supporter as secretary of the city council of Stockholm in 1524. See Strindberg's dramas *Master Olof* (1872) and *Gustav Vasa* (1899).

ACT V

37. See Psalms 139:7-10.

38. Gustav Trolle fled from Sweden for the last time in 1522, stayed in Copenhagen for some time, and was wounded in battle at Öxnebjerg in 1535.

39. Christian failed in this project.

40. Käplinge or Käpplingeholmen is an older name of Blasieholmen. Strindberg refers to the murders of Swedish burghers by German

burghers on that island in 1389. Among the Stockholm merchants were a very large number of German burghers; until 1471 half the members of the council of Stockholm had to be Germans.

41. See note 36, above.

42. The accounts of the imprisonment and treatment of the Swedish ladies in the Blue Tower in Copenhagen coincide with what Strindberg says. Fryxell (II, 219) says: "There [the Blue Tower in Copenhagen] Gustav Vasa's mother and two of his sisters . . . died of starvation, thirst, and cold." Strindberg sometimes refers to "sister" and sometimes to "sisters." I have consistently made it "sisters."

43. Fredrik I became king of Denmark in 1523 when Christian II fled from Copenhagen. Gustav Vasa assisted Fredrik in various ways and was usually on good terms with the Danish king.

Introduction to
'Earl Birger of Bjälbo'

THE HISTORICAL PLAY that Strindberg deals with at greatest
length and with greatest frankness in his *Open Letters to the Inti-
mate Theater* (*Öppna brev till Intima teatern*) is *Earl Birger of
Bjälbo* (1908). In the two letters or essays, "The Historical Drama"
("Det historiska dramat") and "The Concept of Stylization etc."
("Begreppet stilisera m.m."), he discusses frankly the sources of
the historical material; his use of that material, particularly the
limitation, selection, and adaptation of the historical material for
dramatic purposes; and his placement of Swedish history within
the framework of world history.

Without doubt the statement of greatest importance in these letters to anyone who wants to understand the historical dramas is
this:

> Even in the historical drama the purely human is of major interest,
> and history the background; souls' inner struggles awaken more
> sympathy than the combat of soldiers or the storming of walls;
> love and hate, torn family ties more than treaties and speeches from
> the throne [p. 258].

172

For Strindberg's central interest in his historical plays as elsewhere is people; the behavior of human beings rarely if ever takes second place either to historical fact or to detail. That, of course, is the primary reason for the vitality of the historical plays; Strindberg made the historical figures come alive because he saw them as human beings without making use, as many a historian and historical dramatist has, of the blinders of tradition or hero worship.

Strindberg's frank statement that his major sources were such semischolarly sources as Fryxell's *Stories from Swedish History* (*Berättelser ur svenska historien*) and particularly Starbäck and Bäckström's work by the same name, and his equally frank admission that he adapted, expanded, and compressed the historical material as he saw fit in order to present a complex living human being at a time of greatest personal crisis must have been disconcerting to many. For Strindberg admits that in writing *Earl Birger of Bjälbo* he took very great liberties with the details and facts of history. For example: King Valdemar's and Princess Judith's incest probably did not take place until 1273, seven years after Earl Birger was dead. As Strindberg says, "I knew what liberties I was taking, I knew what the drama gains" (p. 257). The accuracy of substantiated detail is of necessity important to the scholarly historian; to Strindberg, the historical dramatist, the historical detail was of minor consequence in comparison to the interpretation of the historical character.

Yet the historian-scholar and the historical dramatist meet on common ground when they interpret the figures out of the past, for the historian as well as the dramatist must use both his insight and his imagination in his attempt to make historical personalities come alive for the reader and (for the dramatist) the audience. It is undoubtedly true that the poet and dramatist Strindberg's insight, understanding, and imagination were so far superior to those of most professional historians that his interpretations of such historical figures as Earl Birger of Bjälbo are likely to become the ones that will live, at least for his fellow Swedes, in spite of minor and major adaptations of historical fact.

Strindberg shared with perhaps most other great writers the practice of using himself as a means of understanding his characters: "When I wrote *Earl Birger of Bjälbo,* I proceeded as usual. I read Starbäck's history. . . . I made the major characters live by taking blood and nerves out of my own life." The simplified, fixed, and static characterizations of Earl Birger and the other characters to be found in the sources has been supplemented, varied, and complemented by Strindberg's interpretation of the earl and the rest as complex beings not unlike himself in his variation and complexity. What the historians have done more or less unconsciously, Strindberg has done deliberately. What the aging Strindberg had to give in the way of blood and nerves to the aging Earl Birger is obvious to any student of Strindberg: the loneliness and frustration of the individual, the unsatisfactory marriages, the imperfections of the parent-child relationship, and the insight into human nature are illustrations.

In so doing Strindberg has again, as in so many of the earlier historical plays, applied so far as it was pertinent the realistic-naturalistic technique that he had discussed in detail in the preface of *Lady Julie* (1888). Theme, plot, characterization, dialogue, and setting (including both local color and the atmosphere of the period) are all realistically conceived and presented in keeping with his conviction that the primarily important is the purely human and that the history is only background.

In his letter on stylization, Strindberg says (p. 299): "The earl is mine, too. He is no teacher of elocution, but a politician and a schemer just as he was in life." What Strindberg has done is to present the aging earl as a family man at the height of his power and on the verge of achieving (or losing) the goal of his ambition. How skillfully he has composed the play can perhaps most easily be observed through an analysis of his presentation of the earl himself.

Earl Birger does not appear in Act I, but in the carefully arranged setting of Birger's Stockholm—fortified and walled on the site of an insignificant earlier village and supplied with the palace, the towers, the Great Church, and a monastery suitable to a medieval seat of government—Birger is most effectively introduced. Everyone who appears is keenly aware of the earl; everyone talks about him; it is as if the earl's eye were on everyone. It is an environment largely dominated by one man.

What he is like begins to become clear immediately. Apparently both a man of ideas and a man of action, Earl Birger has accomplished much: he has established peace and security within the land; he has virtually created a new and strategically placed capital; he has secured peace with neighboring nations through the marriages of his children and through brilliant diplomacy and politics; he has helped establish the civilizing force of Christianity in his own country; he has made Sweden a nation to be reckoned with in Europe. But, great as his achievements have been, he has achieved neither the tranquillity that comes with inner peace nor the crown, the external symbol of power. He still has problems: Lord Karl, one of his ablest kinsmen and claimant to the throne Earl Birger should have had, is still about; the man who for all practical purposes deprived the earl of that throne by securing the election of Birger's ten-year-old son is still active from time to time; the church which has been useful to Birger on many occasions has become so powerful that he no longer can control its influence in his country; guilty of both murder and perjury, he must observe all the outward forms required of the penitent.

Quickly and economically, in the first scene of Act II, Strindberg presents the most pressing and crucial problem of Strindberg's earl: his immediate family. As Hans says, "He manages the kingdom and the council like a groom but keep the boys in line, he can't." The handsome and pleasure-loving oldest son, king in name but still treated by the earl as a child to be sent down into the courtyard to play instead of participating in the conferences with official visitors from abroad; the frivolous daughter-in-law; the second son, who seems contrary and obstinate to the earl; one son who amounts to nothing at all; and a beloved youngest son—all are treated as children, to be used on occasion but otherwise disregarded. It is the sort of family situation not unlike those Strindberg had so often dealt with in his earlier works. The appearance of the earl—on the bastion, observant, watchful, but silent—is very effective indeed. Hans says: "From the roof of my doghouse I can look down at the whole mess—like the earl from his window; and you're my playthings that amuse me."

The second scene of Act II is particularly important for the light it sheds on the central character's thinking, achievements, mode of action, and personality as well as for the light it sheds on Ivar Blå's role in Birger's life. Note that Ivar Blå serves as a sort of nemesis for Birger; it was he who had frustrated Earl Birger's ambition to be elected king years before by securing the election of Birger's ten-year-old son Valdemar, thereby robbing Birger of the crown, the symbol of power, but letting him keep the actual power. Again it is Ivar Blå who suggests and supports the political move that will frustrate Earl Birger's ambition completely. The relationship between the two men is clarified:

> EARL: Do you have important business, or are you just trying to pick a quarrel?
>
> IVAR (*slowly*): Well—
>
> EARL: Since you consider yourself a royal councillor, I want to tell you that the kingdom is in excellent condition . . .
>
> IVAR (*seriously*): I don't doubt that, Birger; I can see the piles of papers on your desk; the country is everywhere at peace; anybody can travel safely on any of our roads; we can sleep in bed without having to be afraid of being burned alive; but, while you manage the kingdom, you mismanage your own house . . .
>
> EARL: Silence!
>
> IVAR: The king is losing his good name, and, when you pass away, not one of your sons will be able to govern the kingdom, and the people will take the most daring first comer!

EARL: Lord Karl?

IVAR: Maybe! (*Pause*) And you won't find him at Herrevad's Bridge!

EARL: Herrevad's Bridge? Still talking about that, are you? I punished the rebels who rose against *your* legally elected king. Isn't that right?

IVAR: In spite of your promise of safe-conduct!

EARL: Safe-conduct! A mere word!

IVAR: I thought you had regretted what you did! The people say you wear a haircloth shirt next to . . .

EARL (*contemptuously*): The people?

IVAR: Well! Then we understand each other! Let's go back to the royal power—Valdemar is disgracing himself!

In his arrogance and pride, Earl Birger thinks of himself as the one man capable of governing the kingdom; he prides himself on his achievements and feels that he understands not only himself but also the people, whom he despises except in so far as they unwittingly wield power which forces him into conformity or hypocritical pretense. Note what Dr. Wilibald, the French astrologer— Birger shared some of the superstitions of his time—says:

Earl, at fifty you face the real goal of your life; an unkind destiny denied you, the worthiest of all, the crown, but now, since you have atoned for your crimes, fortune will turn to your advantage, and your old age will reap what your long years of labor have sown.

Note, too, Earl Birger's frank confession of faith and statement of his concept of life:

EARL: I'll throw my mask away, Wilibald; now I know life and people, and I want to use my dearly purchased wisdom. Human beings? Say scoundrels! Friends? Accomplices in crime—they're friends! Love? Say hate! All people hate each other! My children hate me as I hate them! Every morning they come to ask about my health in the hope that I'm ill. If I ask about something, they lie to me! If I didn't have spies, I'd be deceived every time. On my latest birthday they brought me flowers and filled me with lies! If I ask Magnus how his brother Valdemar is getting along with his wife, he says they're happy, so devilishly happy, though Valdemar is living in open adultery! And these foreign ambassadors, who came to wish me luck—what they wish me is misfortune! But I played the fox with them! The art of governing! Write falsely, promise in order not to keep, fool them into making promises. Business and commerce, deceit! I sat down to eat with Hamburg's and Lübeck's pickpockets today! Bishops? Swine! The pope . . .

ASTROLOGER: People don't say things like that!

EARL (*removes outer garments and takes off his hair shirt*): Yes, in the darkness of the night when the lights are out and people are asleep! Then a person takes off everything and shows himself in all his nakedness. You know, Wilibald, I believe I'm a heathen, and have always been, though I haven't known it! What do I believe in? This! My fist! (*Strikes the table*) But this, my hair shirt, I don't believe in, and never have! Now I'll throw it in the fire!

ASTROLOGER: Earl Birger!

EARL: And, if there are more troublemakers still, they may meet me at Herrevad's Bridge or in hell, and I'll have their heads! With or without safe-conduct . . .

Earl Birger is the great heathen, the great pagan, or, as Bishop Kol says, the barbarian who has the ideas and the ability to realize them, and who pities the people but neither loves nor respects them. The man of power, he has faith in one being only—himself. As he says: "Take a cold bath and then go to work . . . Work is the only thing that gives value to life. It gives appetite and sleep. The rest will have to be as it can."

Scene 1 of Act III gives us a clearer view of Birger's family problems and his techniques for dealing with them. Suspicious even of his son Bengt, "the only human being he can bear," he treats him as a child to be cajoled by demonstrations of affection and promises of rewards into doing what he wants him to do. Respecting his second son Magnus to a degree because Magnus has never been docile and manageable, Birger tries to use him for selfish purposes by appealing to his love for his dead mother, his sympathy, his selfish interests, and his weakness for flattery. A cold, calculating, and hypocritical political manipulator, the earl sows the seed of discord between his two oldest sons in a scheme apparently designed to lead to his own achievement of the crown. In a superb scene, Birger reveals his crippling limitations—his arrogance, his selfish ambition, his distrust of everyone, his inability to understand a thoroughly generous action such as Lord Karl's, and his own lack of inner harmony.

But in scene 2 of Act III Ivar Blå's second thwarting of Birger's ambitions begins to take form. The earl's marriage to Mechtild will be labeled incest by the church—she is too closely related to Birger's daughter-in-law; Magnus has been designated by the church (and Ivar Blå) as regent while King Valdemar goes to Rome as a pilgrim seeking absolution; Birger ceases to be both earl and regent; he loses the support of the church and can no longer count on Norway's support—his son-in-law Håkon the Younger is dead. Again, in the earl's absence, Ivar Blå has frustrated Earl Birger's ambition, this time by providing that the actual power shall pass from Birger to Magnus and that the promise of the symbol of power shall be held out to the successor.

Not yet stripped of his power, and not aware of the implications of the schemes involved in his remarriage and in sowing discord between his two oldest sons, Earl Birger in Act IV is confronted with the Strindbergian and Christian judgment. Bishop Kol says: "The hand of the Lord lies heavy upon you, Birger; your bow has broken, and your arrows go wrong! Your house is falling, and you'd be wise if you withdrew and got ready for the last journey!" and:

> In gambling there are no friends, and you've played for scepters; I believe Valdemar is a better human being than you two are, because he has a sense of shame and a sense of right and wrong . . . Ivar

Blå is a rascal who has lured you into the swamp, and the magician Wilibald is a French bandit who has pulled the wool over your eyes. But that's how it goes when your ways are crooked, and the one who won't obey good advice generally gets bad; the one who wants to rule over everyone often is conquered! That is your case!

But it is not until Act V, when the earl is forced to face the facts of his deception by the astrologer, the loss of his influence in Denmark, the loss of his control of Sweden through Valdemar, the appointment of Magnus as regent, the failure of his last attempt to use Bengt, that the earl is isolated in complete loneliness. In his final exchange with Magnus, the one son capable of matching wits and deeds with him, he is forced to accept being put aside. In weariness and bitterness, he is humbled:

> I am tired of everything, and now I'll go—I'll go to Visingö—I'll walk in the forest, look at the lake, think about what I have lived through, try to be reconciled with the past and to prepare myself for what is ahead!

Strindberg's interpretation of Earl Birger is worthy of its place alongside those in others of his historical dramas—Magnus the Good, Sten Sture the Younger, Archbishop Trolle, Heming Gad, Master Olof, Gustav Vasa, Erik XIV, Gustav Adolf, Queen Christina, Charles XII, and Gustav III. A life spent not in pursuit of power merely for its own sake but primarily for the achievement of the common good—represented by law and order to assure to the Swedes security and opportunity at home and security from foreign aggression—was marred by such basic flaws as the inability to establish adequate and rewarding relations with other human beings, the conviction that he alone could realize his goals, and the pride that comes from the conviction of personal achievement and personal indispensability. Nor has Strindberg neglected the earl's unhesitant use of brute force, hypocrisy, trickery, cunning, and of other human beings as means to an end. The characterization is an application of what Strindberg says in the preface to *Lady Julie* about the characterless character; Earl Birger is anything but "fixed and finished."

Nor are the other characters without interest. Even such minor or incidental ones as the watchman on Brantberg, the fisherman, Peter, the stableman, the Saracen, and the deaf-and-dumb page contribute much to the exposition of Earl Birger's environment of a young but growing Stockholm in a semibarbaric time of great changes both in Sweden and abroad. The somewhat more individualized Dean Lars of Oppunda with his despair and madness stemming from the advent of celibacy in 1248; the knightly Lord Karl of the Folkungs, in whose thoughts, life, and acts the idealism implicit in chivalry has taken firm hold; the royal young people who enjoy the pageantry and language of chivalry but are only superficially gripped by its spirit; Bishop Kol, who takes his Christian vows seriously; the young prince who dedicates his life to the church; and the astrologer who fattens on the superstitions of his day—all have their important roles to play in illuminating the milieu, in interpreting the central character, and, not least, in their own right.

Hans, Magnus' court fool, has a special function, as Strindberg says in his letter on the historical drama (p. 257):

> The fool is the voluntary slave who glorifies the earl's achievement in establishing humane laws; but he is also the *raisonneur* as in Shakespeare, where he sings out what all the others think; he is the voice of the people or the Greek chorus which comments on the action of the drama, warns, and exhorts.

and, in the other letter (p. 299) mentioned above: "But my fool in contrast to other fools (in Shakespeare he is called a clown) got a past, [and] character development." Careful examination of Hans and what he says and does substantiates what Strindberg says about him and his function.

Theme, plot, setting, and dialogue are as realistically presented as the characterization. Note the idea that the human, and therefore finite, chosen of the Lord—from Strindberg's point of view, Birger of Bjälbo is just that—must combat the pride and arrogance that he may acquire because of his own God-given superiority. Strindberg believed that because of the very nature of human life there is no justification for pride and arrogance and that humility and resignation had better be part of the great but finite man's spiritual equipment. Life humbles Birger through his own lack of inner peace as well as through the obvious agency of the people, the scheming of Ivar Blå, and the intrigues of Birger's aptest pupil, his own son Magnus. The setting is, of course, designed to provide color and atmosphere typical of the Sweden of the thirteenth century. The dialogue, on the other hand, is modern, stripped of all attempts at archaisms.

The last of the historical plays, *Earl Birger of Bjälbo* has suffered in Sweden from the fact that critics and scholars have concentrated their criticism and their study on the earlier plays and, as a result, have passed it by with little attention except in so far as they have considered it a reflection of the aging and lonely Strindberg in his self-imposed isolation. They have had little to say about the unusually numerous discrepancies between the historical accounts and the history in the play itself: Strindberg disarmed them by his frank admission that since he was writing a play and not history he took the liberties with history he considered necessary. Perhaps the most interesting fact is that, according to available sources, when the play has been performed, the audiences have liked it.

Earl Birger
of Bjälbo · A Play in Five Acts

Characters

EARL BIRGER (*the earl of Bjälbo*)

KING VALDEMAR, *his son, king of Sweden*

QUEEN SOFIA, *Valdemar's queen and the daughter of Erik Plowpenny of Denmark*

PRINCESS JUDITH (*Jutta*), *her sister*

PRINCE MAGNUS, *Valdemar's brother, later duke and vice-king (Magnus Ladulås)*

PRINCE BENGT, *Valdemar's youngest brother*

IVAR JONSSON BLÅ

DEAN LARS *of Oppunda*

THE SENTINEL *on Brantberg*

HANS, *Magnus' court fool*

PETER, *Ivar Blå's court fool*

MATS, *the stableman*

THE FISHERMAN

THE SARACEN, *the earl's lifeguard (dumb but not deaf)*

LORD KARL *of the Folkungs*

THE ASTROLOGER

BISHOP KOL

MINOR CHARACTERS

Settings

ACT I: *Brantberg (the height later known as Brunkeberg)*

ACT II: *The outer courtyard of Stockholm Castle; the earl's study; the courtyard of the House of the Holy Spirit*

ACT III: *The Great Church; Bjälbo*

ACT IV: *The House of the Holy Spirit*

ACT V: *The earl's study*

ACT I

Brantberg (the heights later called Brunkeberg) with the watch tower. Below the tower is an ale shop, which is kept by the WATCHMAN; *in a hollow can be seen the tower named Kärnan ("The Core") of Stockholm's new palace,*[1] *and the spire of the Great Church. Lights are gleaming from the* EARL'S *windows at the palace. To the left is a badly neglected churchyard; there are flowers on a couple of small graves, and candles have been set in lanterns placed on the ground.*

It is All Souls' Day (November 2). Dull, gloomy weather. Half dark.

To the right is the cave with a crucifix above it in which the HERMIT *lives.*

The WATCHMAN *is standing at the foot of the hill.*

FISHERMAN enters from the right with a basket.

WATCHMAN: Good morning, brother-in-law. Let's see what you caught last night.

FISHERMAN: Nothing much to talk about! Only *one* salmon in the trap, and I have to take that up to the palace—that new mill sort of spoils the fishing. I'll sit here with you until they open the city gate.

WATCHMAN: Are you going up to the palace? *You?*

FISHERMAN: Yes, they'll have to have fish. All Saints' yesterday and All Souls' today. The earl's really strict in his habits—he fasts the whole year through!

WATCHMAN: But King Valdemar lets himself go!

FISHERMAN: He can—he doesn't have murder and perjury on his conscience . . .

WATCHMAN: Sh! The earl's window is open . . . and he doesn't sleep. Do you see the lights in his window down in the palace?

FISHERMAN: My word, there are!

WATCHMAN: And you don't know if he's up early or if he never went to bed.

FISHERMAN: You'll have to call out soon—I can see on the water when it's time—there's a gray light on the water, and the salmon begin to leap.

WATCHMAN: I've a better way: the chimney smoke down at the House of the Holy Spirit [2] . . . the monks on the hill here follow suit. Quiet! (*Goes up on the low tower; then calls out*)
Dominus custodit te,
Dominus protectio tua,
Super manum dexteram tuam!
   (*The* HERMIT *appears at the opening of the cave.*)
Per diem sol non uret te neque luna per noctem.
   (*The* HERMIT *goes in again.*)
   (*The cloister bell rings in the following rhythm.*)

$$- \smile | - \smile | - \smile | - \smile |$$

paus.

$$\smile \smile | \smile \smile | \smile \smile | \smile \smile |$$
$$\smile \smile | \smile \smile | \smile \smile | \smile \smile | - | - | - |$$

paus.

$$\smile - \smile | \smile - \smile | \smile - \smile | - - -$$

   (WATCHMAN *comes down from the tower.* FISHERMAN *sits by the ale shop.*)

WATCHMAN: Want some warm ale, brother-in-law? The old woman's still sleeping, because she's not well, and my boy's up to some mischief in the stables—

FISHERMAN: I don't want anything to drink, since we're going out to her grave—your son's a rascal who fools mine into play-acting

—they were saying yesterday that your Hans is trying to become Prince Magnus' fool.

WATCHMAN: God help me with that boy—he's a fool at foolishness, but, if he's really going to be one, I'll maim him! I'll put a ring in his nose as if he were a pig so that he can't even say mama!

FISHERMAN: He's a regular eel; if you put him on his back, he gives a flip and he's gone . . . and when he's home, he only eats and yells—let him go to court where he'll become the one with the big mouth. (*Pause*) Well, they're opening the city gate—so long, brother-in-law. Greet my sister.

WATCHMAN: You know, I'll have to leave everything I have, too, because they've put a watchman in the tower of the city church, and now they want to cut my wages . . .

FISHERMAN: You're like fleas, all of you; you can't sit still . . .

WATCHMAN: But you can . . . in your boat . . .

FISHERMAN: Because one should! (*Pause*) Here comes—a knight! See him?

WATCHMAN: I wonder who he is. (*Pause*) It's Lord Karl!

FISHERMAN: I think so. He didn't lose his head at Herrevad's Bridge,[3] but, though he's as straight as he can be, he won't be if the earl gets hold of him . . .

WATCHMAN: Lord Karl!

FISHERMAN: I'm going. Good-bye again.

WATCHMAN: Good-bye to you. Come back soon—I won't get old on this hill.

FISHERMAN: The hill's fine—to build on; the sand's looser!

WATCHMAN: The water's loosest, and there's mighty few squalls that haven't come on that!

FISHERMAN: You're envious, brother; you're always after something . . . that you don't have.

WATCHMAN: Like most people! Lord Karl—who wanted to be earl but didn't get to!

FISHERMAN: Poor fellow! Listen! Who's that hermit who has come over here?

WATCHMAN: Well, it's a hell of a hermit! He was a priest at Oppunda, and, when the papal legate at Skänninge⁴ imposed celibacy, they took his wife and child away from him, and then he went crazy. He's a man hater!

FISHERMAN: For something as little as that! If they'd take my old woman, I wouldn't settle in a cave!

WATCHMAN: Say doghouse! Because he leaps and barks like a dog if a human comes anywhere near him. My Hans can really tease him—you ought to hear the two of them!

FISHERMAN: No, now I'm going.

WATCHMAN: Wait a while.

FISHERMAN: No, I won't wait any longer. (*Exits*)

LORD KARL (*enters, points at one of the graves, and asks the* WATCHMAN): Is that *the* grave, watchman?

WATCHMAN: I'm not the gravedigger, but that's *it!*

LORD KARL (*puts a wreath on the grave and prays silently*): Who has lighted the candles?

WATCHMAN: The earl! He does every year on All Souls' Day, the day after All Saints'; that was yesterday. That's penance for the murders at Herrevad's Bridge . . .

LORD KARL: Do you know who's buried here?

WATCHMAN: Yes, I do, but I don't tell every day; I can't afford to tell every day when I have wife and children.

LORD KARL: Then you know it's the son of Magnus Brok,⁵ my kinsman, Knut Folkung. Is it true that miracles take place—here at this grave?

WATCHMAN: Not here, but by Holmger's grave.⁶ He certainly wasn't an angel when he was alive, but after he had had his head cut off, and because he was a wastrel, he became a saint afterward.

LORD KARL: Earl Birger lights candles on his victims' graves—so he does repent!

WATCHMAN: I don't think so—but he has to pretend he does!

LORD KARL: Who can force him to?

WATCHMAN: Well! The one who can't be forced is forced by the people, whom he thinks he controls.

LORD KARL: Is the hermit in the cave?

WATCHMAN: Yes, but he bites!

LORD KARL: He won't bite me, only you! (*Goes up to the cave*) Father Lawrence!

HERMIT (*comes out*): Who called?

LORD KARL: Do you recognize me?

HERMIT: Lord Karl! What do you want, my son?

LORD KARL: Listen to me!

HERMIT: Speak! (*Pause*)

LORD KARL: Peace has come to our country after a century-long struggle between the heathen descendants of Blotsven [7] and St. Erik [8]—Christ has conquered Blotsven. But sacrifices had to be made first, and Earl Birger took his knife in his hand and prepared the sacrifice. He doesn't regret that! But he suffers because of the false oath and the murders—

HERMIT: Pope Innocent IV declared that he should do penance by making a pilgrimage to the Holy Sepulchre, but instead he let the earl go on a crusade against the Finns, and to get absolution he had to live as a penitent. He wears a hair shirt, never eats meat, never drinks wine . . .

LORD KARL: And the poor councillor Bishop Kol [9] had to go to the Holy Sepulchre, which has just fallen into the hands of the Saracens again since St. Louis of France has perished in the sixth crusade. But there's peace in our country—but there's still one seed of dissension.

HERMIT: That's you, my lord!

LORD KARL: Yes, it's I! (*Pause*) When my father, Ulv Fasi, who was King Erik's earl before Birger, died, people looked to me as his successor. Birger knows that, and he knows that, every time he doesn't please them, the people's favor turns to me. But I don't have any calling to govern, I don't want to live like a condemned man, and I love my country above everything. That's why, Father

Lawrence, I want to leave my country, take up the cross, and never come back!

HERMIT: That's a sacrifice pleasing to God.

LORD KARL: But put the insignia on my cape first and consecrate me even if I'm not a knight.

HERMIT: Gladly!

(LORD KARL *gives him a cross of red cloth, which the* HERMIT *fastens on his shoulder.*)

HERMIT: Take up your cross, follow the Saviour of the world, for each and every one who forsakes his home or brothers or sisters or father or mother (*screams with pain and becomes wild*)—or wife or child . . . (*interrupts himself*) for my name's sake . . .

LORD KARL: I have forsaken the woman I love . . .

HERMIT (*beside himself*): But not wife and child! (*Rages as he quotes Lamentations 3:1, 2, 4, and 10*) "I am the man that hath seen affliction by the rod of his wrath. He hath led me, and brought me into darkness, but not into light . . . My flesh and my skin hath he made old . . . He was unto me as a bear lying in wait, and as a lion in secret places."

LORD KARL (*hands a sheepskin document to him*): And I have sold my estates—here are the deeds, which I ask you to deliver to the earl to be distributed among the houses of the Holy Spirit, churches, and cloisters.

HERMIT (*recovers his self-control*): I will deliver them. I will. If you haven't said good-bye to the woman you love, don't do it, for that's the most bitter and the hardest of all! Who is she? What's her name?

LORD KARL: Father Lawrence! Deliver the deeds to the earl and tell him he can sleep calmly so far as Lord Karl is concerned.

HERMIT: But get his answer from me—I'll move into the House of the Holy Spirit today and meet the earl there—go and say farewell to everything that's dear to you, dearer than life itself— (*wildly quotes Job 7:6-7*) "My days are swifter than a weaver's shuttle, and are spent without hope. O remember that my life is wind: mine eye shall no more see good."

LORD KARL: Father Lawrence, have they taken your wife and child from you?

HERMIT: The church has taken them and declared my little son illegitimate . . .

LORD KARL: Say with Job: "The Lord gave and the Lord has taken away; blessed be the name of the Lord!"

HERMIT: I can't! Comforter, you come to me for comfort, but do you have one good word to give me?

LORD KARL: Deliver the message, and I'll come to you in the House of the Holy Spirit! (*Goes*)

(HERMIT *goes into the cave.*)

(HANS, *the* WATCHMAN's *son, comes in.*)

WATCHMAN: How elegant you are!

HANS: Think so, father?

WATCHMAN: When you are, I think so!

HANS: You're so quick-witted that you ought to become a court fool like me. Yes, I've given myself to Prince Magnus, because I played with his stablemen and lost.

WATCHMAN: So you're to end like that . . .

HANS: It isn't ended yet . . .

WATCHMAN: But you wear his collar, you voluntary slave!

HANS: Both fool and dog earn their bread with their mouths!

WATCHMAN: You have a big one, all right!

HANS: Going to live by it, too! Now I can say to the king and princes what no one else dares . . . that suits me.

WATCHMAN: The dog's whip suits you, too.

HANS: Better than mother's stick. You don't dare to strike me any more, now that I'm a courtier—or royal adviser, for they let me give advice which no one asks for. Prince Magnus *is* a man; he can listen to a sensible word without getting angry! You can't, father; Prince Erik agrees to everything; he's a regular yes-man!

And King Valdemar! He only wants to have fun with his Danish women—

WATCHMAN (*begins to get interested*): What about the earl? You don't dare to say anything to him?

HANS: The devil himself doesn't dare to! That's to say, I haven't got any nearer him than his kitchen, and that didn't have anything for me.—Mother's Saturday hash is just as good. But I don't really have anything against the earl except that he's limited in brains! He doesn't understand humor, you see, is always arrogant; the only one who ever gets the best of him is Ivar Blå,[10] the fellow with the cape; when the earl sees the blue cape, he takes a close look to see if it has a king in it; but I will tell you a bit of big news . . .

WATCHMAN: Are you practicing your dinner entertainment on me, boy?

HANS: On you or anyone else! Yes, the earl's thinking of getting married again just to irritate the boys . . .

WATCHMAN: Hush; for heaven's sake . . .

HANS: Hush? Why, I'm paid to be a chatterbox, and I'm one by nature . . .

WATCHMAN: Well, follow your call! You could have ended on the gallows otherwise because of your tongue.

HANS: I think I've found my place in life—as a frank talker—if I only didn't have to wear this collar! There comes a pilgrim as they call them. Do you know why they have snails in their hats?

WATCHMAN: Because they walk so slowly!

HANS: The one who walks slowly ought to have wings—no, they have snails in the hat, because you don't know that they're crabs. Thanks, now you've heard my lesson.

WATCHMAN: Are you going to make me your fool, you selfish idiot?

HANS: Well, I should certainly have one, too! (*Goes*)

WATCHMAN: Yes! That fellow's found his place in life, all right! And that's a good thing!

(BISHOP KOL *enters, dressed as a pilgrim, a withered palm*

branch on his staff, straightens up, puffs, and sits down on a
bench next to the ale shop.)

WATCHMAN: What may I serve you?

(BISHOP KOL *looks at him.*)

WATCHMAN: A drink?

(BISHOP KOL *shakes his head negatively.*)

WATCHMAN: Come a long way? From a foreign country? Saracens?
The Holy Sepulchre?

BISHOP KOL: What grave is that over there?

WATCHMAN: The Herrevad's Bridge grave? That's the grave of
Magnus Brok's son, who was beheaded, by traitors . . .

BISHOP KOL (*makes a movement*): Who has lighted the candles?

WATCHMAN: Earl Birger has had them lighted as a sign of penitence . . . you see, it's All Souls' Day . . .

BISHOP KOL (*notices the castle and the church*): What's this? Am I
dreaming?

WATCHMAN: That's Stockholm Palace, the king's palace, and that's
the city church, St. Nicholas' church.

BISHOP KOL: Who is living in that cave?

WATCHMAN: A hermit, who's sane at times and crazy at times because the church has taken his wife and child away from him!

BISHOP KOL: What is his name?

WATCHMAN: Dean Lawrence of Oppunda, before this—

BISHOP KOL (*gets up*): Lars of Oppunda! (*Goes over to the cave*)

HERMIT (*comes out*): Bishop Kol!

BISHOP KOL: Yes! It's I, Lars!

HERMIT: Back from the Holy Grave?

BISHOP KOL: Eight years, by foot! In prison and shipwreck, with
blows and lashes, I've tried to do penance for Herrevad's Bridge,
and I see Birger still thinks about our crimes. Has he found
peace?

HERMIT: He doesn't have peace, but our country enjoys peace. His
daughter's married to the son of the king of Norway,[11] and his
son with a daughter of the king of Denmark . . .

BISHOP KOL: Take me to the House of the Holy Spirit so that I may meet the earl, after I've rested and have hung my bloody shoes at St. Gertrude's altar.

HERMIT: I'm going up to the House of the Holy Spirit to get a refuge for winter—it'll get too cold up here—

BISHOP KOL: What are you doing here?

HERMIT: I'm hiding myself and my sorrow! (*Wild*) They've taken my wife and child from me!

BISHOP KOL: They took mine first! Bear your cross with patience and punish your body!

HERMIT (*wild*): It isn't my body—it's my soul, it's my heart! Kill me, burn me, and it will still hurt, it will never end, for it will last forever . . .

BISHOP KOL: Will you go now?

HERMIT (*calm*): I'll go, but say nothing; if I should meet them, I'd jump into the stream . . . What was it you wanted? The House of the Holy Spirit? Yes! Let's go! Lord Karl and Herrevad! Let's go! (*They leave*)

CURTAIN

ACT II

Scene 1

Outer courtyard of Stockholm Palace. At the back is the tower Kärnan, in front of it the tourney or jousting course; to the right, a stable and an orchard; to the left, a wing of the palace where the "earl's window" can be seen. Outside this balcony window is a bastion (a low, round tower) with an enclosure for lions.

*Next to the stable on the track's palisade are placed tourney
lances with pennants; shields are hanging on the palisade. There
are two doghouses outside the stable; next to them stable brooms.*

The court fool, HANS, *son of the* WATCHMAN, *in his fool's cos-
tume, comes in from the left and goes up to* MATS *the stableman,
who is standing indolently outside the stable door.*

MATS: Well, Hans, have you been at work?

HANS (*angry and serious*): No, they weren't in the mood, and the
earl can't stand me; you might say we don't have anything in
common, and besides there were so many fine guests—mainly
foreigners, who were speaking foreign languages; they lacked
understanding, in a word!

MATS: Well, it isn't any fun to go through life without being understood.

HANS: Drag together a lot of people like this because the city's got a
charter [12]—the court a roof over its head, and the dean a church!

MATS: Who were they all?

HANS: Can you take the whole list? Archbishop Lars Lilje, Bishop
Lars and Bishop Magnus, the lords Brahe, Sparre, Båth, Oxenstjerna, and Trolle, the Russian prince Andreas, and something
funny ending in "witsch" like a knotted whip! The French ambassador from St. Louis, the English ambassador from Henry III.
Councillors from Hamburg and Lübeck, spies from Christopher
of Denmark and Håkon of Norway ... in a word: it wasn't anything for me! The earl spoke Latin and drank water; King Valdemar got a little tight as early as the soup and didn't get to say
a word. Prince Magnus was quarreling with the Norwegians—it
didn't go, you might say.

MATS: And the ladies?

HANS: They didn't show up since there isn't a hostess.

MATS: Surely the queen's hostess in her own house ...

HANS: In the earl's house, you mean!

MATS: Watch out—the earl's window is looking at us!

HANS: The father's eye! But the curtain's drawn ...

MATS: He's standing in back of it, most likely . . . Watch out!

HANS: He manages the kingdom and the council like a groom, but keep the boys in line, he can't. But the devil himself can't! They get mixed up with the women, and they're cooking a soup that'll have to be gulped down some day . . . A sister-in-law has arrived from Denmark [13]—

MATS: Yes! Who is she?

HANS: The queen's sister Jutta, alias Judith, who's supposed to be an abbess but who's no more holy than I and you . . . but pretty! Beautiful as the day! A beautiful day, that is!

MATS: But you've forgotten Lord Ivar Jonsson, Ivar Blå . . .

HANS: With the cape! He always tags along, for he doesn't know he's not welcome. He's a big rascal, and we get along fine, he and I, but you never know when he's joking or when he's serious . . .

MATS: There comes your master.

HANS: Prince Magnus! And the queen! with her ladies—there'll be an inspection of weapons for the jousting tomorrow. I'll get started on my work, then . . .

MATS: No, they turned into the orchard.

HANS: I don't like this mess . . . getting mixed up with other men's wives; when everyone takes his own, I'm allowed to have mine, in peace! my father said!

MATS: Where's the king, then?

HANS: He's hanging around his sister-in-law, and we've a lot to live through yet . . .

MATS: Are they up to something indecent?

HANS: I don't want to get a stall ready for an unborn creature; but a sow with a yoke and a woman with blue eyes, well, they haven't got them for the sake of decency! What sort of ass is that?

(IVAR BLÅ's *house fool* PETER *enters; he is deformed and is outlandishly decked out.*)

MATS: A colleague, I think!

HANS (*put out*): That fellow?

PETER (IVAR BLÅ's *house fool*): Excuse me.

HANS: What do you want? Who are you?

PETER: My name's Peter.

HANS: Say Petter or Jöns, preferably Jöns from Jönsarbo!

PETER: No, I'm from Gröneborg . . .

HANS: From Ivar Jonsson Blå; then it's right you're from Jonasbo! (*To* MATS) I guess he's one of those objective fools.

MATS: What kind is that?

HANS: A subjective fool is a quick-witted one who kids the rest— I'm one; an objective fool is a dimwit that the others kid! Well, Jöns, where's your master?

PETER: He'll be here right away.

HANS: I asked *where he is!*

PETER: I don't know! What's your name?

HANS: That's none of your business!

PETER (*points at the shields and lances*): What sort of things are those?

HANS: Frying pans and spits!

PETER (*naively*): What are they going to do with them?

HANS: They're going to butcher pigs!

PETER (*points at the brooms*): What are those?

HANS: They're jousting lances! Should we joust a little on the course? (*Gives* PETER *a broom and takes one himself*) *Wollen Sie, mein Herr? Ein, zwei, drei!* The beautiful ladies are watching us from their boxes, the trumpets are blaring, the horses neighing, and the battle cries resounding! Huh, *matador!* Love and beauty! Who is my hero, my lady love? *Allez,* knight! (*They pretend to ride in on the course and joust with the brooms.*) *A vous, monsieur!* (*They salute each other. They tilt.* PRINCE MAGNUS *and* QUEEN SOFIA *have entered with* LADIES *and* PAGES; *they all laugh as they watch the spectacle.*)

PETER: You're hitting, you nag!

HANS: Open visor, knight of the blue cape! Second round! *Qui vive?*

PETER: I can't understand what you're saying!

HANS: *Qui vive? Bête noire, mon joli!* Third round: The ladies' *mêlée! Pêle-mêle!* My lords and ladies! Salute the flag! 'Rah! 'Rah! 'Rah! (PETER *falls down;* HANS *puts his foot on* PETER'S *chest.*) Die, you dog!

QUEEN (*comes up, laughing*): *De grace!* Mercy, stern knight!

HANS: No mercy for the man who has deceived his lady love!

MAGNUS (*frees* PETER): Hold it! Hold it!

PETER (*gets up; flies at* HANS): You'll get it, you, you nag! (*They struggle.*)

MAGNUS (*separates them*): Who is this knight? Let's see your device. Ivar Blå! Good heavens! Let him go, Hans! Or we'll catch it!

    (HANS *lifts* PETER'S *cape.*)

MAGNUS: What are you looking for?

HANS: I'm looking to see if he has a little king under his cape! But carry it on both shoulders, and I'll break a lance for my lady— then it'll be with a knight beyond reproach!

QUEEN: What is your lady's name, Hans?

HANS: *Belle et Fidèle!* Beautiful and faithful!

    (QUEEN *embarrassed*)

MAGNUS (*becomes angry*): Stableman! Tie up these dogs so they won't fight and scold!

    (MATS *ties up the fools, each to a doghouse.*)

MAGNUS: Inspection of weapons, my ladies, for tomorrow's tourney. The shields to be tested to see if they'll resound, and the lances to see if they've knot or splinter that can cause a brave knight harm.

    (*The* LADIES *strike the shields with steel whips, and the* PAGES *inspect the lances.*)

LADIES AND PAGES (*sing as they are doing this; melody: see Bergström and Höjer's* Swedish Folkballads):

And the maiden walks in the flow'ring grove,
There did she see such a lovely linden,
  No sorrow could it ever banish.

And, dearest of lindens, since you can talk;
Is there no one in the world who can comfort you?
  No sorrow could it ever banish.

There's no one in the world who can comfort me,
Save King Magnus, with whom I never may speak.
  No sorrow could it ever banish.

QUEEN (*to* MAGNUS): "Save King Magnus, with whom I never may speak." What king Magnus?

MAGNUS: Who knows?

QUEEN: Does it mean you?

MAGNUS: I'm not king, but, if I were king, my father wouldn't send me down to the courtyard to play.

QUEEN: What's that?

MAGNUS: This: when the earl wanted to be alone with the foreigners, he hinted to Valdemar—*the* king: "Go down to the courtyard to play!" he said.

QUEEN: A toy king!

MAGNUS: But how were the shields? Did the steel resound in a healthy way, or did they sound like treachery? Could the lances sing of honest combat or of murder in ambush?

QUEEN: Ask; I know very little; many a man has fallen in the sport of combat. There are Valdemar and Judith!

MAGNUS: Wearing masks! Valdemar likes what's concealed.

QUEEN: Not always, and, when he conceals, he reveals.

MAGNUS: Let's go. We haven't anything to say to them. Ask them where they've been?

QUEEN: What we already know! Why did I ask my sister to come?

MAGNUS: To banish boredom! "Go down to the courtyard to play," as one tells boys. See! There's Father Earl! He'll soon be lighting a candle in his window up there. Come on, let's go.

(ALL *go*.)

(*The* EARL *comes out on the bastion; looks up at the sky*.)

(KING *and* JUDITH *enter, masked*.)

KING: They were here. They've gone!

JUDITH: Let them go! They prefer to be by themselves!

KING: There! That's how it is for me! Always alone even in their presence . . . I'm not there when they're present. Do you see the earl? He's admiring the lions in the cage. He loves lions—he'd like to be one!

JUDITH: The coat-of-arms of the Folkungs!

KING: He'd like to use *that* weapon! If he could set them loose on his enemies, he'd be happy to look on! They're growling! So he's smiling! Did you know that Richard the Lionhearted brought their parents back from Palestine? [14]

JUDITH: So they have a family tree, too?

KING: Imagine—there stands *my* earl and here stands *his* king!

JUDITH: I can't—even in my dreams!

KING: Judith!

JUDITH: . . . and Holofernes! [15]

KING: Oh, be quiet! There's Magnus' fool on the doghouse gnawing away at a bone. Listen, Hans, what are you doing here?

HANS: I'm playing chess. Watch out for the pawn! The queen's pawn!

KING: There's another fool. Who's that?

HANS: Another! That's an ordinary fool, that one. I'm an artist; he's a dabbler. We're nightingales who can't stand each other's singing . . .

PETER: I'm no nightingale! (*Laughter*)

HANS: That's plain enough, Petter! But there was a bird who was just singing about lions and lionhearted, but he sang about King Magnus first. "Who's that?" said the queen.

JUDITH: Don't listen to him! Why do you keep poisoners at court? At him, Petter! Bite him!

(PETER *bares his teeth at* HANS *and growls.* HANS *lunges with his chain at* PETER *and growls.*)

JUDITH: Get 'im!

KING: Are you that cruel, Judith? I'm not. *Tout beau!*

JUDITH: Why, they're fed to amuse us.

HANS: Can one amuse you, lovely mask? Do you have brains enough to grasp a genuine sally of wit though it's masked like the king . . .

JUDITH: Have respect for the king!

HANS: You should have, not I! I'm outside, below, and consequently above all that. From the roof of my doghouse I can look down at the whole mess—like the earl from his window; and you're my playthings that amuse me. I don't give a damn if it amuses you . . .

KING (*to* JUDITH): You know, I'd like to be a fool sometimes so I could say things like that!

HANS: But you have to be *able* to say things like that, too! And you can't, you dimwit, who can't see that they're taking both your pants and your queen away from you!

JUDITH: I've had enough!—But you're going to get one blow, dog! (*She strikes* HANS, *who sits down and growls.*) Do you bite?

HANS: No, I'm like the king. I just growl because I don't dare to bite yet.

JUDITH: Ugh! Shame on you! I'm leaving! (*Goes*)

KING (*going*): One has to go to the stables to hear the secrets of the court . . .

HANS: There aren't any secrets, master, as long as there are maids and servants in this world.

(*It has darkened, and the* EARL *has gone in.*)

HANS (*to* PETER): This isn't such a good job, and I'm going to apply for retirement with old age benefits. Look, the old man's lighting his paternal eye! So it's bedtime soon. He's like a thief: when the others are sleeping, he stays awake, and when the others wake up, he owns what they miss! Now I'm going to bed, Petter; don't forget to take care of your needs before you creep in.

PETER: I don't need anything!

HANS: Make sure of it, because, if you soak the straw, you'll get a beating tomorrow!

PETER: You rascal!

HANS: Sh-h for heaven's sake! Here comes your master, Lord Ivar Blå. Ivar Jonsson of Jönsarbo!

IVAR (*comes in, accompanied by a torchbearer*): Is there any courtier here?

HANS: Here's one!

IVAR: You?

HANS: Yes, I'm with Prince Magnus and the queen at court.

IVAR: Aren't you a dog?

HANS: That depends on whom I'm speaking with.

IVAR: Mind your manners! Do you know if the earl has gone to bed?

HANS: He? Never goes to bed for either kings or ladies—only for Ivar Blå!

IVAR: A courteous dog! But who's this? Who—is—this? Peter! And who has dared? . . . Are you on a leash?

HANS: Yes, there are couplers here!

IVAR: Choose your words!

HANS: He's engaged, if that's any nicer!

IVAR: Who has dared? . . .

HANS: Prince Magnus is a daredevil . . .

IVAR: Stableman! Get out and unleash my boy!

HANS: Is he your boy? What does your girl look like, then?

PETER: Hans is a rascal!

HANS: Can't you say anything else? Why, you can't scold. Rascal isn't a word to scold with.

IVAR: Stableman!

(MATS *comes out.*)

IVAR: Unleash Peter! And, if you lay a hand on a servant of mine
  again . . .
HANS: There'll be a new king!
  (PETER, *free, goes up to* IVAR BLÅ *and speaks to him softly.*)
IVAR: You do keep your eyes open, though you don't hear well.
HANS: Imagine if that fool weren't foolish!
IVAR: Then you'd be caught, and a lot of others!
HANS: Imagine if that devil weren't a fool!
IVAR (*to the torchbearer*): Take me to the earl!
KING (*enters, masked as before*): Who's shouting in the courtyard?
  Be quiet!
IVAR: What sort of joker is that?
KING (*removes his mask*): The king!
IVAR: Is your father still up?
KING: My father?
IVAR: Don't you know who your father is?
  (KING *remains silent.*)
IVAR: Oh, I'll find him, I suspect.
KING: We should be nice, Lord Ivar.
IVAR: Well! You *are* nice!
KING: What would you like?
IVAR: We'll try to get a change in the sort of life that's led here . . .
HANS: A genuine dog's life!
IVAR: You're right about that, Hans! Now I'll go to the earl.
KING: If he's receiving!
IVAR: I'll take care of that! He always receives me. But "you go
  down to the courtyard to play!"

CURTAIN

SCENE 2

The EARL's *workroom in Stockholm Palace; at the back "the window" facing the bastion and the lions' cage with a view of the city, the stream, and Brantberg.*

A very large desk with maps, sheepskin, paper, manuscripts, writing utensils. Cupboards by the wall. A prayer stool.

A large wax candle is burning on the table. Two unlighted ones are close to it.

A SARACEN *wearing a turban and a scimitar stands by the door to the left; a deaf-and-dumb* PAGE *at the door to the right.*

IVAR BLÅ (*enters from the left*): Is the earl here?

(PAGE *stops him with a gesture.*)

IVAR: Are you deaf?

(PAGE *nods assent.*)

IVAR: Can't you talk, either?

(PAGE *nods "Yes," but is misunderstood by* IVAR BLÅ.)

IVAR (*lifts his hand threateningly*): Are you crazy, boy?

(SARACEN *draws his scimitar.*)

IVAR: What now, you dog! Do you know who I am? He didn't understand! Do you understand this? (*Draws a ring off one of his fingers and shows it to him*)

(SARACEN *becomes calm.* IVAR *sits down at the table. Pause.* PAGE *goes out to the left. Pause*)

EARL (*enters from the left. Pause*): You come very late.

IVAR: No, *you* let me wait!

EARL: It's illegal in the kingdom to force anyone to be your host.

IVAR: You had invited me, and now I've come. You didn't set any time in your letter.

EARL: Within a suitable time, I said.

IVAR: Is the guard at your door deaf and dumb?

EARL: Yes. So I won't have to talk, and he won't have to listen. If you're afraid of the Saracen, I'll have him leave. I got him from the Russian prince—

IVAR: Important company?

EARL: They're finally coming here—and don't stop in Roskilde [16]—

IVAR: And even the Danish women are finding their way up here, too . . .

EARL: Do you have important business, or are you just trying to pick a quarrel?

IVAR (*slowly*): Well—

EARL: Since you consider yourself a royal councillor, I want to tell you that the kingdom is in excellent condition . . .

IVAR (*seriously*): I don't doubt that, Birger; I can see the piles of papers on your desk; the country is everywhere at peace; anybody can travel safely on any of our roads; we can sleep in bed without having to be afraid of being burned alive; but, while you manage the kingdom, you mismanage your own house . . .

EARL: Silence!

IVAR: The king is losing his good name, and, when you pass away, not one of your sons will be able to govern the kingdom, and the people will take the most daring first comer!

EARL: Lord Karl?

IVAR: Maybe! (*Pause*) And you won't find him at Herrevad's Bridge!

EARL: Herrevad's Bridge? Still talking about that, are you? I punished the rebels who rose against *your* legally elected king. Isn't that right?

IVAR: In spite of your promise of safe-conduct!

EARL: Safe-conduct! A mere word!

IVAR: I thought you had repented! The people say you wear a haircloth shirt next to . . .

EARL (*contemptuously*): The people?

IVAR: Well! Then we understand each other. Let's go back to the royal power. Valdemar is disgracing himself!

EARL: How?

IVAR: You don't know!

EARL: His sister-in-law, Judith?

IVAR: Send her home.

EARL: I thought it was innocent.

IVAR: Get Magnus married before it's too late.

EARL: I have a Holstein princess for him. Holstein is the right place —close to Hamburg and Braunschweig and conveniently south of Denmark.

IVAR: You marry off your children by the map!

EARL: A good thing, isn't it? My daughter with Norway, and my oldest son with Denmark! Good security for our new structure.

IVAR: But the children may have another thought about that—

EARL: I won't let them! They'd exchange every other day if they could! Look at Valdemar, who married for love and by his own free will—now it's somebody else. Might as well take the somebody else right away.

IVAR: You lack a stick in this house.

EARL: We lack nothing, but I can't spank grown women.

IVAR: The lady of the house should take care of that.

EARL: Unfortunately, she's in her grave.[17]

IVAR: Yes! (*Pause*) Birger, don't throw me to the lions, don't call for the Saracen if I tell you: Get a lady for this house so that there will be discipline and order in Stockholm Palace.

(EARL *thrusts his compass about on a map on the desk.*)

IVAR: By the map! Let it be by geography—but not too far south!

(EARL *stares at him.*)

IVAR: Do you know Margareta Breakhorse?

(EARL *gives a start.*)

IVAR: You do—since she's the queen of Denmark. But she has a sister-in-law, King Abel's widow [18]—now you've caught on. And

—her name is Mechtild—has two sons, who are dukes in Schleswig.

(EARL *wide-eyed*)

IVAR: Schleswig—look at the map! Very close to Holstein! King Christopher has his Breakhorse and will soon be broken, they think.

(EARL *gets up.*)

IVAR: Earl Birger was once married to the granddaughter of Valdemar the Great . . . Of course, Mechtild is from Holstein—and has something of a bad reputation since King Abel died—Erik Plowpenny's daughter Sofia is queen of Sweden inasmuch as she's married to Earl Birger's Valdemar. The apple's a little sour, but it's a national apple, Birger! There's a worm in the core—but you can cut that away! (*Pause*)

EARL: What are you up to over at Gröneborg?

IVAR: I eat and sleep a year at a time, but I think now and then, and then I have to get out to harry . . .

EARL: Are you ambitious?

IVAR: No, not for myself. But the game amuses me occasionally— until I tire of it again!

EARL (*goes up to the cupboard and takes out a sheepskin document*): Ivar Jonsson! You alone have the right to talk as you have! Here's my letter to the dowager queen, Mechtild of Denmark. Do you want to deliver it?

IVAR: Yes! While I'm in the mood—I'll go to Denmark! and propose to her!

EARL: Mechtild's in a cloister, of course, but she hasn't taken the vows.

IVAR: And you ought to know that there's a hint of sharp mustard about her . . .

EARL: Then she'll be able to manage our young queen, who's beginning to show her claws. And that's my primary reason for writing this letter. There's to be a stepmother and discipline so we get order in this house.

IVAR: It's pleasant that we happened to agree for once . . . I'll go to bed, then, and tomorrow we'll get the fleet ready so we can arrive with dignity. Good night.

EARL: Good night. Now I'll get to work!

(IVAR *nods; leaves.*)

(*Pause*)

EARL (*opens the window at the back. The* ASTROLOGER *can be seen with his alidade*): [19] Dr. Wilibald!

ASTROLOGER: Extinguish the candle!

EARL: What do the stars say on this fateful night?

ASTROLOGER (*enters*): The signs are favorable! Jupiter has entered the constellation of the Lion, and Mars will enter that of the Virgin at midnight—south of the Bear and the Northern Crown.

EARL: The Crown? and the Lion? I can interpret that myself.

ASTROLOGER: Earl, at fifty you face the real goal of your life; an unkind destiny denied you, the worthiest of all, the crown, but now, since you have atoned for your crimes, fortune will turn to your advantage, and your old age will reap what your long years of labor have sown.

EARL: Is Valdemar going to—?

ASTROLOGER: No! The Lion which faces the future is the southern lion, one of the three blue ones that trample on nine red hearts—

EARL: That is Denmark's!

ASTROLOGER: Yes! And to descend to earth—Christopher won't be on his throne for long—Archbishop Jakob Erlandsson is working for Abel's sons—who will be yours soon . . . Then you'll have three crowns on your three crossbeams, Folkung!

EARL: So, it's to be! Heaven has decided it, the earth testifies to it, and hell itself can't prevent it!

ASTROLOGER: *Ite, missa est!*

EARL: Amen! (*Pause*) But you talked of atonement. How's that to be interpreted?

ASTROLOGER: Don't you know that Bishop Kol has returned from his pilgrimage?

EARL: I didn't know.

ASTROLOGER: And, since he has done penance for you, the pope's absolution goes into effect.

EARL: Then my time of punishment is over; life can still hand me a beaker—the wine itself has little attraction for me, but the pearl at the bottom does.

ASTROLOGER: Say the crown!

EARL: We'll say the crown! A blessed night after a glorious day!—I think I can keep vigil until morning.

ASTROLOGER: Yes, keep vigil, Earl Birger.

EARL: I can burn my hair shirt, I can take a bath, sleep on linen sheets! I can drink wine and eat wild game; I can live again when I had thought I had seen the end. Welcome, life!

ASTROLOGER: Earl Birger!

EARL: I'll throw my mask away, Wilibald; now I know life and people, and I want to use my dearly bought wisdom. Human beings? Say scoundrels! Friends? Accomplices in crime—they're friends! Love? Say hate! All people hate each other! My children hate me as I hate them! Every morning they come to ask about my health in the hope that I'm ill. If I ask about something, they lie to me. If I didn't have spies, I'd be deceived every time. On my latest birthday they brought me flowers and filled me with lies. If I ask Magnus how his brother Valdemar is getting along with his wife, he says they're happy, so devilishly happy, though Valdemar is living in open adultery. And these foreign ambassadors, who came to wish me luck—what they wish me is misfortune! But I played the fox with them! The art of governing! Write falsely, promise in order not to keep, fool them into making promises. Business and commerce, deceit! I sat down to eat with Hamburg's and Lübeck's pickpockets today. Bishop? Swine! The pope . . .

ASTROLOGER: People don't say things like that!

EARL (*removes outer garments and takes off his hair shirt*): Yes, in the darkness of the night when the lights are out and people are asleep! Then a person takes off everything and shows himself in all his nakedness. You know, Wilibald, I believe I'm a heathen, and have always been, though I haven't known it! What do I believe in? This! My fist! (*Strikes the table*) But this, my hair shirt, I don't believe in, and never have. Now I'll throw it in the fire!

ASTROLOGER: Earl Birger!

EARL: And, if there are more troublemakers still, they may meet me at Herrevad's Bridge or in hell, and I'll have their heads! With or without safe-conduct . . . Now, astrologer, we'll go down into the dining hall and let the table be set. Light candles and fill flagons!

ASTROLOGER: Earl Birger!

EARL (*strikes the table; the* SARACEN *enters with a flaming torch*): I want meat and blood, wine and ale, after starving for ten years! Ten years—for nothing! Fool that I am! Come, we'll play lions!

(STEWARD *enters; the doors are opened; a cloth-covered table with food, a whole peacock, a hogshead, cans of wine, flowers, and candelabras are carried in by servants. A trumpeter follows.*)

EARL: What's this? Can you perform magic, astrologer?

ASTROLOGER: At your court the art is slight—to produce a banquet.

EARL: Well, then. To the table!

(STEWARD *signals to the trumpeter.*)

EARL: No! Wait! (*Takes a large dish from the table and hands it to the* STEWARD) Let my lions test the food first! (*The* STEWARD *goes out on the bastion with the dish.*) Then I'll get them to sing their songs from the great days of Richard the Lionhearted! (*Pause*) Tonight I dedicate myself to life again, a while to wine and friendship, blended with wisdom! Trumpeter! Say grace: signal "to the table."

CURTAIN

SCENE 3

The courtyard of the House of the Holy Spirit stands open facing Stockholm Stream. A large linden in the middle of the courtyard with a stone chair below; a well to the right. To the right at the back can be seen a part of the palace with "the earl's window."

On the road which extends along the Stream can be seen wanderers now and then.

FISHERMAN, *from Act I, enters from the Stream, carrying a basket.*

WATCHMAN (*from Act I, comes out from the hospital*): Oh, it's you, brother-in-law. Going to the palace with your fish?

FISHERMAN: No, they don't want any fish up there any more—the earl has changed since Bishop Kol got back, and the candles are burning in the banquet hall way into the morning.

WATCHMAN: They say he's thinking of getting married . . .

FISHERMAN: So you're the caretaker here now . . .

WATCHMAN: Yes, I get better pay, but—

FISHERMAN: But you're not happy. Where are you happy, really?

WATCHMAN: Well, where there isn't too much work . . .

FISHERMAN: But too much pay!

WATCHMAN: Maybe so! (*Dries off the stone chair under the linden*)

FISHERMAN: Are you expecting the earl today?

WATCHMAN: Today and every day he sits under the linden like Charlemagne and receives petitions and complaints—he listens to everyone, but doesn't answer everybody—

FISHERMAN: He'll do, as they say, for both big and little. (*Goes into the house*) I'm going in to see the abbess—

(WATCHMAN *sweeps around the stone chair.*)

HANS (*the fool, enters; serious*): Good morning, father.

WATCHMAN: What's wrong with you? What are you looking so sour for?

HANS: I was walking up on Sand Hill, and got to see an execution—ugh!

WATCHMAN: Well, that's everyday fare since the new laws were passed. Was it the robber from Bromma?

HANS: The robber? Why, all he had done was to break into a farmhouse for a little food . . . But how can the earl's Saracen stoop to cutting off heads? See, there he is! With his scimitar! Well, I can't stand the sight of blood!

(SARACEN *enters with his unsheathed scimitar, which he washes at the well; then he stations himself by the linden.*)

WATCHMAN: Then the earl himself isn't far off. He can frighten people out of their wits—and they don't love him particularly.

HANS: There he comes. So I'm off. Is that the stargazer he has with him?

WATCHMAN: Dr. Wilibald—the chancellor—who's both a sacrificial priest and a heathen. That's bad company—

HANS: He could choose better. (*Lifts his cape a little*)

WATCHMAN: You be on your way, and don't rattle your bells, or the earl will be wild!

HANS: Look, how healthy the old man looks! Since he got rid of his hair shirt and has started swimming in the Stream—he dives in in the middle of the night and swims in the moonlight. He'll live to be a hundred!

WATCHMAN: Don't call him the old man! If he heard you, he'd have the Saracen cut your head off.

HANS: The Saracen, yes! Watch out for that fellow! I think he's nothing but—(*softly*) he's a spy!

EARL (*looking very fit, enters, accompanied by the deaf-and-dumb* PAGE *and the* ASTROLOGER): Haven't the people come?

HANS (*in an aside*): Yes, but they left when they caught sight of you! And now I'll go, too. (*Goes*)

EARL (*sits down on the stone chair*): Bring Bishop Kol, and tell him that I won't wait for him!

(ASTROLOGER *goes in and returns with* BISHOP KOL.)

EARL (*rises and comes upstage with* KOL *so that the others won't hear them*): Since our last talk I had expected that you would have obeyed my orders. Why are you staying on here?

BISHOP KOL: To find inner peace.

EARL: Get back to your position; [20] then you'll get peace.

BISHOP: You have an easy time, forgetting!

EARL: It took ten years. A long and a difficult time. But it's over! I'm starting anew, and what's past is atoned for.

BISHOP: It can never be atoned for; swearing a false oath is a deadly sin, and I'll have to stay here suffering for you as long as I live!

EARL: Fool!

BISHOP: You are as irredeemable as the scoffing robber on the cross!

EARL: Are you comparing yourself to the Saviour, then? And you're to do vicarious atonement for me?

BISHOP: For myself and for you! Continue on your robber's way, you barbarian! You're thinking of taking a woman to your bosom, too! May she sting you in your heel!

EARL: Get into the pigsty, and eat with the swine! Try coming afterward to complain!

BISHOP: You've made yourself young again, Birger, and you've taken a bad companion in silken clothing—that puffed-up magician; but, when the stench comes your way and that snake charmer deserts you, you'll have Bishop Kol to creep to!

EARL: Watch out for the Saracen!

BISHOP: I've seen Turks and barbarians before. You've gone on *one* crusade; the last one you have ahead of you!

(EARL *turns his back to the* BISHOP *and goes up to the stone chair.* BISHOP *goes into the house.*)

EARL (*to the* ASTROLOGER): Who's screaming in there?

ASTROLOGER: Dean Lars of Oppunda.

EARL: Bring him to me.

ASTROLOGER: He's coming—voluntarily.

(HERMIT *enters, beside himself.*)

EARL: Why are you screaming?

HERMIT (*wild*): They've taken my wife and child from me!

EARL: Who has?

HERMIT: The church!

EARL: Then they're safe. You mean Innocent IV's bull about the celibacy of the priests. I can't do a thing about that, because I have only worldly power. The church judges what is spiritual. Crucify your flesh with its lusts and desires.

HERMIT: It isn't my flesh; it's my spirit that is in agony!

EARL: Crucify your spirit, then.

HERMIT: Stones instead of bread.

EARL: I am no priest, but for ten years I have starved myself and have worn a hair shirt. Go thou and do likewise.

HERMIT: Earl Birger! . . .

EARL: Lars of Oppunda! I lost *my* wife once, and a little child—in my great sorrow I went to you for comfort. What did you have to say to me then? You said: "It is a sin to sorrow! Put away all that!" And you added: "Your sorrow isn't worth very much! It isn't worth much!" Remember?

HERMIT: Your memory is good, earl! . . . You are slow, but sure!

EARL: Absolutely! Take a cold bath and then go to work, and you'll soon forget all that. Work is the only thing that gives value to life. It gives appetite and sleep. The rest will have to be as it can.

HERMIT: Perhaps you're right.

EARL: To take your mind off yourself, you may do an errand for me. You know where Lord Karl is.

(HERMIT *thinks.*)

EARL: Don't think up any lie, but answer honestly. I know you've seen him.

HERMIT (*admits it unintentionally*): How can you know? . . .

EARL: So you have seen him, since you want to know how I can know that. Where's he spinning now?

HERMIT: Lord Karl has supporters . . .

EARL: Are you thinking of revenge? Only heathens seek revenge. I gave you a cruel word just now; that was not vengeance—just a natural consequence of your action. Where is Lord Karl?

(HERMIT *remains silent.*)

EARL: Well! Go in peace, then! Down into the cellar to cool off! Caretaker, put the priest into confinement . . . When he softens, I'll receive his confession.

HERMIT (*beside himself*): I'm to be judged and sentenced by a spiritual court, I am a priest . . . the independence of the church is still valid . . .

EARL: You have belonged to the priesthood, but, since you ran away from your duties, you're a layman, or, quite simply, a sick man, not to say an insane one. Go with the caretaker, or the Saracen will go with you.

HERMIT (*goes down toward the Stream where he has caught sight of something*): Look! There they are!

EARL (*to* WILIBALD): Is he having a vision?

ASTROLOGER: A woman and a child are walking on the other shore!

EARL: The other shore? Why, you're right!

HERMIT (*beside himself; on his knees*): Margareta, my wife, my child! Lord Jesus! They don't hear me! Hear me, when I call, out of the depths I call, save me, God, for the waters are sweeping over me, I have sunk far down into the mire which has no bottom! Margareta! (*He falls down.*) My child!

EARL (*moved*): Poor people! This isn't right, but—I wash my hands! Caretaker, help the dean to his room, and let the women take care of him. He's a sick man, and he's to be treated as one. (*Gets up*)

(CARETAKER-WATCHMAN *leads* LARS *of Oppunda into the house.*)

EARL: Sick, yes, but he has become mean since they took the woman away from him. (*Pause*) Who's there? Bengt, my son!

BENGT (*the* EARL's *youngest son, has entered*): Is the earl here?

EARL (*gently*): Yes, my child, my Benjamin, the comfort of my old age, my last friend! ... What did you want to tell me?

BENGT: I met Lord Karl.

EARL: That was not well met.

BENGT: Yes, it was! He asked me to tell you that he wants to come to the Great Church three days from now at vespers to say goodbye to you.

EARL: More treason! But I'll meet him—in force. Come!

CURTAIN

ACT III

Scene i

A burial vault under the Great Church. The grave of Queen Ingeborg, the EARL's *first wife, to the right. A little altar to the left.*

Vespers: "Ave Maris Stella" being sung in the church above:

PRINCE BENGT *enters; kneels beside his mother's grave. Pause.*

EARL *(enters)*: Is that you, Bengt? [21] What are you doing here?

BENGT: Praying by my mother's grave. It's the anniversary of her death.

EARL: Well? It's fine to honor your mother's memory, but—everything has its time—mourning the dead shouldn't make us forget the living.

BENGT: The living may not erase my memory of the person dearest to me—no one has taken mother's place in my heart!

EARL: Wait till you get a wife, who'll become the mother of little children!

BENGT: I don't want any wife! I want to be a child all the days of my life, the child of God and the holy church and my mother's son!

EARL: Do you mean—become a monk?

BENGT: That is my calling!

EARL: You may not! You're the descendant of kings, your mother was the daughter of a king, and your father—is more than a king!

BENGT: What is brother Valdemar, then?

EARL *(to himself)*: Now he's biting, too! *(Aloud)* Don't stay down here in the cold and dampness—it isn't good for your health.

BENGT: I always feel stronger when I've visited my mother—she learned so much in the hard school of suffering—

EARL: I don't believe she suffered more than others—

BENGT: They say—

EARL: Bengt! I'm expecting someone . . . You know who it is . . . Go away . . . But don't be angry with me . . . then I suffer . . . for you're the last, the only human being I . . . can bear! Promise me! . . . And whatever happens . . . don't desert me!

BENGT: No, father, not so long as you don't turn your heart away from me, and so long as we can meet beside this grave . . .

EARL: "Let the dead bury their dead!" said the Saviour . . . Go up into light and life, my son . . . your place is there; you are young. *(Sternly)* Go, now! I command it!

BENGT (*submissively*): You have forgotten mother . . .

EARL: Go quickly!

(BENGT *goes*.)

EARL (*to himself*): Everything is loosening at the joints, and breaking . . . Well, let the old break! So that one may renew it!

(PRINCE MAGNUS *enters, a little cold and withdrawn in manner*.)

EARL (*flatters to win*): Magnus, you always come when I ask you to, and you know what is fitting. Thank you for coming.

(MAGNUS *cold*)

EARL: Valdemar doesn't have time, as usual; besides he hasn't a mind for the duties of governing . . .

MAGNUS: You asked him to come to this meeting in such a way that he had to stay away . . .

EARL: Always cold and curt, Magnus! . . . (*Pretends*) Can't the sight of your mother's grave warm your heart? Have you anything to complain about me for? Your position isn't the best imaginable, of course—yours like mine—why, we're nothing, really, you and I. Valdemar is everything!

MAGNUS: Oh, I don't know!

EARL (*forgets himself*): Are you friends again? (*Changes his manner*) It's fine when brothers agree, and to strengthen this agreement, which is as natural as it is necessary for the good of the state, I've arranged to have Pope Clement create—what's new in this country—the title of duke [22] for each of the king's brothers . . .

MAGNUS (*brightens*): What's that?

EARL: But—only you, Magnus, will receive it in my lifetime—your brothers will have to wait. You see, I want Valdemar to have a genuine supporter in you, his sensible brother; an adviser, but one with influence, not to say power . . .

MAGNUS (*strokes his chin whiskers, with an expression as if he understood the deceit*): A duke, eh?

EARL: Duke of Södermanland with Nyköping's fortified castle as your palace! To strengthen the power of the king. You understand?

MAGNUS (*slyly*): Strengthen the king's power! I understand . . .

EARL (*just as slyly*): But you mustn't misunderstand my good will and intentions . . .

MAGNUS (*ironically*): No, not for anything! There's no place for misunderstanding in this!

(*They stare at each other fixedly.*)

EARL: And you're to know the other reason why I asked you to come. I'm expecting to meet the worst enemy our family has— Karl Folkung or Lord Karl.

MAGNUS: What does he want? Is he alive, and with what right?

EARL: You may well ask! New treason, false prospects, empty promises, most likely . . . But I want you to be a witness, an unseen witness, to our talk.

MAGNUS: There aren't any reasons why I can't . . .

EARL: Magnus, I wish I could depend on you—I wish you were my first-born—now that Valdemar has sold his birthright for a mess of pottage . . .

MAGNUS (*wakes up and begins to understand*): Has Valdemar . . .

EARL: I don't say that he has, but that he may if he takes one step more . . . Incest cannot be atoned for even by a ruling monarch, and can only be forgiven in Rome by the Holy Father (*plays the hypocrite*)—but I hope he won't heap that sorrow and shame on my gray head, for then I'll go into my grave before my time . . . Look after your brother, Magnus; your lost, unfortunate brother.

MAGNUS (*unmoved*): Why don't you send Judith home, father?

EARL (*naively; falsely*): I? Who obeys me? What power do I, poor soul, have? Don't you see how the queen behaves? She's impolite; she prefers to do what I don't want her to; she surrounds herself with my enemies . . .

MAGNUS (*forgets himself*): That I don't see!

EARL (*sharply*): Well, you're her confidant, of course . . . (*changes his manner*) but you're the only person close to her I don't need to suspect . . . and that's why I appeal to you . . . Is it right, I ask

. . . is it right that a child—she is a child, of course—interferes in affairs of state . . .

MAGNUS: She doesn't! That's slander; she plays only with the children . . .

EARL (*furious*): And with young lords—with you above all others.

MAGNUS: I am her brother-in-law and her friend . . .

EARL: But she isn't yours—she has a nickname for you that you don't know . . .

MAGNUS: Nickname? What?

EARL: They know it in the stables, in the city, by the Stream, everywhere! (*Pause*) She calls you kettle-mender because you're so dark!

MAGNUS: Kettle-mender! I'll mend her kettles . . . when I'm . . . ready!

EARL: Don't be alone with her! If something happens, you'll be blamed, and it's a good thing to be innocent when the time comes . . .

MAGNUS: What time is it that's coming and that everybody is talking about?

EARL: You'll see . . . soon . . . very soon . . . a day of judgment . . . a great day . . . when you wear the crown first . . . the crown of a duke, of a monarch, perhaps with a seat and voice in the election of emperor—on the electors' day . . .

MAGNUS (*brightens*): The election of emperor?

EARL: The Hohenstaufens are done! It looks like Hapsburg! All votes are welcome, none is despised. The eyes of Europe are on the north: we have Norway as a dowry, and I'm expecting Denmark . . . But hear this last word, Magnus: as a duke, you should have a duchess, and for that reason you should come with clean hands. Undo this loose bond which binds you! [23]

MAGNUS: You mean Karin? That can't be undone . . .

EARL: From your side, perhaps not . . . but she's rather loose . . .

MAGNUS: What's that?

EARL: When she goes with Valdemar, she will soon have left you!

MAGNUS: Death and doomsday! So that's it! Now something broke between us brothers. It hurts, but it feels easier not to have a bond about one's heart . . . everything passes, and the pain will go.

EARL: A crown is worth something, even if it isn't a king's . . . I'll never get any, don't try for any, but you're born to . . .

MAGNUS: You've sown seeds, father; you've soaked them well, so they'll sprout quickly! I used to say to Valdemar: "Touch me; your crowned head is inviolate, but, if you touch my woman, neither crown nor anointment will help" . . .

EARL: Magnus! The table has been set; the way is open . . .

MAGNUS: The way is open, but there is *one* stone left that blocks it . . .

EARL: Lord Karl . . .

MAGNUS (*coarsely*): He should have been at Herrevad's Bridge . . .

EARL (*craftily*): There are other bridges over the brook, and, once you're over, you may say, "Stop!" . . . Here he comes! . . . Step aside, Magnus, but, if you notice the slightest hint of a threat, strike away! You do have men with you, don't you?

MAGNUS (*fully awake*): I have! and I strike gladly! (*Goes*)

(*Pause*)

(LORD KARL *enters, wearing a white cape with a red cross on it.*)

EARL: Well met!

LORD KARL: Earl Birger! You may say that with a good heart and a calm mind . . .

EARL: Really?

LORD KARL: Haven't I shown through my actions that I have only the good of my country in mind?

EARL: Your actions are not all aboveboard. Why are you wearing that cape?

LORD KARL: Hasn't Dean Lars of Oppunda delivered my message?

EARL: Anger or stupidity seems to have kept him silent about your meeting . . .

LORD KARL: Stupidity? . . . Well! I wear this cape because I'm leaving my country to go on a crusade, and I have sold my estates,

so that I'll have nothing to bind me.[24] This is the sacrifice that I
have placed in your hands, although . . .

EARL: Karl Folkung! I am unable to grasp an action that resembles
suicide.

LORD KARL: I want to give up this world; many have given it up;
and I don't want to stand in the way of the happiness of others
who are far worthier than I to enjoy it . . .

EARL: You speak like a knight, but you aren't one. If your sacrifice
is pure, I will receive it, and in return give you this knightly
chain as a token of the knighthood, which only a crowned king
can grant you.

LORD KARL: I take it, but as a symbol that reconciliation has been
attained; now the family tree of the Folkungs has been pruned,
and it can grow straight up through time, spread out over the
north, and flourish, watered by the three waters, the Belt, the
Sound, and the Northern Sea.

EARL: Knight Karl! Go up into the church—perform your knightly
vigil this night. Tomorrow I shall come with the king and give
you the knighthood, in the name of God and of St. Michael, so that
you may be brave, faithful, and just.

LORD KARL (*draws his sword*): By God and St. Michael! (*Goes*)

(*Pause*)

(MAGNUS *enters.*)

EARL: Did you hear?

MAGNUS: Everything!

EARL (*gives him his hand*): The way is free! Take it . . . I shall
tramp it down before you . . . So—straight ahead, Magnus!

CURTAIN

SCENE 2

Bjälbo: The Great Hall. A fire in the fireplace. Chairs in a half circle before the fireplace.

MAGNUS *is standing in front of the fire.*

HANS *comes in with wood.*

MAGNUS: Remember what I told you! For me, you're the squire, to others, the fool. Your natural common sense makes you deserve a better place, and if you serve me faithfully—you understand. I will raise you when the time is right.

HANS (*seriously*): Your Grace, I'm not a comedian by nature—and, now that sorrow has struck me, it's a greater agony than usual to amuse people . . .

MAGNUS (*laughs*): Has sorrow struck you?

HANS: Are you laughing at that?

MAGNUS: Well, it could be a laughable sorrow.

HANS (*as before*): Yes, but one that I don't *talk* about . . .

MAGNUS: Has someone died?

HANS: Yes, so far as I go.

MAGNUS: You mean your heart has been struck! . . . Conceal it well.

HANS: As well as I can.

MAGNUS: Where are King Valdemar—and the others?

HANS: The king's out on the ice fishing—with the others.

MAGNUS: Do you know where the earl is just now?

HANS: Doesn't Your Grace know?

MAGNUS: If I did, I wouldn't ask.

HANS: The kitchen and the stables know everything, first, most, and best! Oh well, the earl is down south at . . .

MAGNUS: In Lund?

HANS: Farther south.

MAGNUS: By the Sound?

HANS: Yes!

MAGNUS: What's he doing there?

HANS: Courting!

MAGNUS: Mechtild!

HANS: King Abel's widow! The murderer's widow!

MAGNUS: Quiet! So it's true?

HANS: Not quite. Lord Ivar Blå did the courting and got the "yes"!
    I think the earl's down there getting married, a little on the quiet
    —the match isn't the best—and there's unrest in Denmark—
    Bishop Erlandsson is applying the brakes—Queen Mechtild has
    prospects of seeing her two sons get the crown—the earl will be
    stepfather to the Danish king just as he is father-in-law to the
    Norwegian one . . .

MAGNUS: You know all that down in the kitchen? . . .

HANS: And in the stables . . . Does Your Grace know why you get
    to know so little up here? . . . Well, because no one dares to tell
    you anything unless he's asked. And, when you do ask on rare
    occasions, they have to agree with you or just tell you what
    pleases you. You see, that's why you don't know anything . . .
    Down in the kitchen we sing out even if we risk getting a slap!

MAGNUS: I suspect you're right.

HANS: And I'm sure Your Grace doesn't know the people about
    you . . . not the ones closest to you . . . doesn't know what hap-
    pens in the house . . .

MAGNUS: And I'm to learn this from you . . . by way of the kitchen!

HANS: I'll keep still, then. (*Pause*)

MAGNUS (*struggles with himself*): Hans.

HANS: You'd like to know, but not from me. I understand that, but
    ask Karin, the queen's maid; she knows for sure that it's so!

MAGNUS: Now you've told me everything. Thank you for not mak-
    ing me ask . . . You're a bright boy, and I'll remove your collar at
    the earliest opportunity . . . (*Pause*) Where is Ivar Blå?

HANS: His Peter shows up now and then. He's a spy, so I pour into him everything I want to get rid of . . . Lord Ivar can't be far off, for he's busy as the pike after midsummer . . .

MAGNUS: The earl can't surprise us here, can he?

HANS: You can never be sure about him . . .

MAGNUS: Where is Princess Judith?

HANS: Where she is? How she is? In what condition? In what year? In what month she is?

MAGNUS (*strikes him in the face*): Don't act the fool in my presence!

HANS: Then I'll keep still, and Your Grace won't learn what you want to know.

MAGNUS: Now I know everything . . . Go! . . . No, stay here and tend the fire . . . I'll be in the secret chamber; knock two times twice if you have something to tell me.

HANS: That's worth thinking about . . . and I believe I won't have anything to say. After that slap!

MAGNUS: Do you resent it?

HANS: No, but I can correct myself.

MAGNUS: Is it Else that's troubling you?

HANS: One doesn't talk about things like that. Your Grace knows by experience that you don't hang your dishonor on a pole outside the window . . .

MAGNUS (*gives him another blow*): Watch out!

HANS: Strange time to say, "Stop it," when the shot has been fired!
    (MAGNUS *goes. Pause.* JUDITH *enters, in despair, paces back and forth, throws herself into a corner bench to the left and hides her face in her hands.* HANS *coughs to make his presence known.*)

JUDITH: Who's there? . . . Hans! Help me! Will you?

HANS: Yes. What can I do to help?

JUDITH: Take a message from me to the dean's house . . .

HANS: And I should go to that rascal's den! . . .

JUDITH: I don't know what it is, but I see you mean something ugly by it, and I don't want to ask . . . Can you be serious for a minute?

HANS: This is serious, and I'm not a joker by nature, least of all in love affairs like this . . .

JUDITH: Is it far to Alvastra Cloister?

HANS: There are only monks there, and they don't understand things like this, and neither do nuns. Send for the midwife. That would be best.

(JUDITH's *face in her hands*)

HANS: Yes, I put it as it is, and in circumstances like this you can't smuggle it away, because, if the child disappears, you'll be buried alive!

JUDITH: God, my God!

HANS: There, there! We'll talk like human beings though I'm not considered one. We're at Bjälbo, but it isn't far to the outlying farm. I can take horses in the stables, and, when I've peeled off these clothes, I'll be ready . . . You can depend on me, even though I'm not a knight . . .

JUDITH: If I can only hide myself . . .

HANS (*acts as if he were old*): Yes, poor child, that's what you get for your foolishness. What did I say down by the stables? It will turn sour, I said, but it was like talking to deaf ears . . . Quiet, a horn is sounding . . . Company coming! It's too late! . . . I know who it is . . .

JUDITH: The earl?

HANS: No! Lord Ivar Blå!

JUDITH: What shall I do? What . . .

HANS: Do as I do . . . act . . . pretend . . . Can't you? Oh yes, you can! I've seen you! . . . Receive him with open arms. He's as easy to fool as all other foxes . . . I'll help you . . . One, two, three! (*Pause*)

(PETER, IVAR BLÅ's *fool, enters.*)

HANS: There's that devil! . . . Well, you stupid dog, where do you have your Bluebird? Are you out courting?

PETER: You are a real rascal!

HANS: Haven't you got beyond rascal? You're supposed to be witty

even if you're here only to spy. Go ahead, spy! Or maybe you
want to joust for the lady, *monseigneur* . . . *fendez-vous! Un,
deux, trois!*

(IVAR BLÅ *enters.*)

HANS: See, there we have the knight Blue—beard!

IVAR: Is the king here?

HANS: No, he's out on slippery ice and is fishing in muddy waters—

IVAR (*to* JUDITH): Princess Judith! (*To the* FOOLS) Out! Quickly!

JUDITH: Lord Ivar . . . I welcome you to Bjälbo . . .

IVAR: I'm usually not welcome at Bjälbo, but this time I have to
force myself in, welcome or not, for I'm here on matters of the
greatest importance! . . . May we sit down?

JUDITH: Do sit down, Lord Ivar. (*Pause*)

IVAR: Where is the king?

JUDITH: He's out fishing with Sofia . . .

IVAR: Where's Prince Magnus?

JUDITH: In his room.

IVAR: Prince Erik at Hova, and Prince Bengt at Årsta!

JUDITH: What are you getting at?

IVAR: Well! Big things have happened!

JUDITH: Is the earl . . . married?

IVAR: The earl is married . . . very quietly.

JUDITH: To the widow of Abel, who murdered Erik Plowpenny,
my father and Sofia's!

IVAR: That has not been proved, and Abel swore himself free of the
accusation.

JUDITH: But all Denmark says he is guilty!

IVAR (*rises and goes up to the door*): Call Prince Magnus! (*Comes
back to* JUDITH) Abel's sons claim the Danish crown! (*Pause*)
How is your health, Princess Judith?

(JUDITH *stares at him.*)

IVAR: We'll wait until Prince Magnus comes. (*Pause*) It'll be a cold
winter since there are plenty of rowanberries, the people say.
Haven't you heard that saying? (*Pause*)

JUDITH: Did you cross the ice on a sleigh?

IVAR: No, I rode horseback on the country roads, and in Holaved
Forest we ran into robbers . . . (*Looks at the door*) They were
outlaws from Småland. (*Pause*) Don't you get bored out in this
country district? How do you amuse yourselves?

JUDITH: Is the earl coming here?

IVAR: I don't think so.

JUDITH: Is he happy?

IVAR (*smiles*): What a question, little child. Why, he's a newlywed!

JUDITH: Why do you smile?

IVAR: I was thinking about something . . . forgive me . . .

JUDITH: Wouldn't you like something to eat and drink, Lord Ivar?
After your trip . . .

IVAR: Thank you, later. First what's most important . . . This is a
fat and prosperous country, Östergötland, and the people here
certainly aren't getting thin . . .

(JUDITH *embarrassed*)

IVAR: I didn't mean . . . (*Looks toward the door*)

HANS (*enters*): Prince Magnus will come as quickly as time and circumstances . . . permit.

IVAR: Who are you? Aren't you . . . Hans the fool!

HANS: I'm Prince Magnus' appointed squire.

IVAR: Yes, but you have been a fool?

HANS: My past is as shadowy as my descent, but the future will
show that you have been completely mistaken about my humble
person.

IVAR: I think the squire's funnier than the fool.

HANS: Am I funny, too?

(JUDITH *rises in order to go out.*)

IVAR: Stay, Princess Judith; we have to speak with you.

JUDITH (*frightened*): With me?

IVAR: Yes. (*Comes up to her*) But we're not cruel . . . we're not
without sympathy, and as a knight I defend the defenseless and
the unfortunate . . . For that reason I speak in this way: Take

my horses and servants . . . go to Kungslena Manor. Hide yourself there until it's all over . . . at Bjälbo there's going to be in-
vestigation, and fixing of guilt, and punishment of the guilty
man. Go in peace. God be with you!

(JUDITH *bows her head and goes.*)

IVAR (*to Hans*): Tell your master to come at once . . . Ivar Blå has
a gift for him!

(HANS *hurries out. Pause.* IVAR *goes up to the window and looks
out. Pause*)

MAGNUS (*enters, stiff and haughty*): You wanted to see me, Lord
Ivar?

IVAR: Yes, my boy . . . Your father greets you and sends as a gift
this new headpiece he bought in Roskilde on his wedding trip . . .

MAGNUS: That trip would be better . . . undone!

IVAR (*opens a casket*): You can't know that. (*Takes out a duke's
crown and shows it to* MAGNUS) Here you have a little crown!
It looks like a king's, but there's a hood underneath—a child's
cap that you grow too big for with the years . . .

MAGNUS: You handle crowns like other fools' caps, Lord Ivar. Don't
you have any for yourself?

IVAR: I'm above that sort of thing . . .

MAGNUS: I don't understand that . . .

IVAR: I don't doubt it! But I have a bride for you, too, a Holstein
princess, the daughter of Count Gerhardt.[25]

MAGNUS: Then I'll be related to my father . . .

IVAR (*smiles*): Aren't you already?

MAGNUS: Why do you treat everybody like a stupid ass?

IVAR: Because I find them very foolish . . . That was the lightning!
Now comes the thunder! . . . Valdemar, your brother, is guilty of
incest, since as a married man he has possessed his sister-in-law,
who has taken her initial vows, and for that reason Pope Clement
IV has sentenced him to appear in Rome to be heard and judged.

MAGNUS (*strikes the table with his fist*): And then?

IVAR: The next oldest brother becomes regent with royal prerogatives . . . You, Magnus!

MAGNUS: And the earl?

IVAR: The pope's letter says nothing about him.

MAGNUS (*bites his beard*): Then he'll go to Norway to get reinforcements!

IVAR: He can't, for his son-in-law has just . . . died.

MAGNUS: Is Håkon dead?

IVAR: Yes! . . . Now you have the steak on the spit . . . turn it, but don't let it burn.

MAGNUS: So there *is* justice in this world!

IVAR: Didn't you know that before this?

MAGNUS: But the earl?

IVAR: He's done for. Has gone into the wrong barrel. Yes, he has got a devil of a wife, just between you and me!

MAGNUS: Who fooled him?

IVAR: Who knows? However, I believe I've performed my errand well, and I'm not anxious to repeat this litany to your brother Valdemar . . . I'll leave that to you! *Is fecit cui prodest.* He who gains may take the harsh words!

MAGNUS: But the earl?

IVAR: He's done for. Worked out. Needs to rest and to age in peace . . . Now I'm going home to wait for next year, hibernate for the winter, put up my ship. Ask Valdemar not to be angry with me; he got the crown from me, but he was to keep it clean; he didn't, so I take back the loan . . . And Magnus! Be a ruler! But not a tyrant! Protect the weak when they deserve it, otherwise not; and keep after the mighty when they misuse their power, otherwise not! . . . Be brave, faithful, and just, and it will go well for you all the days of your life! People love themselves most and . . . those who serve their selfishness. Amen! And may this be granted by God! (*Shakes hands with* MAGNUS *and leaves*)

(MAGNUS, *alone, thoughtful, places the crown on his head.*)

HANS (*enters*): Is it the king?

MAGNUS (*removes the crown*): Come here, Hans.

(HANS *comes up to him.*)

MAGNUS: Now I remove your collar, and you are free!

HANS: Free?—To walk the highways like a tramp! No! I'd rather be a servant!

MAGNUS: Be my squire, then. But consider yourself a human being in the future . . .

HANS: I always have.

MAGNUS (*gives a friendly blow*): And spare your tongue! (*Takes off the collar*)

HANS (*looks at the collar*): Freedom's fine, of course—but the food wasn't bad.—May I keep this thing?

MAGNUS: What do you want it for?

HANS: I was thinking I'd give my sweetheart a collar . . .

MAGNUS: You ought to have a lock for your mouth . . .

HANS: Then I'd be like the rest of you . . .

MAGNUS: But how does it feel to be a human being?

HANS: Is this being a human being? May I feel? (*He touches his body.*) There's no difference!

MAGNUS: Where's the king?

HANS (*serious*): He just got home.

MAGNUS: Where is he?

HANS: In the great hall.

MAGNUS: Tell him I'm coming.

(HANS *goes; serious. Pause.* MAGNUS, *alone; puts the crown back in the box; becomes thoughtful and seems to be thinking out what he is going to say. The door is opened wide.* HANS *appears in the doorway.*)

HANS (*seriously*): The king awaits Prince Magnus!

(MAGNUS *pulls himself together and goes out through the door at the back.*)

CURTAIN

ACT IV

The chapter room of the hospital (The House of the Holy Spirit). At the back a large window with a grillwork of bars, where visitors can be received without being allowed to enter. To the left at the back an archway with a Christmas manger, the Star, the shepherds, the Child in the manger, the Three Kings, etc.

Doors at the right and left.

An altar with a crucifix at the right.

When the curtain goes up, the stage is empty and dark except about the Christmas manger, which is brightly lighted.

In back of the manger, a trio (not a quartet) is singing "O! sanctissima," avoiding tierces in so doing.

CARETAKER *enters; trims the candles.*

HANS (*enters; serious; clad as a squire*): Merry Christmas, father.

CARETAKER: Merry Christmas to you.

HANS: How do you like your new job, father?

CARETAKER: Oh, there's such a lot of sickness here.

HANS: There usually is in hospitals.

CARETAKER: How are things going up at court?

HANS: Miserably! The new lady is out at Årsta and doesn't want to be seen.

CARETAKER: Has she met her stepchildren yet?

HANS: Oh, yes! There was quite a set-to. When Sofia, the queen, saw Abel's widow, she screamed and fell to the floor! In a word: it wasn't a successful meeting . . . What are you people going to do here to celebrate Christmas eve tonight?

CARETAKER: Terrible things! . . . Bishop Kol's going to receive King

Valdemar's confession before he goes to Rome, that is to say, before they ship him to Danzig—after that he'll have to walk.

HANS: What about the poor princess? Judith . . .

CARETAKER: Since her child was born, she's been here as a penitent nursing the sick.

HANS (*points to the barred window*): What are those bars for?

CARETAKER: That's where they may receive visitors—see but not touch!

HANS: Do you know if the earl is coming?

CARETAKER: He usually does come on Christmas eve to comfort the sick and the poor—he wants to show that the fatherly eye watches over the humblest . . .

HANS: But the fatherly eye is an angry one; he's harder than ever, since he lost his hold on Norway [26] . . . The people hate him, as they did, but aren't afraid of him any longer . . .

CARETAKER: Do you have anything special to do here?

HANS: I have a letter from my duke to deliver to Bishop Kol—Duke Magnus is coming, too—later on, to take over the government . . .

CARETAKER: There come Lars of Oppunda and Bishop Kol—put the letter down and go . . .

(HANS *puts the letter on the table.* LARS *and the* BISHOP *enter.*)

BISHOP: The canonical law and the papal decrees apply everywhere in Christendom . . .

LARS (*calmly*): I admit that, but the national laws, the people's laws, cannot be abolished by decrees from Rome . . .

BISHOP: Yes, for members of the spiritual estate and for crimes that concern the moral law . . . Even King Valdemar had to lift off his crown before the miter . . .

LARS (*beside himself*): But you certainly don't call a priest's marriage a moral crime?

BISHOP: Yes! It is adultery if a priest lives with a woman, and it has been for a hundred years—ever since the great days of Gregory VII . . .

LARS (*furious*): You ought to be ashamed! You have never had wife and child; you don't know what a real marriage is . . .

BISHOP (*immovable*): It is adultery!

(HANS *covers his ears with his hands.*)

BISHOP (*speeds up*): St. Chrysosthom says: "What is woman but an enemy of friendship, an unavoidable punishment, a necessary evil, a natural temptation, a desirable misfortune, a flowing spring of tears, an evil work of nature, covered with shimmering varnish!"

LARS: What do you know about the highest good in life, about wife, about children, about a home? . . .

BISHOP: I know more than you do about that matter, for I have been married myself—and I have been a father confessor and have had charge of penitents. If you just get the highest good, it turns into evil which you want to escape. That's why we'll jerk out the tooth so it's settled once and for all . . .

LARS: Dear God, Kol, my brother, my friend, let me see them, see them, it's Christmas; let me go out into the market place for only an hour . . .

BISHOP: Go out? Are you crazy?

LARS: Kol, in the name of Christ and that of the Holy Mother . . .

BISHOP: You may greet them through the bars over there.

(LARS *looks closely at the bars.*)

BISHOP: But if you howl, we'll lock you up!

LARS (*flies at the* BISHOP): You angel of Satan . . .

(CARETAKER *hurries up and separates them.*)

LARS (*calm again*): Not through the bars, then I'll die; take me to my cell in the darkness . . . I expected light, and the darkness came!

BISHOP: Go to your cell! The earl is here!

(LARS *is taken out by the* CARETAKER.)

(*Pause*)

BISHOP (*to* HANS): Out, fool!

HANS: I'm a messenger from my master, with a letter!

BISHOP: Leave the letter. Out!

(HANS *leaves*.)

(*Pause*)

(EARL, *accompanied by the* SARACEN, *enters*.)

BISHOP: Merry Christmas, Earl Birger, but leave the heathen outside.

EARL: What, do you dare?

BISHOP: You associate with heathens and magicians, Birger, and for that reason your power is at an end, within these walls at least . . . Get the heathen out of here, or you'll be stoned by the people!

(EARL *dismisses the* SARACEN *unwillingly*.)

BISHOP: The hand of the Lord lies heavy upon you, Birger; your bow has broken, and your arrows go wrong. Your house is falling, and you'd be wise if you withdrew and got ready for the last journey.

EARL: Are you a judge?

BISHOP: Here is spiritual judgment since the worldly lords have given way after the fall of the last Hohenstaufen . . . there aren't any emperors any more . . .

EARL (*hesitantly*): Do you want to talk about Valdemar?

BISHOP: I will speak with him, but privately, here.

EARL: Will you speak kindly?

BISHOP: No, not about ugly matters. I believe you already regret you stirred this up.

EARL: Do I have Rome above me?

BISHOP: You were always the first to appeal to Rome—this is what you get for it! And one fine day a bolt from the Lateran and St. Peter's will strike Stockholm Palace!

EARL: What now?

BISHOP: Your new wife is too closely related to your son's wife— you're living in incest, Birger. But you married out of hate, not for love, and you took a wife for the sake of revenge . . .

EARL: Is this a confessional?

BISHOP: There's confession here all day long . . . and, if you want absolution, leave Mechtild *de facto* . . . It *is* incest, and you're guilty of the same crime as Valdemar!

EARL: I'll move this controversy to a basis I know; I'm not holding court here any more . . .

BISHOP: If you do, Birger, you'll meet the right one. You don't know Magnus yet!

(JUDITH, *dressed in penitent's garb and hood, enters with a moneybox; stops by the door without being noticed.*)

EARL: Magnus is my friend . . .

BISHOP: In gambling there are no friends, and you've played for scepters; I believe Valdemar is a better human being than you two are, because he has a sense of shame and a sense of right and wrong . . . Ivar Blå is a rascal who has lured you into the swamp, and the magician Wilibald is a French bandit who has pulled the wool over your eyes. But that's how it goes when your ways are crooked, and the one who won't follow good advice generally gets bad; the one who wants to rule over everyone often is conquered. That is your case.

EARL: Merry Christmas! And thank you for your entertainment!

BISHOP: Present your Christmas gift first.

EARL: To whom?

BISHOP: The sick and the poor. You are no joyous giver, and you'd prefer to see all the poor in the abyss.

(EARL *throws a pocketbook into* JUDITH's *box.*)

BISHOP: Don't you want to greet the child Jesus in his manger?

(EARL *crosses himself carelessly before the manger.*)

BISHOP: One does not walk by the cross without kneeling . . .

(EARL *struggles with himself.*)

BISHOP: The people see you through the bars . . .

EARL (*nods slightly toward* JUDITH): Who is that beggar?

BISHOP: You may not ask.

EARL: Is she dead?

BISHOP: Buried alive! But in her lifetime she was Princess Judith,

daughter of Erik Plowpenny, who was murdered by his brother
Abel . . .

(EARL *stares at* JUDITH.)

BISHOP: Perhaps you two want to receive each other's confession?

(EARL *intends to say something but keeps still.*)

BISHOP: Who is the judge, and who is the plaintiff?

(EARL *moves his lips as if ready to speak, but checks himself.*)

BISHOP: Give her your hand! It's Christmas! The reconciliation fes-
tival of the Christians! Give her your hand, Birger!

(EARL *turns and goes slowly out.*)

BISHOP (*goes up to* JUDITH): Go in peace, my child; your sins will
be forgiven you, not by me, the greatest of sinners, but by your
repentance, your obedience, and your faith.

(JUDITH *goes.*)

(*People appear behind the bars of the window.*)

BISHOP (*at the bars*): Woman, whom are you and your child seeking? I know—the dean of Oppunda! Eternal God! You human
beings are tearing me to pieces! Christmas Eve? Yes! Your
child? Yes, I admit that! Yes!—But I'm not hard. No! I too have
been disciplined, I have suffered what I deserved for my sins,
why should I spare you? Innocent? Yes! One must suffer for the
other. We must help each other. Go home to the inn, sweep and
straighten it, have a little candle ready on the table, prepare dinner, buy a toy, a Christmas tree, be happy and praise God for the
little child that is born this blessed night. He will come, yes, he'll
come! (*Pause*)

(VALDEMAR *enters, dressed as a pilgrim but without a staff.*)

BISHOP: King Valdemar!

VALDEMAR: Speak, Bishop Kol; I shall gladly listen . . .

BISHOP: What your sense of right has said to you I do not want to
repeat. Go to the Holy Sepulchre, but you may not speak on the
way either with your tongue or with your eyes—in solitude and
silence you will hear new voices; listen to them and come back
with a strong heart. You were born with a good spirit. (*Hands*

his own pilgrim's staff with its palm to the KING) Take my pilgrim's staff on your journey—it supported me and guided me—the palm of peace has withered, but it can turn green again, and then it will be the staff of victory.

(VALDEMAR *receives the staff, kneels before the crucifix, and goes.*)

BISHOP: Go in peace.

(*The people outside the barred window move.*)

BISHOP (*now notices the letter on the table, picks it up thoughtfully, opens it while he goes to the door at the left*): Caretaker! Bring Dean Lars of Oppunda! (*Fingers the letter. Pause*)

LARS (*enters*): St. Augustine says in *Civitate Dei* . . .

BISHOP (*while he reads the letter*): In my capacity as disciplinarian of penitents and with regard for the significance of this holy evening, I grant you a dispensation of three hours to visit—in the company of the guardian—your wife and child . . .

(LARS *falls to his knees in ecstasy.*)

BISHOP: Wait a bit! What's this? In this letter from Pope Clement IV to—what's this?—King Magnus Birgersson, complete license is granted to secular priests to continue throughout their lifetime a legal marriage.[27]—There's a Christmas present for you from King Magnus! Don't run as if the house were on fire! They won't desert you . . . They're waiting at the inn . . . You're an old fool, Lars . . . Well, Merry Christmas to you and yours!

(LARS *has been behaving as if he were crazy, has kissed the* BISHOP's *garments, run to the door, and come back.*)

BISHOP: "A time to weep, and a time to laugh; a time to mourn, and a time to dance."

LARS: "Do not be too righteous, and do not be too wise if you do not want to destroy yourself."

BISHOP: "A merry heart maketh a cheerful countenance." Now your light shines upon my darkness, Lars!

CURTAIN

ACT V

The EARL'S *study as in Act II, scene 2.*

Dark and cold, the EARL *is sitting at the table, has a book before him and a large candle near him.*

The ASTROLOGER, *who is standing in front of the* EARL, *looks frightened.*

ASTROLOGER: There was a mistake in the calculations last time—the tenth sign isn't the Scorpion exactly, but it's the Scale—the Scale is a lucky sign; and the person who's born under the sign of the Scale becomes an honest person without deceit, but he's quick to anger.

(EARL *coughs impatiently.*)

ASTROLOGER: He has to wander through many countries, but he will die in the land of his fathers. The time of his greatest good fortune comes when he has lived through half his lifetime— (*Becomes dismayed by the* EARL'S *coldness*) And if he lives to be forty-four, he'll be alive at seventy-five. (*Pause*) You are not listening to me!

(EARL *stares fixedly at him.*)

ASTROLOGER: In the Virgin he'll get a fair amount of wealth (*hesitant*)—and in the Twins he'll get anguish and adversity. (*Pause*) Don't you believe what I'm saying?

EARL (*strikes out*): No!

ASTROLOGER (*winces*): You don't believe what I'm saying?

EARL: I don't believe one word!

ASTROLOGER: Well, then—

EARL: This book says the exact opposite of what you've said . . .

ASTROLOGER: What book?

EARL: *The Ancient Chaldeans' Interpretation of the Stars . . .*

ASTROLOGER: That's no good!

EARL: Wilibald! You have been a poor councillor for me, but you may have been led astray. For the sake of my honor, not for yours, you may retire from court . . .

ASTROLOGER (*sharply*): Do you think I want to?

EARL: If I command it, you'll want to!

ASTROLOGER: Would it be wise to let a man wander about the country with secrets?

EARL: You're right. That could be unwise. Secrets should be concealed . . .

ASTROLOGER: But secrets can be kept—better still, if one makes himself their owner . . .

EARL (*looks toward the left door*): Speak a little more plainly. I don't quite understand you!

ASTROLOGER: A person can sell secrets . . .

EARL: If there are buyers! Otherwise there's a very sure way of concealing treasures like that—a person buries them, in the depths of the earth; then they're entrusted to silence—the eternal silence . . .

ASTROLOGER (*reaches for a dagger concealed in his garments*): The way is approved and can be used when it's necessary . . .

(EARL *strikes the table with his gavel.* SARACEN *enters behind the* ASTROLOGER, *takes the dagger away from him, and, holding him by the throat, leads him out.* EARL *alone; unmoved; cold as ice. Pause*)

(IVAR BLÅ *enters.*)

EARL: Was the door unguarded?

IVAR: Yes.

EARL: What do you want?

IVAR: Can't you guess?

EARL: I don't want to.

IVAR: You had a friend who prophesied you'd have three crowns on your crossbeams; the first, the Norwegian one, has gone; the second, the Danish one, has also gone . . .

EARL: What's that?

IVAR: Christopher of Denmark has been poisoned, and Margareta Breakhorse has taken over the government.[28] That was crown number two that went. The third one, Valdemar's, is just going.

EARL: Christopher? Poisoned?

IVAR: Step aside, Birger; you've done enough for the kingdom, and your name will be revered if you don't destroy it by staying on too long as an uninvited guest . . .

EARL: Who'd govern, then?

IVAR: Magnus!

EARL: He can't!

IVAR: Are you sure?

EARL: Why, he doesn't know anything!

IVAR: More than you think. His first act as ruler honors him . . .

EARL: Which act?

IVAR: Magnus wrote to Pope Clement IV and got the decree about the celibacy of the priests modified, and thereby the general lamentation of deserted women and children no longer darkens the land.

EARL: Did Magnus dare to do that?

IVAR: The duke has been appointed regent by the pope in Rome.

EARL (rises; then collapses in his chair): I believe that . . .

IVAR: Further! Do you really intend to enter Stockholm with your consort—at the head of a procession?

EARL: Tomorrow I will bring my bride into Stockholm Palace.

IVAR: Then the murderess will be stoned at the City Gate as Queen Jezebel [29] was . . .

EARL: Shame . . .

IVAR: Stoned by the people, and you will be excommunicated by the pope for committing incest!

(EARL throws a book at IVAR BLÅ.)

IVAR: You're done, Birger, and you'll destroy your beautiful story if you keep at it. All your wise and just laws you wrote for the people, but you yourself do not keep them. Go to Visingö,[30] that's a good lion's cage; that's a beautiful foundation for your statue, a verdant frame for your portrait. There you'll have forest and lake, field and meadow; there live good, simple people, who honor your name for the good you have done; live out your saga, old heathen, you who have made your country Christian; and have the courage to go living into your grave as Håkon the Red did.[31] Take the lions with you as a memento of your victories in Finland and as a token that the Folkungs have now become kings.

EARL: Have you finished?

IVAR (*rises and opens the door to the right*): Now I have finished! And Magnus will have to begin! (*Goes*)

(*Pause*)

(MAGNUS *enters from the right; courageous.*)

EARL: I don't want to talk with you! I want to find my Bengt!

MAGNUS: Good luck!

(EARL *goes out at the left.*)

MAGNUS (*calls*): Hans!

HANS (*enters*): *Durchlaucht!*

MAGNUS: You're to be serious.

HANS: It's very boring to be serious. I think I'll go back to my job as fool.

MAGNUS: Why?

HANS: Why, a person may never say a sensible word when he has a regular job.

MAGNUS: I believe you're right. And, if I weren't what I am, I'd want to be a fool. Follow your calling, then, and be a fool!

HANS: I might almost as well, I guess. This royal stuff is too fine for me.

MAGNUS: Clear that table first. But let the candle be!

HANS: What'll the old man say about that? He'll go crazy, I think!

MAGNUS: Put that chair at the short end . . . But let the candle be!

HANS: Is he going to rule—and attack it?

MAGNUS: Put the gavel there. But don't touch the candle!

HANS: The paternal eye!

MAGNUS: Put the writing utensils here. (*Pause*) Go!

HANS: Now I understand. Farewell, Your Majesty; now I'll return to the kitchen and the stables. But give me a blow first!

(MAGNUS *strikes him and then goes out on the bastion.*)

HANS: That one was royal! Shoemaker, stick to your last; *Valdemar* and I should never have forgotten that.

EARL (*enters with* PRINCE BENGT; *does not notice the changes as he comes downstage*): You're to be a duke and get a little duchess . . . Would you like that?

BENGT (*childishly; precociously*): Yes, father—but Magnus is king!

EARL: Is he king? You've misunderstood that—there won't be any king here as long as I'm alive, but the one I want will become king. And . . . you should watch out for Magnus! He isn't our friend . . . I have a princess for you!

BENGT (*as before*): Father! I have made up my mind never to marry!

EARL: Really, have you? Why don't you want to get married?

BENGT: I've seen so much misery in marriages. They're so rarely happy . . . and besides! (*Pause*)

EARL: Bengt, my beloved son, my hope, the only one on earth who's dear to me, don't you want to meet your new . . . your stepmother?

BENGT: No, I can't!

EARL: You, too! (*Angry*) Who has taken you away from me? Who has separated us from each other? Who stands between our hearts?

BENGT: The memory of my mother! If my sorrow could only bring her back from the grave!

EARL: So you're still avenging yourself, Ingeborg, from the other side. Cursed be the hour when I became unfaithful to your memory! Everything is going to pieces! But, Bengt, you'll be a knight, you'll get a crown and a dukedom . . .

BENGT: The best of gold crowns wouldn't do for me . . .

EARL: And perhaps . . . a kingdom sometime in the future, a whole kingdom . . .

BENGT: Father, I've seen so many crowns and kings fall into the pit —and, so that you won't tempt me any more: I have promised God to serve Him—whose kingdom is not of this world—

EARL (*beside himself*): What's that?

BENGT: I have given my promise . . .

EARL: What promise?

BENGT: To enter the priesthood. I want to become a servant of the Lord!

EARL: Before you've had a chance to be young! Give up everything life has to offer . . .

BENGT: Was it so much? And what there was, did it keep its promises?

EARL (*collapses on a chair at the end of the table. Pause*) Isaac was to be sacrificed! A priest! (*Pause*)

BENGT: Do you have anything else to say to me, father?

EARL: You want to go; I weary you; you're tired of me, you, too— Go, dear child; I'll be alone anyway.

(BENGT *goes out very slowly, hesitantly.*)

EARL (*alone*): The minute they lose their baby teeth, they bite. (*Pause*) Three crowns, and not one left! (*Pause. Gets up and listens as if he has heard something on the balcony, where* MAGNUS *is making a noise*) What's that? It can't be (*draws his sword*)— my lions? Or is it a ghost? (MAGNUS *appears.*) Is it an animal? The devil! It's a human being! (*Puts his sword in its sheath*)

(MAGNUS *sits down at the short end of the table; unabashed.*)

EARL (*notices the changes that* MAGNUS *had made for the first time*): What's this? Who has . . . (*They stare fixedly at each other.*)

MAGNUS: I have!

EARL: Are you sitting in my chair?

MAGNUS: It's mine!

(EARL *moves his hand as if to draw his sword.* MAGNUS *draws his sword; remains seated. Pause*)

EARL: Who do you think you are?

MAGNUS: I happen to be in the king's place!

EARL: But I am the earl!

MAGNUS: We have abolished the position of earl!

EARL: We?

MAGNUS: We, by the grace of God and the good judgment of Pope Clement IV!

(EARL *looks toward the door to the left in order to find the* SARACEN.)

MAGNUS: Don't look for the Saracen—he has already been executed —in the lions' den! (*Pause*) You, who have gone on a crusade, shouldn't keep heathens in your court. Yes, he's lying in the lions' pit!

EARL (*looks at* MAGNUS *threateningly, but also with a certain admiration*): *You* do have courage!

MAGNUS: *Your* son can't be a lamb!

EARL (*gulps*): The truth! . . . Will you honor my wife's entry tomorrow?

MAGNUS: It has been canceled . . .

EARL: That depends on me!

MAGNUS: No, on me! I have forbidden the entry, because—Lady Mechtild would be killed if it took place . . . And she has returned to her own country!

EARL: Has she?

MAGNUS: Yes! (*Pause*)

EARL (*listens*): Who's singing?

MAGNUS (*listens*): That's in the stables.

EARL: What is he singing?

MAGNUS: Well . . . I don't want to expose my father's shame.

EARL: What is he singing?

MAGNUS: Hear it for yourself!

EARL (*listens*): "Lord Ivar Jonsson . . . who fetched the earl's bride —" Dastards! Magnus, I curse you!

MAGNUS: Don't do that, father! Remember, you were the one who began the struggle between us brothers—you taught me to plot and intrigue—you did the plowing, I will harvest. But don't be concerned: Valdemar *had* to go. Now I have come. You yourself placed a crown on my head; I was born to the scepter!

EARL (*struggles with himself*): I'm beginning to believe—I see that I have fathered a king—I didn't know, though I hoped—now I know that the Folkung dynasty has come into being . . .

MAGNUS: You knew that at Herrevad's Bridge!

EARL: Herrevad's Bridge? It wasn't my youngsters! Not mine! And as long as Lord Karl is alive, I alone can keep the kingdom going!

MAGNUS: Lord Karl stepped aside—sacrificed himself for peace within the country. Do likewise . . . father!

EARL: As long as I'm alive and stand upright, I'll sacrifice nothing; and, as long as Lord Karl can avenge himself, our country will have no peace.

MAGNUS: Lord Karl never avenged the massacre of his kinsmen— he forgave, and so there was an end to the feud. You know, of course, that he's dead.[32]

EARL: Dead? I didn't know! Is he dead?

MAGNUS: On a crusade in Russia. That innocent man went into death for the common good.

EARL (*after a long pause*): Are you a Christian, Magnus? I mean, in your very heart!

MAGNUS: I am a Christian, and so I feel justified!

EARL: Karl Folkung is dead. Herrevad's Bridge is atoned for! My saga is over! (*Pause*) Magnus, take the inheritance of the first born; be master and ruler. My son, I forgive what you have done to your father this hour. My king, I hail thee! (*Bows*)

MAGNUS (*rises, uneasy; gives his father his hand*): Father, Earl Birger, you have never spoken like that, and you must not . . . Are you tired? . . .

EARL: I am tired, of everything, and now I'll go—I'll go to Visingö. I'll walk in the forest, look at the lake, think about what I have lived through, try to be reconciled with the past and to prepare myself for what is ahead.

MAGNUS: Go in peace, father; conceal your wounds; you will never
be forgotten!

EARL (*doubtingly*): Never?

MAGNUS (*moves the candle on the table*): No! Never! You have
made laws, I shall enforce them!
And from this window your paternal eye
Shall glow forever over land and city!
For I, your son, shall keep your light burning—
And, when night rests on Stream and shore,
The watchman on the heights shall see
That not he alone keeps watch and wakes,
For, when the sun has gone to rest,
The earl's light shall gleam from Stockholm's palace!
And foremost in the list of Swedish kings, though not a king,
Shall be your name that you have made as ruler!

CURTAIN

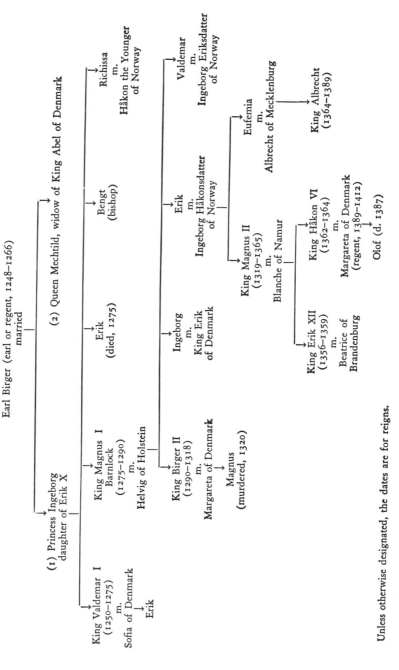

THE ROYAL BRANCH OF THE FOLKUNG FAMILY

Earl Birger (earl or regent, 1248–1266)
married

(1) Princess Ingeborg daughter of Erik X

(2) Queen Mechtild, widow of King Abel of Denmark

King Valdemar I
(1250–1275)
m.
Sofia of Denmark

Erik

King Magnus I Barnlock
(1275–1290)
m.
Helvig of Holstein

Erik
(died, 1275)

Richissa
m.
Håkon the Younger
of Norway

Bengt
(bishop)

King Birger II
(1290–1318)
m.
Margareta of Denmark

Magnus
(murdered, 1320)

Ingeborg
m.
King Erik
of Denmark

Erik
m.
Ingeborg Håkonsdatter
of Norway

Valdemar
m.
Ingeborg Eriksdatter
of Norway

King Erik XII
(1356–1359)
m.
Beatrice of
Brandenburg

King Magnus II
(1319–1365)
m.
Blanche of Namur

King Håkon VI
(1362–1364)
m.
Margareta of Denmark
(regent, 1389–1412)

Eufemia
m.
Albrecht of Mecklenburg

King Albrecht
(1364–1389)

Olof (d. 1387)

Unless otherwise designated, the dates are for reigns.

Notes on
'Earl Birger of Bjälbo'

THE TIME

THE PERIOD from Birger's election as earl (commander of military forces, director of the national defense, and, for all practical purposes, actual ruler of Sweden) in 1248 to his death in 1266 is an exceedingly important one in Swedish history. A loose confederation of semi-independent folklands or provinces under a king with little power was replaced by a strong centralized kingdom; national laws took the place of provincial laws; the church was firmly established through agreements with Birger; peace permitted the country to develop its cities (Stockholm began to come into its own during Birger's rule); Hanseatic merchants, welcomed to Swedish cities, did much to initiate commerce. A unified nation, gaining swiftly in international power and prestige, was the result of Earl Birger's years of labor as an administrator.

The earl's dream of a strong Sweden which would hold a superior position in northern Europe included not only friendly relations with Denmark, Norway, the German cities, and Russia through state marriages and conferences but also strengthening of the country itself. This was accomplished by issuing decrees concerning the rights and security of Swedes: security in the home, in church, at the *Thing;* protection of women; women's rights to inherit; the elimination of trial by fire; and the elimination of voluntary slavery. Earl Birger established peace and justice in his day by gaining recognition for the principle of the ruler's responsibility for preserving order and punishing lawbreakers. In these efforts, Earl Birger was imitated by his brilliant son, King Magnus, who gained the happy nickname of Barnlock (Ladulås) because he guaranteed the farmers security from enforced hospitality—the lords and their followers had been in the habit of putting up at farmers' homes and helping themselves to what they needed without paying for it. It was during this period that chivalry was introduced (note that in Sweden only the king could dub anyone knight) and that nobility in the continental and British sense came into being in Sweden.

Earl Birger's period of power also marks the beginning of the Folkung Period (1250–1389), during which members of his dynasty ruled Sweden (see the table on p. 248). It is a story of ambition and struggle for power between members of the clan, treachery, murders, and civil war. Birger's consolidation of power in himself through the massacre at Herrevad's Bridge (1251 or 1252) of most of his Folkung rivals was merely the first act in a tragic drama of intrafamily or intraclan rivalry. Strindberg's drama *Saga of the Folkungs* (1899) is the finest literary interpretation of this story.

THE CHARACTERS

Earl Birger of Bjälbo (died 1266) was a member of the powerful and numerous Folkung clan which played a dominant role in Swedish history from the twelfth to fourteenth century. Born on the estate Bjälbo in Östergötland, the son of Magnus Månesköld Folkung and the famous Ingrid Ylfva, Birger became prominent early in his life as a supporter of King Erik the Lisper and Lame in that king's struggle for the throne with King Knut the Tall. Birger married Princess Ingeborg (died 1254), the sister of King Erik. During the earlship of his kinsman, Ulf Fasi, Birger served in the king's military forces and is said to have been primarily responsible for breaking the Danish siege of Lübeck, an achievement that led to close relations with the Hanseatic city that were to last, with some interruptions, into Gustav Vasa's time. On the death of Ulf Fasi in 1248, King Erik passed by Ulf's son, Lord Karl, and appointed Birger earl. From that time until his death, Birger dominated Sweden. In 1249, he established peace between Sweden and Norway, became the good friend of King Håkon the Old, and arranged with him for the marriage of Birger's daughter Richissa and Håkon the Younger. While Birger was on a crusade in Finland, childless King Erik died. To forestall civil war among the powerful Folkungs, Ivar Blå quickly summoned a *riksdag* and secured the election of Earl Birger's ten-year-old son Valdemar as king. The earl hurried home when he heard the news, but had to reconcile himself to having the actual power. To secure power for himself and to assure that his dynasty would keep the throne, Birger as regent liquidated most of the pretenders at Herrevad's Bridge (see note 3, pp. 253-254). To atone for this crime, as Strindberg says, Earl Birger had to undergo penitence. The remaining pretender, Lord Karl, voluntarily left Sweden (see the note on him below).

Ambitious, brilliant, forceful, and, when he deemed it necessary, ruthless, Earl Birger quickly became the most powerful ruler in Scandinavia and strengthened Sweden in the ways that have been indicated (see pp. 249-250). In 1261, he married Dowager Queen Mechtild of Denmark, one step of many to increase his own power and to strengthen the kingdom. Perhaps his greatest political mistake was to grant duchies to his younger sons—Magnus, Södermanland; Erik, Småland; and Bengt, Finland. In this division lay the foremost cause of the struggles between King Valdemar and his brother Magnus. In Strindberg's sources Earl Birger is interpreted as a combination of the man of action and the man of ideas, whose personality was such that he dominated his environment.

King Valdemar I (*ca.* 1240–1302) was a mere child when he was elected king and apparently never had much to say about the affairs of his kingdom until his father died in 1266. The sources agree that he was exceedingly well built, extraordinarily handsome, lively, and gay; they agree, too, that Valdemar was a frivolous subject of his own desires and passions; pleasure seems to have been his greatest goal in life, although recent historians suggest that he was a far abler king than Strindberg's sources admit. Married to the beautiful Sofia of Denmark as a result of his father's political maneuvering, Valdemar proved anything but a faithful husband; his best-known extramarital affair was his incest with his sister-in-law Judith of Denmark, a relationship that led to his pilgrimage to Rome to get absolution from the pope and that perhaps provided his brother Magnus with his best opportunity to gain the throne. By 1275 Magnus was king, and by 1278 Valdemar was completely without royal power. In 1289, on the advice of their brother Bengt, King Magnus imprisoned Valdemar in Nyköping House.

Queen Sofia was the daughter of King Erik Plowpenny (Plogpenning) of Denmark. She is remembered for her beauty and her frivolity; Strindberg's sources speak of her thoughtlessness and her addiction to making fun of others without attempting to spare their feelings. Thus she labeled her brother-in-law Magnus "Kettle-mender" (*kittle-botaren*), because he was exceptionally dark, and her brother-in-law Erik "Nothing-at-all" (*alls intet*), because he let himself be led by Magnus in everything and therefore seemed to her to signify nothing.

Princess Judith, Sofia's younger sister, entered a cloister when she was twenty; whether she had taken her final vows is uncertain. In 1269, when Queen Sofia visited her homeland, the beautiful young princess decided to leave the cloister to go to the Swedish court. There she fell in love with her brother-in-law. In 1273, she became the mother of his son, who, incidentally, according to Fryxell (II, 46), became the forefather of the prominent Lejonhuvud family. Shortly after the child's birth, she entered a convent, where she stayed until her death in 1284.

Prince Magnus (ca. 1241–1290), dark and not particularly handsome, was in many ways the direct opposite of his older brother. He did inherit the qualities that made Earl Birger one of Sweden's greatest rulers, and he himself is recognized as one of Sweden's greatest kings. Note his nickname Barnlock (Ladulås). In general, Strindberg has given an interpretation of the brilliant and worthy but not saintly Magnus that is in keeping with that of the sources.

Prince Bengt (died 1291), the youngest of Birger's sons, became a monk and, in 1286, bishop of Linköping. SB (I, 456) makes this typical comment: "He was a pious and well-meaning man. His generosity was great, even too great. He gave of his large inheritance to churches and cloisters and individuals so much that he became overburdened with debts which were not becoming to a bishop."

Ivar Jonsson Blå was, as has been stated before, the prominent lord who maneuvered Valdemar's election as king. SB (I, 403) says: "He was an experienced, wise, and careful man as well as powerful and highly respected within all the folklands." Legend has it that he told Earl Birger, who had wanted to be king himself, that, if he was not satisfied to be his son's regent, Ivar Blå could easily enough shake out a king from below his blue cape.

Bishop Kol of Strängnäs was not only a bishop but Earl Birger's chancellor as well. It was Kol who delivered Birger's promise of safe-conduct to the rebellious Folkungs at Herrevad's Bridge. The bishop, overcome by his apparently unwitting share in the crime, spent the rest of his life atoning for it. He did give up his responsibilities as bishop and set out on a pilgrimage to the Holy Sepulchre.

Lord Karl (Junker Karl) was the son of Ulf Fasi, Birger's predecessor as earl, and because of his royal ancestry had as good claims as Valdemar to the throne. Not present at Herrevad's Bridge, Lord Karl was a constant source of fear for Earl Birger until, in the 1250's, Lord Karl decided to give away all his possessions, leave Sweden, and join the German Order of the Knights of the Sword in its crusade against the Lithuanians. He died in the first engagement in which he participated. In the sources, Lord Karl is presented as an idealistic, chivalrous knight.

ACT I

1. Earl Birger began the construction of Stockholm Castle on the site of the present royal palace but did not live to see it completed. The castle, both a fortress to defend central Sweden and a residence for the royal family as well as the seat of government, survived as part of the royal palace in spite of later rebuilding until fire destroyed the palace in 1697.

2. The Gray Friars (Franciscans) apparently constructed their first cloister building on Kedjeskär or Riddarholmen in the middle of the thirteenth century; at any rate, according to SB (I, 465), the whole island was given to the Gray Friars in 1270 and a hospital became part of the quickly expanded cloister. Riddarholm Church, the burial place of King Magnus Barnlock and many other Swedish monarchs, was the Gray Friars' cloister church.

3. When King Erik XI died in 1250, there were many candidates for the throne—most of them members of the powerful Folkung clan. The election of Valdemar, son of Earl Birger—who was then in Finland

—as king led to no settlement; the rival kinsmen marched against Earl Birger and King Valdemar only two years later; the two forces met at Herrevad's Bridge (probably in Västmanland). Fearful of the outcome because of his rebel kinsmen's numerical superiority, Earl Birger sent his chancellor, Bishop Kol of Strängnäs, to ask for a meeting, assuring the rebel leaders safe-conduct if they would come unarmed to his side of the stream. They had hardly crossed the bridge when Earl Birger had the defenseless men seized and beheaded. Only one among the many was the son of Magnus Brok mentioned by Strindberg. Lord Karl (Junker Karl), the son of Ulf Fasi, Earl Birger's predecessor as earl, was not among the rebel lords at Herrevad's Bridge. See the note on Lord Karl on p. 253.

4. In 1248, the papal legate Wilhelm of Sabina called a church council at Skänninge in Östergötland. Present were not only the archbishop of Uppsala, the bishops, and many priests but also many lay leaders, headed by Earl Birger. The most important decision of the Skänninge Council was the obligatory and immediate introduction of celibacy among the Swedish clergy. Strindberg's short story, "Högre ändamål" ("Higher Goals"), in *Svenska öden och äventyr* (*Swedish Destinies and Adventures*) (Stockholm, 1882–1892), gives a more detailed analysis of the effects and real purposes of the edict of celibacy. This edict continued as a source of difficulty and embarrassment as well as gain in power to the Church of Rome in Sweden.

5. Magnus Brok, nephew of King Knut Eriksson and consequently a pretender to the throne, was the father of Knut Folkung, a leading rebel who lost his life at Herrevad's Bridge. See note 3.

6. Holmger, the son of King Knut the Tall (reigned 1229–*ca.*1234) and one of the leading Folkung lords, was imprisoned in 1234 in Sko Cloister (Sko kloster). Shortly after Birger became earl, he had Holmger beheaded. According to Strindberg's sources, the earliest accounts say that many miracles occurred by his grave.

7. The Swedes of Svealand were the most faithful to the old pagan religion. About 1100, Sven, the brother-in-law of King Inge Stenkilsson, was made king of the pagan Swedes when King Inge had been driven out of Svealand because he refused to sacrifice (*blota*) to Odin and the other pagan gods at Old Uppsala. According to Strindberg's sources,

Sven was elected king when he offered to take charge of the pagan sacrifices. Hence, his name Blotsven or Sven the Sacrificer.

8. St. Erik (Erik IX), the patron saint of Sweden and a grandson of Blotsven, was a devout Christian who is remembered for his contributions to the establishment of law and order, his crusade to convert the Finns about 1158, his establishment of the church throughout most of Sweden, and his martyrdom outside Holy Trinity Church in Östra Aros (present-day Uppsala) on May 18, 1160.

9. After the massacre at Herrevad's Bridge, Bishop Kol gave up his bishopric and went on a pilgrimage to the Holy Sepulchre in the hope of finding inner peace. The archbishop fined Earl Birger and prescribed the sort of penitence that Strindberg mentions. St. Louis of France perished while on a crusade in 1170.

10. Ivar Blå of Gröneborg, a powerful lord but not a pretender to the throne, forestalled immediate civil war upon the death of King Erik XI in 1250, by summoning a *riksdag* (parliament) and securing the election as king of ten-year-old Valdemar, son of Earl Birger who was then absent in Finland. The accounts state that Blue Cape was one of Lord Ivar's nicknames because of his usual garb. Strindberg's treatment of Ivar is very much like that of his sources.

11. Earl Birger's daughter Richissa (1238–1288) was married to Håkon the Younger, the son of King Håkon the Old (reigned 1240–1263); although given the title of king, Richissa's husband never became the reigning monarch; he died in 1257. King Valdemar was married, of course, to Princess Sofia of Denmark.

ACT II

12. Stockholm received its charter in 1252.

13. Princess Judith (Jutta) had entered a Danish cloister but, after Queen Sofia's visit to her homeland in 1269, decided in 1272 to visit Sofia. Handsome King Valdemar and beautiful Princess Jutta fell in love, and in time the Princess became the mother of an illegitimate child; she spent the rest of her life in a cloister (she died in 1284). King Valdemar had to make a pilgrimage to Rome to receive absolution for incest from the pope. Strindberg has obviously taken great liberties with the historical material.

14. Richard I (1157–1199) of England, one of the leaders of the third crusade.

15. See the Apocryphal book of Judith for this allusion. Judith delivered her people by killing Holofernes, Nebuchadnezzar's general.

16. Roskilde, the cathedral city and one of the seats of the Danish kings in the middle ages.

17. Earl Birger's first wife, Princess Ingeborg, the sister of King Erik XI, died in 1254.

18. King Abel of Denmark, "the fratricide," may have caused the death of his brother Erik Plowpenny in 1250. It should be remembered that Queen Sofia of Sweden was the daughter of the murdered king and the niece of the man accused of murdering him, and that her uncle's widow Queen Mechtild, who became Earl Birger's second wife in 1261, the same year in which Sofia and Valdemar were married, was suspected of having egged her first husband on to murder Sofia's father. King Christopher was a younger brother of Abel. King Christopher's queen Margareta was called Margareta Spränghäst (Breakhorse) because of her hard riding. The struggles for the Danish throne were as complex and violent as those for the Swedish one.

19. Astrology played an important part in medieval life. For centuries to come, astrologists and stargazers were to "cast horoscopes" for the powerful and learned even as they do for the ignorant and gullible today. See any encyclopedia for an account. For Dr. Wilibald's instrument, see "alidade" and "astrolabe" in any unabridged dictionary or encyclopedia.

20. As bishop of Strängnäs. See note 9.

ACT III

21. Prince Bengt (died 1291), Earl Birger's youngest son, became a monk and, in 1286, bishop of Linköping.

22. In 1255, Earl Birger secured the pope's approval for assigning control of parts of Sweden to his younger sons—after his death. Magnus became duke (*hertig*) of Södermanland about 1266; he may have received authority over his duchy shortly before the earl died.

23. Magnus did break his engagement to a Swedish girl when he found it advantageous to marry Helvig (or Hedvig) of Holstein. Karin was either the queen's maid of her lady-in-waiting.

24. In the early 1250's, Lord Karl, perhaps the most dangerous pretender to the throne, disposed of his property as Strindberg says, joined the Knights of the German Order of the Sword, and died in their crusade against the pagan Lithuanians.

25. See note 23. Magnus' queen was the daughter of Count Gerhardt of Holstein.

ACT IV

26. With the death of his son-in-law, Håkon the Younger. See note 11.

27. Special concessions were made for a time. Magnus did not become actual king of all Sweden until 1275.

ACT V

28. See note 18.

29. For information about Queen Jezebel of Israel, see I Kings 16:31 and II Kings 9:30-37. See note 18.

30. Visingö is the largest island in Lake Vätter in south central Sweden.

31. Håkon the Red, king of the Swedes (*Svear*), reigned from 1066 to 1079.

32. See note 24.